TOMORROW THE TRAIN

JOURNEY TO THE WORLD RECORD

By Mona MacDonald Tippins

Edited by Jane Gowan

1999

Copyright © 1999 by Mona MacDonald Tippins

ISBN 0-7414-0330-7

Published by:

Infinity Publishing.com
519 West Lancaster Avenue
Haverford, PA 19041-1413
Info@buybooksontheweb.com
www.buybooksontheweb.com
Toll-free (877) BUY BOOK
Local Phone (610) 520-2500
Fax (610) 519-0261

Printed in the United States of America

Printed on Recycled Paper

Published November-1999

To my grandchildren: Christine Lila Dalton, Kamie Lee Tippins, Shane Michael Tippins and Ian Christopher Tippins.

To the memory of my beloved brother, Rex Brindley McDonald.

Family reunion - Aug 11, 2001

To Uncle "Al"
   Roderick Albert MacDonald

Mona MacDonald Tippins

Jack's daughter

Acknowledgments

I owe a debt of gratitude to many, and I list them in alphabetical order in each category. I thank the following railways and companies for complimentary rail passes:

British Rail International (the Regional Office in Denton, Texas) for a 15-day BritRail Pass.

CIE (Irish Rail) for an Irish Rover ticket.

Rail Europe for a 15-day Eurail FlexiPass.

Swiss National Tourist Office for an 8-day Swiss Pass.

Touch N' Go Travel for a 30-day PolRail Pass.

Thanks to these businesses for contributing services to expedite my travels: Arkansas State Bank, Cindy's Unique Boutique, and Fitzgerald-Olsen Real Estate.

I thank these businesses for travel items and gifts: Big World Drug Store, Booneville Chamber of Commerce, Booneville Human Development Center, Cheryl's General Store, Dollar or Two Store, and Hicks' Quick Mart.

Thanks to the following people for cash donations: Joan Collins, D.R. "Randy" Dalton, Loretta Tippins Dalton, Tim Tippins, Crissy Tippins, Skip Wofford and Nancy Wofford.

I am grateful to those indefatigable souls who assisted in the preparation of this book: D.R. "Randy" Dalton and Tim Tippins.

I thank Jane Gowan for her gentle criticism and suggestions, which improved my manuscript immensely.

I thank Janie Mashburn for her timely suggestions and her encouragement.

Thanks to Leslie Oliver. Her scrutiny of my manuscript caught many discrepancies. Her genuine interest in my book gave me the inspiration I needed to finish the book.

I owe a special thanks to Rosi Paulun, who provided me with a haven in her home in Bad Kreuznach, Germany. And to Erich Heitbrock, who became my private chauffeur in Bad Kreuznach.

I am grateful to all of the conductors, assistant conductors, and other crewmembers that signed my documents.

Contents

Prologue

Trains and train stations were to be my home and my life. For much of the time, I ate, showered and slept on trains, or in the stations. Sometimes I had to forgo food, showers or sleep. I was robbed, beaten, and spit upon, and I was mistaken for a spy, a prostitute and a beggar.

My journey of 79,841 documented rail miles became an odyssey. I set out to beat the existing Guinness World Record of 76,485 unduplicated rail miles. Uncooperative conductors and a few extenuating circumstances prevented documentation of a portion of the 100,000 miles I traveled. In the beginning I had a plan; I would sweep across Europe, North America and part of Asia. I spent months working with train schedules and maps, but was able to adhere to the plan for only one week, before natural and unnatural events plagued my way. Railway strikes, cholera epidemics, floods, snowstorms, bombings and threats of bombings, and train wrecks intervened. And then, there were my own bouts with illness and a few injuries. My travels took me through thirty-three countries and along the coasts of ten major seas, and the Atlantic and the Pacific. The total documented mileage was enough to have circled the globe three and one-fifth times. It was not, as they say, a "journey of a lifetime," but later it seemed a lifetime of journeys.

Introduction

THE GUINNESS BOOK OF WORLD RECORDS! These words comprise a title, a book, a collection of astonishing facts and amazing records, and for many of us, a dream. I dreamed of being in that book.

One night I was struck with the idea of combining my love of train travel with my dream. I had a goal then, not just a dream. For a time, the ordinary business of living and a few emergencies kept my goal somewhere out there... just out of reach. It was tomorrow the dream, tomorrow the train. Finally, the dream became reality. Tomorrow had become today. It was time to test my plan and my fortitude, and perhaps my courage. I arrived in Frankfurt, Germany, armed with an array of rail passes, my mileage notebook, rail maps and my only traveling companion, the *Thomas Cook European Timetable.* In keeping with my endeavor, I was wearing a T-shirt that reads "Breaking the World Record on Train Travel." I traveled on to Bad Kreuznach, Germany. My friend, Rosemarie "Rosi" Paulun was keeping a room at my disposal, a place to recuperate and to receive messages. My husband and I lived in Bad Kreuznach in 1953 while he was serving with the 31st MASH in the United States Army. It is fitting that I begin my journey here, the terminus of my first European train journey, from Le Havre and Paris, France, on the way to join my husband, so long ago.

Chapter 1
The Journey Begins

Today I had a free day, tomorrow the train. It was a pleasant October day, the kind that only furthered my fit of nostalgia. I stood on the small bridge that straddles the *Muhlenteich,* an arm of the Nahe River that courses through Bad Kreuznach (shortened to BK by Americans) on its way to meet with the mighty Rhine at Bingerbruck. As always, I felt young again. Traveling almost anywhere in Europe is like stepping into a fairy tale or a storybook from the past. In Bad Kreuznach, I step into my own past.

From the small bridge, one can see the old stone bridge built in the year 1311. Its arches span the *Muhlenteich* and the Nahe River. The *Bruckenhauser* (Bridge Houses) that nestle along one side of the bridge were added in the sixteenth century and used as toll houses. A cannonball from the war with Sweden in 1632 remains embedded in the front wall of one of them. The Bridge Houses are in use today as businesses. Looking across to the *Wortherinsel,* a small island between the *Muhlenteich* and the Nahe River, one can see the fourteenth-century church, *Pauluskirche.* Only the East Choir was left intact after the assault by France's Sun King, Louis XIV in 1689. It was rebuilt in the eighteenth century. Karl Marx married Jenny (Jannie) of Westfalen in the church in 1843. Now it rests serene in rose-colored brick.

There are several ways to the *Kauzenburg,* the thirteenth-century castle that sits high above the town. I walked through the pedestrian zone, over the old stone bridge, and into the medieval part of town. A narrow alleyway leads to the steep steps that spiral up to the castle grounds. At each landing I paused, savoring views of the bridges over the Nahe River, half-timbered houses, high-steepled churches and an occasional train. The castle was built in 1206 and destroyed in 1689 by the troops of Louis XIV. It has been rebuilt over the ruins several times, always in a different style. Now it is topped with a shockingly modern, glassed-in upper half that serves as a roof for a restaurant. Looking up at it from below, I can only describe it as garish. Nevertheless, from the inside, the panoramic view of the town and its surroundings is fantastic; I can forgive the architects. The old dungeon is intact, and serves as a medieval banquet hall. The huge stone lion still guards the castle from a vestige of the wall, and in May, the lilac tree will bloom, just as it has through the ages.

It was time to begin my expedition. The first destination was Italy.

Although I could have taken a "through" train all the way to Rome, I opted to begin with an old "friend," the *Holland-Italian Express,* train # 201, with a change of trains at Milan. Boarding at Mainz (about forty kilometers from my base in BK), I approached a conductor and explained in German that I needed his signature on my document to verify my kilometers. I smiled, anticipating a warm, "Welcome to the German Railways," expressed in a congratulatory way. He refused me in no uncertain terms. When we stopped in Frankfurt I asked another conductor, who also refused. I followed him down the corridor; he signed just to be rid of me. Was this the way it was going to be?

So I began my journey, innocently unaware that I would jump from a moving train in Poland, be chased by drug addicts in Denmark, or cross the border between Kazakhstan and Russia without a passport. Nothing could have prepared me for the adventures, good and bad, that lay ahead.

In a compartment alone, I raised the arms of the seats on one side, making a narrow bunk to sleep on. Sleepers were not considered as part of my plan. With a little luck, one can have a place to stretch out for the night in a regular compartment, although not often in second class.

We crossed the Italian border at Chiasso. The train stopped in Milan at 7:40 a.m., and ten minutes later I was on board a train to Rome. Foiled again! The conductor wouldn't give me his signature, because he was afraid I might forge his travelers' checks in the future. He spoke English, so I knew he understood. I walked the length of the train, but found no one to sign for me. In the snack bar, even the waiter refused to concede that I was on the train. A few minutes later I found another conductor. He signed my document, and asked about my journey.

The famous tower in Pisa is not the only one in Italy that leans. Bologna has two leaning towers, and the Garisenda Tower leans over the other, the Asinelli Tower (which also leans). The leaning towers in Bologna were the first of many wonders I was to see from the window of a train.

My sister Joan was spending a few days in Rome, and I had arranged to spend the night with her. On arrival in Rome I had 1,363 kilometers (847 miles) to my credit. Only 75,638 miles to go! Joan was waiting for me in the hotel lobby after my wild taxi-ride from the station. It was our first meeting in two years. We had a lot to catch up on.

Lines were long at each information window in Rome's Termini Station; I didn't have time to wait for a letter in Italian, requesting a signature for my documents. I hurried to the platform, sans the hoped-for paperwork, and boarded a "through carriage" to

Lourdes, France for connections to Bordeaux. The rest of the train would travel on to Spain. Many long-distance trains begin the journey with one or more carriages that will be uncoupled and hooked to another engine somewhere along the line, going to a different destination. Passengers must check the metal plates on the side of the carriage before boarding. The final destination is printed on the plate.

From the train I saw the Castel Sant' Angelo in the distance. It was built in the year 138 as Emperor Hadrian's tomb, and later transformed into a citadel, due to its position on the Tiber River. The statue of its namesake, the Archangel Michael perches at the very top. It was added in 1753. The famous Coliseum appeared, much closer outside my window.

The coastline along the Mediterranean Sea afforded some fantastic views. My window formed a frame around each scene; I was riding a rolling art gallery. At Pisa I saw the famous leaning tower, the *Torre Pendente,* but from the train it didn't look as spectacular as the two towers I had seen in Bologna.

I consulted my phrase book and wrote a note in Italian, requesting a signature. Although it wasn't perfect, it worked. When the first conductor came to check tickets I showed him my note. He laughed at the wording, but understood, and signed. *"Por favor Graczie. Il firme + timbre por record por il treno kilometers. Guinness Libro. Tren KM."*

When we stopped at Las Spezia, a long-forgotten fact popped into my mind. My father told me about an old manuscript in the library at Las Spezia that was written in the 1500s, stating that on several occasions peasants had reported seeing a disc in the skies over the town, with lights that changed from red to yellow, with red glowing from beneath.

At Ventimiglia, just before the French border, customs officials checked passports on the train. We traveled the French Riviera in darkness. I caught only shadowy glimpses of the long coastline. Sleep was not horizontal; four passengers shared my compartment. One man snored most of the night.

In Lourdes, I was appalled by the crass commercialism. Merchants accosted the tourists as they passed the stores, beseeching them to come in and buy. One woman was particularly aggressive. She said, "Come, I speak English! French! German! Dutch! All languages!" Somehow I found it hard to imagine her speaking Kazakh or Pushtu. When she saw that I was not really interested she practically shoved me aside, and started on the next passerby.

Lourdes is a small town that became famous after a peasant girl, Bernadette Soubirous, professed to have seen apparitions of the Virgin Mary in 1858. The *Grotte Massabiele* marks the site.

The Gave de Pau River takes a detour, allowing room for an asphalt floor between the basilica and the grotto. A huge castle rises from a crag above a row of old houses.

Pilgrims flock to Lourdes by the thousands to join the candlelight procession. Nurses and volunteers push invalids in wheelchairs.

I suspected that a few of the tourists were filling their water bottles from the "healing waters," just to use as free drinking water while traveling. Not a bad idea. Many have been healed, and miracles have been attributed to the waters and the prayers at Lourdes. I met a "miracle" myself. A man from Florida told me his story on a train in the Rhine area of Germany. He was not Catholic, and didn't go to Lourdes with healing in mind. An acquaintance talked him into going into the healing baths. The man continued on his European holiday. Several days later while undressing in his hotel room, he noticed that a hole in his foot had closed up. The hole had baffled doctors. It wasn't a wound; it was a deep, pocket-like space in his foot. The spontaneous closing was nothing short of a miracle.

The conductor to Bordeaux wouldn't sign; I got off and took another train. Another refusal. I jumped off the train at Pau and caught a train to Bayonne. The conductor signed. If he understood my note, I'm sure the others did. *"S' il vous plaît. Je voudrais votre signature, appelle est timbre sur ma livre journaux Guinness pour le Guinness Livre du Recorde du Monde pour le Chemin de Fer kilometers avec Chemin de Fer. Merci."*

I changed to a Direct Express to Bordeaux. The conductor didn't sign, but he stamped my document with his employee number. Because of the refusals I had taken four trains. One should have been enough.

Finally, I made it to Bordeaux. I walked across the street from the station and checked into the Hotel Faisan. It had been thirty-one hours since I left Rome.

Breakfast was continental. I felt a bit awkward drinking coffee from a large white bowl (a custom in the area), but soon got the hang of it after the initial chin dribbling.

On the way to Peregueux city scenes faded away, and the tracks wound through woodlands, then fields of vegetables. As we passed a cornfield I observed a large gray goose pecking at a dried stalk. Determined to reach the uppermost ears of corn, he tried to bend the stalk down with his beak. His life was much happier than that of the goose I had seen yesterday. A woman was force-feeding the poor thing to fatten up its liver for the famous *pate de foie gras;* the liver spread passed off as a gourmet food. It translates to the unappetizing name of "paste of fat liver." The geese (and ducks) are kept all of their lives in a small wooden

4

crate, confined to it for all of their needs, including the bodily functions. It is torture, in the name of "good taste." The only time they leave the crate is for the guillotine.

From Peregueux I returned to Bordeaux by a different route, adding to my mileage.

After a leisurely morning in Bordeaux the next day, I took a train to Rennes, where I changed to a "TGV" *Train a Grande Vitesse* (Train of Great Speed) to Paris. "TGV" also stands for *Tres Grande Vitesse* (Very Great Speed). First class on the TGV is a misnomer. I call it world-class. The seats were plush and comfortable; I was sitting in the "lap" of luxury. I had no difficulty getting a stamp and a signature from the amicable conductor.

We pulled into Paris in the late evening. It was standing room only on the bus from Paris Montparnasse Station to Gare de l' Est (the East Station) for my overnight train to Germany. Outside the station I saw two Gypsy children (a boy and a girl) approaching an elderly couple. Both of the children began kicking the older couple in the shins. I ran over to them, and grabbed the children by the hair, and held them away from the couple (I received only a couple of minor kicks) until several other people stopped to help. The victims were American tourists in their eighties. They thanked me, and said they were so surprised by the attack they couldn't respond. The girl had asked for money, pointing to the cardboard sign she was holding with one hand, while the other hand tried to grab the woman's purse. In the confusion, the boy tried to steal the man's wallet. When they failed, they began the attack. I knew the plan; I have heard the same story from several tourists.

The train wasn't crowded. I had a compartment to myself. Just out of Paris I saw what looked like a fairyland with multi-colored lights and castle-like buildings. It was EuroDisney, the Disney amusement park at Marne-La-Vallee. The overnight ride was easy; I folded down the arms of the seats on one side and slept until twenty minutes before time to take my next train.

Back at base, I went to the pedestrian zone to do my errands in preparation for my next rail trip. A Turkish man stopped abruptly in front of me. He shook his finger at me, and spoke harshly to me in Turkish. The woman with him stopped too, pointed at my head, and spit on me. The man tried to spit on me, but missed. Because of my dark hair they must have thought I was Turkish, and that I should have my head covered. I yelled at them in German, "I am not Turkish! I am an American and I am free! I don't have to hide my hair!" I wanted to say more, but I had to hurry back to the apartment to shower and wash my hair; I wasn't sure where the spit had landed. If I had been wearing my blue contact lenses, I might have frightened them; some Turks still believe in the

"*Nazar*," the evil eye. Blue eyes are the most feared, and suspected of the capability of giving the *Nazar*. I wonder how they manage to look all those blue-eyed Germans in the eye.

I was confused. Many Germans have dark hair, and some Turkish people have light hair. Could there be more to the threats? Is the new wave of Islamic Fundamentalism spilling over into Europe? Some of the younger Turkish women no longer cover their hair or wear the long, cover-up coats, but women of my age are expected to do so, even when living in a Western country. Many Turkish women still wear the *chador*, the veiled, cloak-like ensemble, or the *charshaf*, a black headpiece that covers all of the head and the hair. Some wear the *yasmak* (*yashmak*), which covers the head, and is wrapped around the lower and upper parts of the face, leaving only the eyes visible. I couldn't believe anyone would go so far as to spit on a woman in Germany because her hair wasn't covered. In the Middle East or North Africa I wouldn't have been surprised at all. I've heard many horror stories about the self-appointed "religious police" hassling (and sometimes flogging) women who don't follow the Islamic dress code.

After World War II the German Government invited Turks, along with Greeks, Italians, Yugoslavians and Portuguese to become "Guest Workers" in Germany. Now several generations of each nationality are living and working in Germany, causing some resentment among the natives. More foreigners are pouring into Germany now, uninvited, claiming to be political refugees, Russians, Romanians, Poles, Africans, Gypsies and Kurds (to name a few).

I had promised Rosi's twelve-year-old son, Dirk, that he could take a part of my journey with me. After our evening jog, Dirk and I discussed our forthcoming adventure. I suggested a few places, not too far away, as he had only a few days off from school and I would have a long journey ahead of me when we returned. We agreed to go by ship and train to Trier, near the Luxembourg border, and return by train.

Dirk woke early, excited about our trip. We started our Rhine cruise from Bingen. My Eurail Flexipass is valid on the KD (*Koln-Dusseldorfer*) Line. Castles were in view before the ship pulled away. Across the river, above the vineyards I could see the ruins of Ehrenfels castle, and nearby, much higher on a hill, the Niederwald Memorial of "Germania." It stands thirty-four feet tall, on a base that measures eighty-two feet. Adding the height of the hill it rests on; the monument is almost one thousand feet above the river. It was erected in 1871 to commemorate the revival of the German Empire. As Emperor, William the First, King of Prussia, dedicated the monument in 1883, narrowly escaping assassination during the ceremony. It seemed that the explosive used by the assassin included a wet fuse.

Almost as soon as the ship sails away, the three castles at Trechtinghausen come into view on the left side of the river. All three were havens for medieval knights to rest from their plundering. The eleventh-century Stahleck Castle sits on a ledge above the town of Bacharach. Now it is a popular youth hostel.

Two Australian women embarked at Kaub, and we watched from the deck together. One of them was a descendant of the Prussian Field Marshall, Gebhard Blucher (also called Prince Blucher von Wahlstatt). The Australian women had been to visit the museum and monument honoring Blucher at Kaub. I told them about the *Blucher-Haus* in Bad Kreuznach, where he had stayed overnight on New Year's Eve, 1813. He and his men were en route to fight yet another battle against Napoleon. The building was named after his visit. One wonders where Blucher's 90,000 troops slept. The *Blucher-Haus* in Bad Kreuznach is now a Greek restaurant. We discussed the importance of tracing one's ancestry, and I remarked that I hoped to see the spot in Scotland where the Campbells massacred members of the MacDonald Clan. My family is descended from the Glencoe MacDonalds, the victims. The other woman hadn't said much, but then she reached over, took my hand and said, "Glad to meet you, I'm a Campbell!"

As we approached the famous Lorelei Rock, above the town of St. Goarshausen, the Loreley song was playing. The author of the lyrics, Heinrich Heine, has been honored only recently. Because he was Jewish, his lyrics were listed as "author unknown" through the war years and beyond. The lyrics are based on an old legend that tells of the enchantress, "Lore" (also called Loreley and Lorelei), who sat atop the mountainous rock above the river, combing her long golden tresses. The sight of her supposedly drove the sailors to distraction, causing them to crash their vessels into the rocks below.

Saint Goar, on the left side of the river, is still watched over by Burg Rheinfels, once the most massive fortress on the Rhine. In modern German, *Burg* means castle, and *Berg* is a mountain, but at one time the two meant the same (the spelling just varied). Castles were called *Burgs* because they were built on the mountains to guard against invasion. The townspeople lived as close as possible to the castle walls for protection. So the word *"Burgher"* (sometimes spelled *Burger*) became the word for "citizens."

There are more than forty castles (some in ruins) between Mainz and Koblenz, a one-hundred-kilometer stretch known as the Middle Rhine.

Dirk and I checked into the Hotel Hochwald near the station in Trier, then spent the rest of the day sightseeing. The *Porta Nigra* dominates the entrance to the town square. Built in the second century, it served as the city gate on the northern side of the city walls during Roman times. The ancient structure appears to be out of its element, although Trier is the oldest town in Germany (16 BC). *Porta Nigra* means "Black Gate," so named because of the dark patina accrued over the ages that covers its stone. Once part of the city walls, it was built of blocks made of sandstone mixed with lime. Mortar was not used; the blocks were held together by crampons, a kind of iron clamp, similar to those used by mountain climbers. It was a remarkable feat for the times, and the size (118 feet wide and 98 feet high) of the building. We climbed up to each floor and read the historical information posted on the walls inside and viewed the town from the arched, unglazed windows.

The remains of the Roman Amphitheater that held up to 25,000 spectators are very impressive, but perhaps the most striking Roman edifice in Trier is the *Romerbrucke,* the bridge across the Mosel River (Moselle, in French) that still rests on Roman foundations.

Although it was late when we headed back to the hotel, the pedestrian zone had a festive air about it. The tables at the outdoor cafés were filled with customers. Children played ball in the middle of the walkway, and a few toddlers rode tricycles. I heard German and Turkish being spoken by the children. Soft, lilting music was being piped from some hidden source for the enjoyment of the customers and the pedestrians. At night, the bright lights on the dark *Porta Nigra* give it an eerie glow. We walked through its arched gateway, and back to our hotel.

Within an hour after breakfast, Dirk had a craving for a Turkish *"doner,"* pita-like bread filled with chopped raw vegetables, meat and a creamy dressing. We stopped at a Turkish restaurant up near the castle. The Turkish waiters spoke German, so I let Dirk do the ordering. I felt he hadn't stressed the fact that I wanted no meat or fish on my *doner*, so I said, *"Ich bin vegetarisch, ich mochte keine fleisch oder fisch auf mein brot."* The cook came out of the kitchen and convinced me he understood. We sat down at the first table, facing the counter. As soon as we began eating, a white delivery van pulled up, blocking the door of the restaurant. Two men in white, bloodstained aprons came in carrying a whole animal carcass, right over our table. I screamed my "vegetarian-sees-bloody-meat" scream and Dirk laughed. No one said a word, but I got a few quizzical looks, and every now and then Dirk would snicker.

It was time to go "home." We boarded an express train, and changed in Saarbrucken to a little aqua *Regional Schnell Bahn* (Regional Fast Train). The driver signed my document, and let Dirk drive the train. It was the highpoint of our trip. When rounding curves, Dirk sounded the horn. He was elated.

My plan to take on Italy again was canceled after Rosi gave me the news that a cholera epidemic had struck Italy. Many were dead, and more were dying. I had to reconstruct my plan. Back to the drawing board. I decided to play it by ear, and plan one trip at a time. It was the first of three cholera epidemics that would cause me to change travel plans.

Before dawn I was on a *Regional Schnell Bahn* (RSB) to Bingen Hauptbahnhof (the main station), a new name for the old Bingerbruck station. I changed to an InterRegio and traveled along the Rhine. My plan was to go as far north in Germany as I could before catching a night train to either Poland or the Czech Republic, depending on the available overnight connections. On the InterRegio I sat in a first-class compartment with four plush seats and one child-size seat, which converts to a table. Since I was alone in the compartment, I felt comfortable using my micro-mini recorder rather than writing in my journal. I quote my recorder:

"I have been seeing a lot of freight trains on the other side of the Rhine, and sometimes, another passenger train. There is no shortage of barge travel either. From my `window on the world' I can see castles up on the hillsides along the river. The trees on the hills are beautiful in their autumn colors, a panorama of green, goldenrod, rust and scarlet.

"We are coming into Boppard now. Many of the houses are built over, or as part of, remnants of the old town walls. A few are built into the stone towers of the walls. Most of them have white lace curtains on the windows and geraniums (in pots or window boxes) on the windowsills. In one open window, a large orange cat was sitting on the sill, surrounded by pots of geraniums, watching the train go by. I waved at him.

"We just passed a KD *(Koln-Dusseldorfer)* passenger ship. The train tracks are so close to the river that I can see passengers sitting at the dining room tables. We are passing another ship now; its Swiss flag is slapping the wind. Some of the passengers are standing on the deck in the rain, waving.

"The tunnels we go through are designed to blend with the Rhenish scenery; the openings have castle façades over them.

"It's about ten o'clock now and we are stopping at Remagen, once the Roman Citadel of *Rigomagus.* The Remagen Bridge played an essential part in the history of World War II. After most of the bridges across the Rhine had been destroyed, the Germans attempted to blow up the bridge at Remagen, but the Americans arrived just days before it collapsed. They were able to cross the Rhine, thus shortening the war. Remains of the famous bridge are visible from the train. A museum is housed in the surviving bridgehead, dedicated to peace, and honoring all the Nobel Peace Prize recipients. Our own *Old Glory* flies above the bridgehead, in memory of those who died for Europe's freedom. It is a piece of America, a gift from the German people.

"We have stopped at Cologne *(Koln),* and from the train I can see the Gothic cathedral. It looks as though its dark web-like spires are piercing the blue sky. As I look through the side of my window to take a picture, it seems as though the cathedral is falling. We are crossing the Hohenzollern' Bridge now, and I can still see the cathedral through the black iron braces."

At Hamburg's main station, I went to an information window and asked the agent about an overnight train to Poland. "Where in Poland do you want to go?" I paused for a moment to think, but she became annoyed and grabbed a map of Poland, and stuck it in front of my face. "Now, there is Poland! Where do you want to go?" She was so rude; I didn't want information from her. I said, "You are too young to have become so grumpy. I can find a train to Poland on my own!"

I went outside to find some fresh air. What I found was an assortment of punks, Neo-Nazis, and crazies. As I turned to the right, and down the walkway, I couldn't help noticing a young redheaded woman in front of me, walking between two men. She was wearing a black leather midriff vest and tight leggings of sheer black lace with the "F" word printed on the rear end of them. Or it might have been a tattoo showing through the sheerness; it was hard to tell. Then a 'crazy' wearing black leather (including a black, spiked collar) walked toward me, leading a Great Dane. The dog was wearing a matching collar. As they came nearer, the man bared his teeth at me; they had been filed to the sharpness of fangs. He snapped a chain toward my face. I turned and ran into the station.

I read the schedules and elected to go into the Czech Republic from Stuttgart. InterCity Express (ICE) # 795, the *Munchner Kindl* was leaving at 4:00 p.m.; I had less than an hour to wait. *Munchner Kindl* means Munich Child, a name they use for the little brown-suited monk that is the symbol of Munich. The German name of Munich is *Munchen,* which means "Little Monk."

France's answer to Japan's "Bullet Train," is the TGV, and the ICE is Germany's answer to both. The *Munchner Kindl* travels at high speeds from Hamburg to Munich and vice versa. The restaurant car and the Bistro are done in pale lavender, black, white, and silver.

Because all my trains had been a few minutes late, in Stuttgart I had to run down the stairs, through a tunnel, and back up the stairs to Platform 5 to catch my overnighter to Prague. I sat in a first-class compartment in a Czech carriage with the "CSD" logo of the Czechoslovakian Federal Railways. The initials stand for *Ceskoslovenske Statni Drahy,* the collective name before the Czechs and the Slovaks divided. Some of the carriages have the new logo of the Czech National Railway, "CD" *(Cesky Drahy).* The red vinyl seats in my compartment were the high-backed theater types, usually found in second-class, older trains. I saw only one other person in the carriage, a woman two compartments down.

When we reached Aalen, I could see a luxurious old tourist train sitting two platforms away. Victorian lamps were glowing softly on each table of the restaurant car. The tables had been set for the next meal, but there were no passengers on board. I thought of writing a story about a Ghost Train, the passengers mysteriously vanishing before they could partake of the meal.

At the Czech border I was surprised at the quick check of passports. I remembered the first time I had crossed this same border. It was before the "Freedom," and it was my first visit to an Eastern Bloc country. After the border guard checked my passport he reached in his jacket. I thought he was reaching for a gun, so I held my hands up, but he was only reaching for his stamp to validate my visa. Now I don't need a visa.

In Prague, I caught a local to Bakov nad Jizerou. Just as I climbed up the steep steps of the train, trying to shove my satchel into the hallway, two little girls spilled a big bag of red apples right in front of me before I could get all the way into the train. I didn't want to step on the apples, but I had to move before the train took off. The girls managed to pick them up just as the train was pulling away. I barely stepped all the way into the train before the doors closed. The carriages were all second class, and crowded. A group of schoolgirls sat on the floor, in the aisle.

I was hungry, but all I had left from my early lunch on the Rhine yesterday was a plastic packet of peanut butter (about a teaspoonful). When some of the girls began eating sandwiches and fruit from their lunch bags, I became even hungrier. I opened my peanut butter and sucked it right out of the packet. That didn't take long.

At Bakov nad Jizerou, I changed to a local to Ceska Lipa (Bohmischer Leipa). The seats were like those in the third-class carriages used in the 1950s, green vinyl double banquettes with separate headrests and arms between them. The banquettes weren't built into the wall; they were fastened onto the floor with braces and screws. Beige linoleum covered the floors.

A conductor signed, and even wrote the time and number of the train for me. The beautiful old green train twisted through mountains and woods. Little streams rushed along near the tracks, and ferns were growing on the banks.

From Ceska Lipa I went on to Nymburk, but the new conductor wouldn't sign. I caught a train to Kolin, encountering another "refusenik." In Kolin I tried to find a hotel for the night. Although it was only late afternoon, I was tired and hungry and felt as though I couldn't go any farther. The only hotel close to the train station was a large several-storied one that catered to business people, mostly Germans. The price list was printed in Czech and in German. When I asked for a room, in English, the receptionist quoted me a price five times of that on the sign. I waited until a German man was charged the right price, then I spoke in German, letting the receptionist know that I understood what was going on. He answered in German, "We have more than one thousand rooms in this hotel, but not one for you!"

I could see there were not that many rooms, but if there had been, I didn't want one. I would rather sleep on a train again, although I was tired and ill. One has to have a little pride. I was so proud, in fact, that I became the Ugly American. My retort was, "Have you forgotten who was on your side in the Second World War? Do you favor the Germans above Americans now? Yes, I think you cheat only us. But I am a big girl. I can sleep on the street!"

I walked back to the station to catch a train back to Prague. I still hadn't eaten, but was beginning not to care. Oh well, starve a cold and feed a fever. Or is it vice versa? I had a cold *and* a fever and was starving them both.

A man in his late teens sat across from me, holding a Michael Jackson record album in his lap. Although his skin was extremely white, he seemed to think he looked like Jackson. He was wearing a suit that resembled the one Jackson was wearing on the album cover. Slyly, he looked at the album and then at me, repeating the looks several times. I smiled, acknowledging the album, and pointing at the young man's long, black hair, I said, "Michael!" He seemed pleased, and began humming. I didn't recognize the tune, but I suppose it was one of Jackson's. When he got off the train, I called out the corridor window, "Good-bye Michael!"

EuroCity # 170, the *Comenius* travels from Prague to Dresden. The conductor didn't sign, but stamped my document with her employee number, the date and the number of the train.

My carriage was next to the restaurant car. It had been thirty-two hours since I had eaten, but it seemed longer. I had a salad plate, and two cups of coffee.

We soon crossed the Czech border at Decin (Tetschen), and then the German border at Bad Schandau. From the window I caught dark flashes of deep gorges. At times we followed a river. It was getting late, but sleep would have to wait until the next train. According to the schedule I could change in Dresden to an overnighter to Frankfurt.

In Dresden, a "D" (Direct Express) train was ready to board; I made it just in time, jumping onto a Polish carriage. I fell into a deep sleep, and slept until dawn.

In Frankfurt, as I was walking down the platform to board my train to BK, I noticed a blind woman with a white-tipped cane, tapping the carriages as she passed. Positioning myself beside her, I spoke in German, explaining as we walked, "This is a second-class carriage, and this is a non-smoking carriage." She didn't say anything; she probably wondered whom I was talking to. Pausing as we came to one of the carriages, she stepped up onto the train as quickly as anyone could. I followed her back through the automatic doors to the next car, still thinking she needed help finding a seat. It was the mail car. I said, "No, no, this is the mail car. You can't sit here!" One of the workers at the mail desk said, "It's OK, she works here." Unsaid, I suspect, was "Crazy American!"

By the time I got to my base in BK I was exhausted. Rosi was still sleeping; I left my backpack in the hall by the door so she would know that I had come home safely.

In the early evening Rosi tapped on my door; she was bringing me a huge plate of steaming vegetables. Although I am older than Rosi, she tends to mother me. She brought me a cup of tea and took away my empty plate. I was feeling much better and I felt like going out on the town. Rosi didn't want to go out; I walked to the *Liedertafel*, a nearby dance *"Lokal."*

I'm not a good dancer; I usually only dance when they play a favorite of mine, "Spanish Eyes." Sometimes I will join in a folk dance like the "Chicken Dance" (which is really a Duck Dance). I was wearing my black 'dancing boots' just in case.

A young man I didn't want to see walked in, so I paid for my drink, made my excuses for the short visit, and went for a pizza. I couldn't face the man (Heinrich) because I was afraid he would remember an embarrassing (to me) situation. He was at a party Rosi had thrown for me at her apartment. Some of the guests were telling off-color jokes. I was glad they were speaking German, because I could pretend I didn't understand. Following a joke that got a lot of laughs, someone asked Heinrich to repeat it to me in English. He used a kitty-cat word for the female genitals; it really embarrassed me. I told him I didn't want to hear his joke if he was going to talk that way. He apologized, and said that was the only name he knew for it. He asked me what the proper word for it was. I couldn't bring myself to say "vagina" to this man, so I wrote it down. In German, "I" is pronounced "EE," so when he read it, he said, "Oh, I know the word! You have named two states after it." I gasped! He said, "Yes, Vageena and West Vageena!"

Chapter 2
The *Chopin Express* and Poland

EuroCity # 25, the *Franz Liszt* begins in Dortmund, Germany and ends in Budapest, Hungary. I boarded in Mainz, planning to detrain at Wien West, Vienna's West Station. EuroCity (EC) trains are fast and comfortable. About 160 ECs cross Europe daily, linking countries and cities. Border checks are handled on the train and are cursory (in the West) except for an occasional spot-check.

I arranged to have lunch in the restaurant car during the time we would be passing the Rhine-Main-Danube Canal (also called the Main-Danube Canal). Charlemagne began the building of the canal in the year 793, but his plan was unsuccessful. In 1837 King Ludwig the First succeeded after nine years of building, and the canal was used for shipping until 1940. Horses towed the barges from the shore. The present route of the canal deviates slightly from the old *"Ludwigskanal."* Completed in 1992, the canal links the North Sea to the Black Sea by way of the Rhine, Main and Danube rivers. The Rhine alone connects the inland ports of Duisburg and Dusseldorf in Germany with those of Basel, Switzerland and Strasbourg, France. It seems odd that one usually thinks of Germany when speaking of the Rhine, yet it begins in Switzerland. Although the Danube conjures up visions of Vienna, Austria, it begins in Germany. I could see the canal from the window of the restaurant car.

Many medieval buildings in Regensburg can be seen from the train. I saw several old stone bridges; one of them dates from the twelfth century. Regensburg was first a Celtic settlement, and then a Roman fortress called *Castra Regina.* Today I felt more like a tourist than a traveler with a goal in mind, not only because Regensburg seemed too perfectly medieval to be real, but because I was so comfortably ensconced in the restaurant car while viewing perfection.

In Vienna's West Station I stood gazing at the departure schedule, with no idea where I was going, only that I needed a night train to sleep on. The *CHOPIN EXPRESS!* It would leave at 10:20 p.m. from Wien Sud, the South Station, to Warsaw. Never mind that I'd heard that the *Chopin* was not so clean, or so comfortable anymore; I never met a train I didn't like.

On the *Chopin* I sat in a first-class compartment with an Austrian couple as the only other occupants, which meant space for all to stretch out. When the conductor came by to check tickets

I showed my EurailPass, valid in all classes, but the couple had second-class tickets. The conductor had no choice but to send them packing. I now had the compartment to myself. The rumors were true; the *Chopin Express* wasn't so clean. "It's a dirty train, but somebody's gotta ride it!"

It wasn't long until we came to Hohenau, where the Austrians checked passports before the train went into the Czech Republic. I asked the Austrian official to stamp my passport. The Czechs stamped for me at Breclav (Lundenberg). I validated one day of my Czech FlexiPass for the short distance on to Poland. The conductor smiled when I told her about my Guinness Record, and signed my document. Passports were checked at Petrovice (still on the Czech side), and checked again at Zebrzydowice (Siebersdorf), on the Polish side. I managed a stamp at each place; I was beginning to feel like a world traveler already. My PolRail Pass had been validated at the information window in the station in Vienna. I used three different passes on this one journey from Germany to Poland.

Although it was difficult to sleep with all the border checks, it was exciting. I slept about three hours, but not in succession.

The *Chopin* pulled into Warsaw, Wschodnia (East) Station at 8:00 a.m.; I had five hours before my train to Wroclaw would depart. I was tired, but I stored everything in a locker and took off to see the city. Warsaw was almost completely demolished in World War II, but it was rebuilt as closely as possible from old photographs and paintings (many by Canaletto, the Italian artist). I strolled through the cobbled market square among the reconstructed medieval buildings and houses. It was crowded with locals and tourists. Wandering down to the sixteenth-century city walls tired me; I turned back toward the station.

There was much more to see in the area, but I was determined to go as far as Wroclaw (Breslau) before stopping for the night. Wroclaw is near Sniezka, a special place I have wanted to visit since I first read about it in 1975.

Sniezka (Schneekoppe, in German) is the highest peak in the Giant Mountains (the highest range in the Sudety Mountains), which form part of the border between Poland and the Czech Republic. The Giant Mountains are called the *Karkonosze* in Polish, and the *Riesen* in German. Sniezka has a sub-arctic climate. The temperature goes below zero for about 185 days of the year, and snow covers the peak for close to 200 days in the year. I wanted to see the fog and the clouds around the mountain, and the lightning flashing between the zenith and the clouds. Sniezka, at 5,257 feet above sea level, is in the lower troposphere, where all of Earth's weather begins.

I had hoped to visit Sniezka before they demolished the old

weather station, built in 1900. The wind had caused a permanent tilt in the old wooden one, and the plan was to replace it in 1977.

In 1976 I tried to reach Sniezka from a chair lift in the resort town of Pec Pod Snezkou, Czechoslovakia, near the Polish border. After taking several buses and trains from Prague to Pec Pod Snezkou, I hired a man to drive me in a jeep to the lift that would take me to the top of Sniezka (Snezka, in Czech). The names for Sniezka in all three languages mean "Snow Peak." The Czechs call the Giant Mountains *Krkonose*. Crossing into Poland at Sniezka was reserved for Czech and Polish citizens, but I didn't know it at the time. When I bought a ticket for the lift, one of the workers asked if I had a visa for Poland. I showed him my passport and Polish visa. He put my suitcase beside me on the double seat of the lift. After I was already seated, one of the young women called the police and they said I couldn't go. Just as the lift began to move, a man came out, seized my chair, and pulled me, along with my luggage down and off the lift. I stumbled as I touched ground, but I wasn't hurt.

A man carried my suitcase and walked with me to the nearest bus stop. It started to rain lightly. The path led us over little streams that we had to jump. When we got to the bus stop the man spoke to the driver about me, bowed, tipped his hat and vanished. I was driven up into a deep forest, at the end of the bus line. It was a different border crossing into Poland. When I asked to go through on foot, the border guards forbade me. The crossing was for vehicles only, and not for Americans, with or without wheels.

It was difficult finding my way to the border to get back into Germany; I didn't have a dual visa, so I had to exit Czechoslovakia at the same border I had entered. By then, it was dark, and I had to catch several buses and six trains. On the first train, the conductor spoke German. He told me when to change. I was the only passenger detraining at the little station in the woods. It was closed. There were no houses or people in the area; I was alone on the wooden platform, waiting for the next train. It was kind of scary; I imagined that wild animals were watching me. I had read about all the wild creatures that lived in the area, including a mythical giant called *"Rubezahl"* by the Germans, and *"Krakonos"* by the Czechs. His spirit is said to live there yet. Hence the name, the "Giant Mountains."

I saw the light on the train before I heard the whistle. Stepping out a little further on the platform to make sure I was seen, I was almost hit. The engineer passed the station before he could stop. I felt the hot, wet steam from the engine as it passed. I jumped onto the nearest carriage. There was dead silence as the other passengers stared at the American who appeared out of nowhere.

I found one young man who spoke a little English; I still have the note he wrote, listing the changes I would have to make to get back to the border.

On arrival in Prague, at one o'clock in the morning, I had changed trains four times, and needed two more trains to make it to the border.

At the border I sat on an old wooden bench in the waiting room. The man who was sweeping the floor came up behind me and whispered in German,

"They will come for you soon."

"Who? Why?" I was a little apprehensive.

"The border police will come to take you into the customs office. You are going to the West."

I said no one knew I was there, or where I was going. He said, "They know."

A middle-aged East German woman, wearing a gray suit and a black porkpie hat with a green feather came and sat next to me, and also warned me. She said a doctor had examined her internally, but that I, as a Westerner would not have to go through it.

Two solemn-faced soldiers appeared, and without a word motioned for me to come with them. I walked between them out of the station, across the cobbled square and through a huge double door. As they marched me down a long hall, I saw a doctor in a long white coat. I was afraid he was coming for me, but he went into one of the rooms. We entered a large office with a wooden floor. I stood with the soldiers until an officer called me to his desk. He asked how much money I had, and checked my passport and visa. One of the other soldiers pointed out that according to my visa I was leaving a day early. It must have been allowed; the same two soldiers escorted me back to the station. When I finally boarded a train for the West, I felt a great sense of relief.

Attempting to reach Sniezka again in 1978, I approached it from the Polish side, taking a Polish ship from Copenhagen to Swinoujscie (formerly the German port of Swinemunde). I traveled all around Poland with a PolRail pass, saving Sniezka until near the end of my trip, as a grande finale. However, it was not to be. I was prevented from reaching my goal, because I was from the West. Now, many years later, I have another chance.

I snapped out of my reverie. It was time to head back to the station for my train to Wroclaw, and plan my third try up to Sniezka. I had five more hours to travel before my overnight stop. It had been thirty-four hours since I left BK, and I was tired.

In Wroclaw I could see several large hotels across from the station. I took the nearest one, the Grand Hotel. I was charged the equivalent of only twelve American dollars, including breakfast.

The "Grand" must have been grand in its heyday, but now it is just old. A restaurant with a stage and a dance floor is just off the lobby. The stairs from the lobby to the upper floors are carpeted in a dark wine color. Each one has a brass rod bolted across it to hold the carpet down. One of the rods is loose near the top of the first landing, and I slipped on it. I have to remember to kick it back each time I use the stairway. The wood under the carpet of one of the stairs on the next landing is split or warped. When I stepped on it, it made a loud cracking sound. I thought someone had shot at me from the lobby. My room is small, but adequate. The bath and the WC are down the hall; the huge old claw-footed tub is equipped with a hand-held showerhead.

The hotel has a clinical feeling about it. A sign on one of the doors in my hallway says something about stomach X- rays. Some of the landings on my floor are roped off. In the hall, I noticed a metal cart like those used in hospitals for medicine. At first I thought it could be for room service meals, but the empty containers I saw on the cart were not for food. Visions of Frankenstein danced in my head.

No heat came from the narrow pipe where a radiator once had been, and I was awakened in the wee hours of the morning by the cold. I added my jacket to my covering and slept until dawn.

At the currency exchange desk in the lobby the exchange rate was 23,000 Zlotys for each dollar. Fifty dollars and I would be a millionaire. I converted one hundred dollars and received two million, two hundred and ninety-nine Zlotys. I felt rich.

A local train to the town of Jelenia Gora (Hirschberg) was ready to board. From there, I could get to Sniezka, *my* mountain peak. I was the only passenger in the first-class carriage. The springs were sticking out in some of the seats, but I loved the old train; I felt like I was an actor in a class-B spy movie.

The view quickly changed from the cityscape to a wooded, mountainous area. There were no stations. Passengers detrained alongside a gravel embankment. We stopped briefly at a small rural village. An older couple hadn't been able to get off the train before it pulled away. The man jumped off before it picked up speed, but the woman was not so lucky. When she jumped, she fell onto the gravel, and began rolling down the embankment toward the wheels of the train. I was standing in the corridor, near the door; I jumped off to help her. I landed on my feet, but fell from the momentum (the train was going a little faster by then). Somehow I managed to turn her to a vertical position, keeping her from rolling under the wheels. With my assistance, she stood up. By that time the engineer had stopped the train. The woman began shouting at the conductor, who had also jumped from the train (after it had stopped). She was still shouting at him when the train pulled away. Luckily, I wasn't seriously injured. My arm was bleeding, and there were a couple of pieces of gravel I had to dig out. The sleeve of my blouse was torn. Then I felt like I was a stuntwoman in a class-B spy movie.

Arrival in Jelenia Gora was without further incident. Buses were waiting outside the train station; I bought a ticket and boarded one of the buses through the rear door. "Sniezka?" I was speaking to anyone who could understand me. The bus was filled with teen-agers on their way home from school; I was answered with giggles. I walked up the aisle to the driver and repeated, "Sniezka?" He must have thought I was Russian. *"Da!"* Yes, the bus would take me to Sniezka. I asked, in English, if he would tell me when I should get off. When the kids heard me say that I was an American, they suddenly stopped chattering, and stared at me until they reached their stops. I was the only passenger who remained on the bus until the end of the line. The driver had forgotten me. He told me to walk three kilometers back down to the town of Karpacz, and ask for directions to the chair lift to Sniezka. That sounded easy, although I was a little sore and stiff from my jumping fall, or was it a falling jump?

Karpacz is a ski resort. The summer crowds had gone and the ski buffs had not yet arrived. I didn't see anyone on my walk back down the hill. Near the path to the lift I met a group of high school students who had been up to Sniezka with their teacher. One of them spoke to me in English. He said I would miss the last trip back down the mountain. I walked back to the bus stop with them. My sister had given me some Elvis Presley postage stamps to give as souvenirs on my journeys. The students loved them. I stayed, talking with them until the bus came, but I had decided to walk back to Jelenia Gora. Once more Sniezka had eluded me.

The road narrowed after a couple of kilometers; I had to walk in a ditch to keep from being hit by the autos that were speeding by, too close for comfort. I boarded the next bus that came along. Fortunately, it went to the train station in Jelenia Gora.

I wasn't sure where I would go next, but it would have to be a night train again. The schedule listed an overnight train to Szczecin, a port up near the Baltic Sea, leaving at 10:20 p.m.; it would do. There was plenty of time before the night train, so I took a short trip to gain a few more miles. The conductor wouldn't sign. Several stops later, I got off the train and found a worker that spoke German. We walked up the platform to the engine, and he asked the engineer to sign for me. The conductor overheard and shouted in Polish at the engineer, who repeated to the worker, who told me in German (I translate to English), "No one will sign anything for you. Get away from the train, off the platform and out of the station!" I answered angrily, in German, and the linguistic process was repeated. "I don't have to leave the platform or the station. I have a rail pass!" Defiantly, I stayed on the platform until the train and the conductor left. I caught the next train back to Jelenia Gora, thinking I would get the conductor on the return trip to sign. He didn't, but only because he didn't understand.

In Jelenia Gora I went into the snack bar in the station. A homeless old man with long white hair and a beard sat at a table by the window. His eyes were the shade we call "China" blue. He wasn't dressed too shabbily, but I knew he was homeless because I had seen him sleeping on a wooden bench in one of the waiting rooms earlier. We tourists sleep on the benches in stations sometimes, but I could tell he was not waiting for a train. He kept all of his belongings, including an old wool army overcoat and a dark-blue toboggan hat on the bench, as if to mark his place. After he peeled an apple, he walked over to the wastebasket, took out a paper cup, and filled it with water from the fountain. He was keeping his food warm in a paper bag on the radiator.

A young Gypsy mother sat on the other side of the room with a little girl about six years old and a boy about ten years old. Both of the children spent most of their time running around the station, to the gift shop, restaurant and snack bar. The mother just sat with her several skirts tucked under her, staring at the TV screen. Her only movements were to adjust the tan cotton scarf tied tightly over her head. Every now and then one of the kids would come back and show her an ice cream cone, a soda or a sandwich before they consumed it. I surmised that other passengers were buying them the food or that one of the vendors had given it to them.

I watched as the boy went over to the little girl and hit her on the arm. She ran to her mother, crying loudly, while the boy made faces and shook his fist at her behind the mother's back. I went to the gift shop and bought a little doll in a woven basket. When I gave it to the girl she stopped crying, smiled, and ran to show her mother. She was a carbon copy of her mother. The boy came to me, and I knew he was asking for a toy, but I shook my head. Through gestures that resembled a game of Charades, I made him understand that because he had hit the girl, I would not buy him a toy. He began to cry, but I didn't weaken.

I took a light-blue turtleneck sweater from my satchel and the scarf from my neck, and laid them on the coat that marked the old man's place on the bench in the waiting room, before going to the platform where the train to Szczecin was waiting.

Initially I was alone in a compartment, but was soon joined by a Polish woman about forty-five years old. She spoke no English, but knew a few words of German, so we almost had a conversation. The conductor had already checked my pass and signed my document before the woman had boarded. When he passed by the compartment the woman hid behind the curtain, a sure sign that she had a second-class ticket, and had come to first class because second class is often crowded, making it difficult to find enough room to stretch out to sleep.

Even in the early morning darkness the port of Szczecin (Stettin) was beautiful. A cold, damp wind blew steadily against me as I walked along the platform to the station. It was crowded with commuters.

I was beginning to feel the effects of yesterday's mishap; I was hurt after all. I had injured my rib cage, back, and shoulder. Although I felt I should check into a hospital, or at least a hotel, I boarded Express train # 8502, with some distress. The train steps were so high I had to haul myself up, not easy with my sore back. I was on my way to Gdynia, a resort on the Baltic.

When the mini-cart came by I showed the vendor a note I had written (from a phrase book) in Polish. *"Mam jarzyny damska. Nie mieso, nie ryby, nie jajka."* All the sandwiches on the cart were made with meat, but the young man went to the kitchen and fixed me a delicious sandwich on a soft roll with cheese, tomatoes, cucumbers, green peppers and pickles. I couldn't have asked for more. Not just because I didn't know any more Polish, but it was just what I needed. The veggie note I had written was almost childlike in its structure, but I couldn't find all the right words or phrases in my book. There wasn't even a word in it for vegetarian. I thought my note translated as, "I am vegetable lady. No meat, no fish, no eggs." But, checking further, I discovered a mistake. *Mam* means, "I have not." *Jestem* is "I am."

Since the waiter with the cart understood, I decided to write a note for the conductors about my record and the need for a signature. After considerable searching, I came up with *"Damska Ameryki panni. Guinness Ksiazke do pociag jedziemy. Proze podpisiac. Proze dziekuje bardzo."* All of the words hadn't come from a book; I had seen some of them on signs and hoped I had used them right. As near as I could tell, it translated more or less as, "Lady American person. Guinness Book for train kilometers. Please signature. Thank you very much." I couldn't wait to try it on the next conductor. My chance came. The conductor came to check my pass and I handed her the note and my document. Of course she laughed, but she signed.

There was a red rug on the floor of my compartment; it skidded every time I stepped on it. The brown-plaid seat backs were covered with white antimacassars. I just call them scarves at home, but I like using the old word that always seems to be used when referring to a scarf on an antique chair, or on a train seat. The word antimacassar has a certain fascination about it, despite

21

its mundane meaning. I looked it up in the dictionary; it means "anti-oil." Macassar is a type of oil, named for the city of Macassar (formerly called Ujung Pandang), on the Indonesian Island of Sulawesi (Celebes), where the oil was manufactured and imported for use in hair creams and hair oils. Thus, the antimacassar protects the upholstered seats from the oils of passengers' hair. The pleated curtains on my window were embossed with "PKP," the initials of the Polish State Railways *(Polskie Koleje Panstwowe)*, pictures of the station in Szczecin, and the words *"Szczecin Glowny"* (main station in Szczecin).

By the time we reached Gdynia I ached too much to go sightseeing. I sat in the station until time for my next train, the 12:00 p.m. train to Bydgoszcz (Bromberg).

In less than four hours I was in Warsaw, with about two hours to wait for an overnighter to Berlin. I put my gear in a locker; I was unable to wear my backpack. The pain in my back had worsened, and I was tired from all the trains and the waiting.

The train left from the lower level. I could hardly make it down the escalator. A young man was watching me candidly, so I walked to the other end of the platform to wait.

I found an empty compartment and tried to make myself comfortable. Minutes later the young man came in. He was Polish, but he spoke to me in German, asking if there was a seat free. When I answered in German, he knew it wasn't my native tongue. His next guess was right.

"You are an American! I knew you were not Polish. Where are you going?"

"Germany."

"How long have you been traveling?"

"A long time. Where are you going?"

"Berlin. I have an old wife there and a young wife in Poland."

He waited for my reaction. I laughed.

"You don't believe me! I don't lie! I am going to Berlin now, to see the old one. She makes better love than the young one!"

I was spared a reply; the conductor came in to check tickets. He signed my document and wished me well. When he left the compartment I quickly folded up the arms of the seats on one side of the compartment and propped my feet up, pretending to look out the window. The young man prepared the seats on the other side for sleep, turned out the light, and said goodnight. Then he sat up suddenly and asked me to help him get across the border. He had no "papers" for Germany. I said I had only my own passport and couldn't help him. He then asked me to get off the train one stop before the border and go across with him on foot. If we were stopped, I should tell the patrol that he was my husband. I was astounded; he already had two wives! He didn't take my refusal lightly. "Madam, I think you must be a Jew!"

"No, my ancestors came from England, Wales and Scotland."

"Jews can be from any country, even Scotland!"

Although I felt a little threatened, I couldn't resist, "Are you a Jew, sir?"

"*Hasslich nicht!* (Hatefully not!) I am Polish!"

"Jews can be from any country, even Poland."

At that, he began squealing like a pig, slamming his pillow against the wall. Then he threw it on the floor. I had the last word, but I knew when to quit; I left my satchel and backpack on the overhead rack, taking only my document notebook and went to another compartment.

When the train stopped at Rzepin, still on the Polish side of the border, I saw the young man detrain and walk over to a small stone building. As the train pulled away I could see him in the shadows, hiding behind the building, his blond hair shining in the moonlight. Once I was certain he did not get back on the train, I went back to the compartment where my luggage was. I was surprised to find a Polish person so full of hate. Poland suffered so much in World War II because of Hitler's hatred for its people.

I opened my sliding door and moved to the seat closest to it; I could hear the border guards coming down the corridor. The first to enter was a German shepherd dog. He immediately stuck his nose in my jacket pocket. I was wearing the jacket. He was trained to sniff out drugs. A border guard came in right behind the dog. We stopped for border checks at Kunowice (Kunersdorf), still on the Polish side and the officials stamped my passport, but when we crossed over to Frankfurt an der Oder, in the former East Germany, stamps weren't given. The "an der Oder" (on the Oder) is used because the town is on the Oder (Odra) River, and to distinguish it from Frankfurt am Main (on the Main River), a city on the Main River, in Western Germany. It doesn't mean that the river is the main one. The name of the river is *"Main,"* pronounced "mine." On maps or schedules the names may be written as Frankfurt (Oder) and Frankfurt (Main).

After my arrival in Berlin I boarded an InterRegio to Erfurt. In the last five nights I slept in a bed only once. I was tired and I ached from taking showers in the damp stations. Two more trains and I would be back at base to sleep in a bed again.

I had planned to wake early and do my laundry, but I overslept. When I woke, Rosi had coffee ready for me, and she had done my laundry. Our friend, Erich Heitbrock drove us to a neighboring town to shop. We came out of the shopping center into a storm. Back at the apartment, I ran to the balcony to get my clothes from the line. My custom-made T-shirt was missing; no doubt it had blown off the line. Somewhere in BK someone is wearing a T-shirt that reads, "Breaking the World Record on Train Travel."

Two days of rest, and I was ready to tackle Poland again. I was tempted to wait one more day, because today is *Mantelsonntag* (Coat Sunday), a traditional holiday in BK. More than one hundred years ago, when BK was given Market Rights, the farmers from the neighboring towns came once a year to buy their winter coats. Since the farmers worked six days a week, the market was held on Sunday. They still celebrate it every year (except during World War II and for a few years after). *Mantelsonntag* is celebrated on the last Sunday in October or the first Sunday in November; whichever is closer to the end of October. It's just like a fair, with rides for the children and lots of food and merchandise in the wagons and booths set up in the pedestrian zone and the market squares. Most of the stores are open too. On ordinary Sundays the shops and markets are closed. Live bands render folk music under tents and canopies that serve beer, wine and food. Naturally, there is a cotton candy *(Sussewatte)* machine twisting out the irresistible fluff in pink and white.

I walked to the station in a gentle rain, rolling a huge brown suitcase called "World Traveler." It was filled with clothing for the homeless people I had seen in the train station in Wroclaw, Poland. We gave the suitcase a name because it had become a legend. It originally belonged to my sister, but it was passed around within the family, and used for so many trips to so many places that we named it World Traveler. I caught an early train to Mainz and another to Frankfurt to board InterCity # 653, the *Georg Philipp Telemann*. It would take me to Dresden, with credit for only a portion of the way, but it was a quick route into Poland, where I would accumulate more mileage, and perhaps make it to Sniezka.

My train from Mainz was late; I thought I had missed my InterCity, and must wait two hours for another train. I glanced over to Platform 4. A sign said the InterCity was delayed. I ran down the stairs, through the tunnel, and up another flight of stairs to the platform. I had heard the train pull in when I was in the tunnel. The conductor saw me running, and waited until I hoisted my luggage aboard, then gave the signal for the train to leave. He didn't expect me to be so slow. The doors slammed shut on my shoulders. I twisted myself free, but my backpack was holding the doors slightly open as the train pulled slowly out of the station. I finally forced my backpack out of the doors, almost falling in the process. Later, I was in almost as much pain as I had been after I jumped from the Polish train.

There was only one other passenger in my first-class parlor carriage, the last carriage on the end of the train. I could see clearly out the wide rear window.

Briefly, I watched the rain from my window before beginning my bookwork. It was hard to keep my mind on my work; the passing towns were so interesting. In Bad Hersfeld, the old *"Kurhaus"* is built on top of a hill. *Kur* means cure, and *Kurhaus* is a hotel with a bathhouse, or medical treatments, or a combination of both. Or, it can be a building without the hotel, just the treatments. In German-speaking countries, any town with the prefix or suffix *"Bad"* or *"Baden"* is a spa town. *Bad* means bath, and *Baden* means bathe.

I was in Dresden by 3:30 p.m. On my platform, seven little kids were doing the European version of the "Achy Breaky" Western dance. They mixed it with disco and other fast dances from the sixties, with a few modern moves thrown in. I had seen the same version performed at the *Liedertafel* in BK.

Train # 457 was a Direct Express to Gorlitz (Zgorzelec) on the German/Polish border, but there was a *"Kurswagen"* (through carriage) to Wroclaw, which I settled into.

At the border the officials on the German side checked, but didn't stamp my passport. The Polish officials stamped "Zgorzelec," for me. Although both are called Gorlitz (with different spelling), the towns are almost two kilometers apart. The Polish town of Gorlitz (Zgorzelec) was the eastern part of the German city until 1945, when the Oder-Neisse line was designated as a provisional border between postwar Germany and Poland. The line was named for the rivers that form the border. The suburb of Gorlitz-Moys that had been part of prewar Germany is now called Ujazd, and is south of the Polish Zgorzelec.

It was slightly after ten o'clock at night when I arrived in Wroclaw. Fortunately, the Grand Hotel was still open. They gave me room # 235 again. I paid for two nights; I planned to try again to reach Sniezka, and needed a base.

I went back to Jelenia Gora. Perhaps I will fulfill my dream of reaching the summit of Sniezka. Today is a holiday in Europe, All Saint's Day. There was a brisk business done in flowers and wreaths, both fresh and plastic. Vendors were sitting by the roadsides and at the gates of the cemeteries we passed.

A beautiful young woman sat across from me in my second-class compartment. Dark brown hair framed a round, fair face. Her large brown eyes were heavily made-up with blue eyeshadow. She was wearing a tan suit with a short skirt, and clutching a small bouquet of pastel flowers. I asked her if she spoke English, and she answered in German. She was on her way to take the flowers to her grandmother, and I wondered if her grandmother was alive or if she was going to her grandmother's grave to give her the flowers. I gave the young woman a sample vial of Elizabeth Taylor's "Passion" perfume fastened in a folder that was printed with an autographed picture of Elizabeth. Although some perfumes manufactured in the West are available now in the Eastern European countries, one seldom sees the samples. She stared at the picture and the autograph, smiled and said "Leestabet!"

There was a different bus outside the station in Jelenia Gora this time. I asked my standard question, "Sniezka?" The driver answered in German, *"Ja, Ja."* I was optimistic when I asked if he would show me where to exit the bus, and the answer was affirmative. But he forgot, and took me to the end of the line, which was much farther up the steep winding road than I had gone before. He told me he was "closing" and I'd have to walk back down to the town of Karpacz. Not again! "How far?" I asked. "Three kilometers." (He suddenly could speak English.) I had mistakenly thought the bus went all the way to the top.

I came to a spot on the road where I had a clear view of Sniezka and the weather station. It was so exciting. There it was, so near, and yet so far away. The weather station looked like a space ship, with two others sitting on top of it. There was a road leading to the top, but I couldn't judge how long it would take to walk up to the peak. I didn't see any vehicles using the road, so I continued on my way back to Karpacz. From the road I saw a wooden church that looked very old, and definitely not Polish. I recognized it as the thirteenth-century church brought from Norway by the King of Prussia in the early 1800s. I had read about it, and wanted to see it someday. How odd that I should find it purely by chance.

The air was much colder than the last time I was here, and the wind had become a monster. It was much more than three kilometers. Without luggage it would be easy, so I thought, but the 'monster' huffed and puffed, and blew my earmuffs off.

I saw no one for several kilometers; then I came to a little gift shop. I bought some postcards and a child-size walking stick for my granddaughter. In Europe people use them when hiking in the woods and mountains. They decorate them with tiny metal plates imprinted with pictures and the names of places they have been. The plates come with tiny nails to fasten them to the walking stick. The pictures are either painted in bright colors on silver or gold colored metal, or etched in copper or pewter. I chose a copper one that reads "Karpacz."

The wind diminished as I descended, making my way easier. As I neared Karpacz, I saw several people get off the bus at the stop below the gift shop. One of them was a stocky, red-faced man in a brown suit, and a brown Homburg hat; he carried a brown overcoat across one arm. He mistook me for a German and asked me where I was from. When I answered in German, saying I was from America, his face actually lit up. *"Amerika! Amerika! Sie ist vom Amerika!"* Everyone who had gotten off the bus spoke to me, either in Polish or German. For a moment, I thought they were going to ask me for my autograph.

When all the others had gone, the stocky man lingered. He told me he had fought the Germans in World War II and he had met many American soldiers, but he had never seen an American in these mountains. Then he asked me to walk with him to a café and have a beer or a coffee. I think he wanted to show off his American "friend." I should have gone with him; he seemed so happy to talk with me, but I had a goal. " *Ich muss zum Sniezka gehen.*"

When I got almost down to the turn for the chair lift, a Doberman was running ahead of his master. The dog snarled ferociously. He leaped on me, and began gnawing at my sleeve. I yelled and tried to pull away, but he held on. The dog was big and heavy; he almost knocked me down. Although the thick quilted fabric of my coat saved me from his bite, my sleeve was wet with his saliva. The owner of the dog finally spoke to him and he let go. I wanted to ask why it had taken so long for him to control the dog, but I had to hurry on. I should have had that drink.

As I was getting close to the chair lift, two women stopped me. One of them asked, in German, if I was going up to Sniezka. She warned me that the weather on the mountain was changing quickly to a snowstorm and advised me not to go. I thought of taking a chance; I was so close. But when I pictured myself as an icicle, trapped on a stalled chair lift, thousands of feet high in the frozen air, I gave up. Perhaps I was never meant to reach my mountain.

Back in Wroclaw at the Grand Hotel, I washed out a couple of items and hung them on the narrow pipe that passed for a heater, hoping it would be turned on later.

I walked across to the station to give the clothing to the homeless I had seen there. Many homeless people spend most of their time in train stations. For some, the station is their only source of warmth and rest. A little Gypsy girl was playing a flute in the main hall. She wasn't trying to collect money; she was just walking along playing. Suddenly, about six little Gypsy kids started following her, single file. I couldn't get my camera out fast enough; I wanted to take a picture, and caption it "The Pied Piper of Wroclaw."

In the Italian café in the station, I ordered a small cheese pizza, in Polish. *"Mala pizza, pomydory, ser"* (small pizza, tomatoes, cheese). I was proud of myself. *"Kava"* is coffee, so I managed a meal. As I sat at a round table facing the large picture window, the radio was playing "What a Wonderful World." A man who sounded like a hillbilly with a Polish accent was whining the English lyrics. I could see nine homeless people sitting on a bench outside the window. They were watching me eat. Their world was not so wonderful. I ordered ten hamburgers to go, one for everyone on the "homeless bench," with one extra, just in case. As I walked away, I saw another homeless woman, sleeping on her back under a table, so I put hamburger # 10 on her chest and returned to the hotel, wondering if any of the homeless ones were vegetarians.

The mystery of the "clinical feeling" about the hotel was solved. I approached the hotel from a different direction and saw a sign on one of the outside walls that said something about it being a gynecology clinic. My feeling was correct. But was it still a clinic? Perhaps it's better if I don't know.

There was a bit of warmth coming from the heating pipe when I returned to my room, enough to dry my clothes. I slept soundly all night.

Breakfast was upstairs in the bar this morning. There must be fewer guests or the restaurant would have been used. I was the only guest so far, and perhaps there were no other guests; I didn't hear a sound all night. If I had thought I was alone in the spooky hotel, I wouldn't have slept so soundly. I might not have slept at all.

Each table was covered with a cloth of lime-green linen and set with a small white cream pitcher of white and reddish-rose flowers. The chairs and booths were upholstered in brown velour. Checkout was easy; my World Traveler suitcase was empty.

Train # 73102, the *Slazak* travels to Krakow via Katowice. The conductor gave me her signature and a smile. I had added more words in Polish to my document pages. Time is *"godzina"* and *"pociag numer"* is train number. She filled those blanks in too. I even wrote the day and the month in Polish. Tuesday is *"Wtorek"* and November is *"Listopad."* I think she was impressed. I know I was. A man and a teen-aged boy sat across from me, and a woman sat beside me. When the man and the boy prepared to leave, I gave the boy one of the Stars and Stripes pens I had brought from home. He thanked me in English, but I think that was the only phrase he knew. The woman used German, Polish and a few gestures to tell me that the boy would be happy to show his friends the pen from America. A few minutes later the woman reached into her purse and handed me a pen, and I gave her one from America. When she was leaving the train, she said good-bye in German, and I tried to say it in Polish, but it sounded more like Russian.

When the train stopped in Katowice several winos got on the train to search for bottles of wine or beer left by detraining passengers. Some of the glass bottles can be recycled; the winos can earn a little cash.

Katowice is a large industrial city, the center of the Silesian coal district. At one time, Silesia was divided between Czechoslovakia, Poland, and Germany, but not in equal portions. The Germans had the biggest slice, most of which was given to Poland in 1945 at the signing of the Potsdam agreement.

In Krakow I opted to take the first train that would travel a new route for me. A train was leaving for Przemysl, on the Poland/Belarus border in one hour. It was only a four-hour ride; I could return to Krakow for the night if I couldn't get a transit visa through a part of Belarus, or catch a train in another direction in Poland right away. The young conductor understood my note and sat down to sign, but then had a change of heart. He threw his arms up in the air, sneered at me and said, *"Nie!"* I saw another conductor walking down the hall. He looked at me, and shook his head *"nie"* before I could show him my note. In the restaurant car *"BAR· WARS,"* I asked the waiter to sign. He didn't sign, but stamped my document with his employee number. It was a *BAR WARS* stamp, but it would do. *WARS* is short for *"Przedsiebiorsewa Wagonow Spialnych i Restauracyjnych."* I'm glad they shortened it. Another conductor came into the restaurant while I was eating, and the waiter asked him to sign for me. He obliged.

I was unable to cross into Belarus (also called Belaruse, Belorussia, and Byelorussia) to take a new route right away, so I caught a second-class train back to Krakow. Among my seatmates was a young blonde-haired woman who spoke fluent English. It had been a long time since I had an opportunity to have a conversation in my own language. She lives in Przemysl, and was returning to the university in Krakow following a holiday at home. As the train pulled away from the station she pressed her forehead to the window and waved good-bye to her mother as we passed her house. This was a ritual with them. Her slim face and straight, chin-length hair gave her a girlish appearance. She kept pushing her hair away from her face. We talked politics and tried to come up with solutions for the world's problems. She has high hopes for Poland's future, now that it is free. Having had so little freedom, for so long, the Polish people treasure what we have taken for granted.

I hoped to find a connection somewhere along the line where I could change to an overnight train going over a different route. The young woman volunteered to check the possibilities with the conductor. When she returned, she was angry. The conductor had said, "You ask too many questions. Don't bother me now." She had answered, "It is your job to help the passengers." But he told her it would take away from his personal time. She did find out I was out of luck, though. There would be no connections for me; it was back to Krakow.

When we arrived in Krakow, I went over a small bridge to the Hotel Europejski, checked in, and hurried to find something to eat. It was close to eleven o'clock at night; the hotel restaurant had closed. Back near the station I found a small café and ordered a pizza. The waiter and the cook wanted to close for the night, so I took my coffee back to the hotel. Instead of crossing the bridge again I went through the underpass. It was a mistake; three young men edged close to me in a threatening manner. A group of people came through just at the right time. I hurried out and up to the street without looking back. My hotel was in view. I was safe, but I had spilled most of the coffee.

I love the Hotel Europejski. The curtains on the tall window at the beginning of the first landing are of white lace with a bouffant valance, and the drapes are deep red velvet; the kind you might see in a castle. Oval mirrors framed in gold rococo decorate the walls.

My room only cost fourteen dollars, without breakfast. It's furnished with a single bed, dresser, wooden-slatted suitcase bench, and a sink with one of the rococo mirrors above it. The walls are papered with an old-fashioned print of stripes and flowers in soft gold, gray and peach.

The total price for my breakfast in the hotel restaurant was 49,000 Zlotys, a little over two dollars. I had heard there would soon be a change in the Polish currency. They would drop some zeros, but the old money (which I had) would still be valid. A group of Swedish teachers sat at a large table across from me. Some of them spoke English, so we exchanged travel stories. They were going by taxi (it would take at least six taxis to transport the group) to Oswiecim, the former Nazi concentration camp of *Auschwitz*. One of the taxi drivers approached me and asked if he could drive me there. I know that someday I must go. But for now, I had seen so much sadness; I couldn't handle a visit to a concentration camp.

Tomorrow is the last day on my Eurail FlexiPass; I'll barely have time to get into Switzerland with it to begin my Swiss Pass. If I start back to base immediately, traveling all day and all night, I can make it. I have plenty of time left on my PolRail Pass.

I took the first train heading west. With a couple of changes of trains I'll arrive at my base by morning. I sat in a compartment alone. The curtains were wine color with "PKP" embroidered on them, and the seats were orange-and-gray tattersall. My carriage was old, with wood veneer on the walls and the ceiling. It squeaked constantly. I stood in the corridor for a few minutes talking with a young Polish woman who spoke English.

Later in the evening I was writing in my journal when the train stopped and a lot of people detrained. When the two conductors left the platform, I figured it was just time for a crew change, but then, a few minutes later, the young woman with whom I had been conversing came aboard. She said, "Hurry, you must leave. The train is not going!" She helped me gather my things and transfer them to another train several tracks over. The carriages were not yet hooked to an engine, but I boarded anyway. I wasn't sure if something had gone wrong with the other train, or if I had misread the schedule back at the station. Luckily, she remembered me, or I might have sat on the siding alone all night on the other train, in the middle of nowhere (I always wondered where that was).

A few minutes later the train took off abruptly. I was on my way again. The lights on the front of the train were shining brightly on both sides of the track, but there was nothing to see except deep ditches, and the dark, blurred shapes of the trees in the woods above them. My light wasn't working properly; it winked off and on constantly. I couldn't turn it off; it was the light on the ceiling that remains on, without a switch. It was giving me a headache. Suddenly, there was something to see. Cars and trucks were lined up for more than a mile, waiting to cross the Polish/German border. For some it would take hours. Train travelers cross easier and faster. Unless there is a problem, trains are never delayed more than thirty minutes. I loosened my shoestrings. My ankles were swollen from all the train riding, but I didn't want to take my shoes off, because we were close to the border. I wanted to be ready if I had to leave my seat or the train. Before we stopped at the border the customs officials walked along the corridors, looking into each compartment, to spot any suspicious-looking characters that might warrant closer checks. At the border, one of the guards asked me to move from my window seat. There is a small compartment on the floor, under a seat, on some of the older trains that holds some kind of an electrical connection and they sometimes lift the cover of it to check for contraband. The train sat at the border for thirty minutes while workers checked under all of the carriages. They stood on ladders in the halls and compartments and unscrewed the light bulbs to check. All the carriages were searched thoroughly, as the borders between Poland and Germany are prime routes for smugglers. The guard dog didn't come into my compartment, but I had hung my coat up, and sat by the window instead of the door, just in case.

Chapter 3
The *Glacier Express* and Switzerland

I had five hours in BK to shower, wash my hair, repack and call home. It was time to get into Switzerland on my Eurail FlexiPass before it expires. Tomorrow I'll begin my Swiss Pass.

In Mainz I boarded an InterCity to Basel. As soon as I had settled into the compartment, a tall dark-haired man came in, put his briefcase up on the luggage rack and went out again.

I was checking my mileage documents after the conductor had signed for me when the man came back into the compartment. He sat across from me, watching as I slipped my documents into a folder.

"Are you traveling all the way to Basel?"

Not mentioning that I was going on to Lucerne from Basel, I said, "Yes, I am going to Basel."

"Are those the documents?"

"Yes, do you want to see them?" I assumed the conductor had told him about my travels after he left the compartment.

"No, I just wanted to know."

He didn't say anything for a few minutes, then he said, "Do you have anything for my side?"

I figured his side was hurting and he needed a pain pill or something, so I said I had only aspirin.

"Do you have anything for my side, my government? We will pay you well."

He must have mistaken me for someone else. *His* government? I thought he was Swiss. We were supposed to be on the same side. Hesitant to explain my "documents" to him, I went along with it, whatever it was. I said, "Not at this time, but soon." We were coming into Heidelberg. I started to gather my things; I wanted to get off the train, because I was afraid of him. He was either crazy or in a business I didn't want to know about. But then, he said good-bye and stepped out into the corridor to wait for the train to stop. He got off the train and never looked back. What a relief! I was glad I wasn't traveling overnight, in case someone on the train had a "mission," and was wondering what happened to their "contact." Later I wondered why the man had mistaken me for someone else; the conversation we had couldn't have caused the confusion. Do I resemble the other person? I didn't feel completely safe, after all. I tried to convince myself it was a coincidence.

From Basel, one more train would take me to a night's rest. I wanted to spend the night in Lucerne, everybody's favorite tourist town. The lake and the river are just outside the train station. Just across the street you'll find the old wooden covered bridge, the famous *Kappellbrucke* (Chapel Bridge), with a hundred paintings on the ceiling, depicting scenes of local Saints and some of the history of Lucerne. The water tower was attached as a stronghold. The other covered bridge, the *Spreuerbruck* (Mill Bridge) is known for its ceiling paintings, the *Totentanz* (*Dance of Death*). The bridges were built in the 1300s, but the paintings were done in the late 1700s.

The hotel *Zum Weissen Kreuz* (To the White Cross) is just over the *Seebrucke* (Lake Bridge). I checked in and immediately went back out to jog over Lake Bridge. There are walkways on both sides of the black lacy wrought-iron rails. Lake Bridge spans the Reuss River at the point where it joins the *Vierwaldstattersee* (Lake of the Four Forest Cantons), better known to us as Lake Lucerne. The many neon lights cast shimmering streaks of blue, green, yellow and pink across the lake. Churches on shore and the small castle hotel on the hill were illuminated, adding a golden glow to the sky. I felt like I was jogging in a dream.

After breakfast I had a few hours to spend before my train to Interlaken. I walked across the covered Chapel Bridge that was damaged by fire in 1992. The bridge and the paintings have been restored. Assuming it was too late in the season to take the steepest cogwheel railway in the world, the Pilatusbahn, up to Mount Pilatus, I hurried to catch a bus to Kriens, where I could take a cable car up instead. There is a legend claiming that Mount Pilatus was named for Pontius Pilate, whose spirit was banished to the top of the mountain.

Snow covered the peaks, and it was cold at the top. The views from the lookout point were magnificent. It looked as if the Alps were pressed against the sky. I was sorry when it was time for me to head back down to Lucerne to catch the train to Interlaken, my next overnight stop.

In Interlaken I checked into an inexpensive hotel, near the station. From the main street I can see the snowcapped peaks of the Eiger, the Monch and the Jungfrau.

The solar-powered revolving restaurant made famous by the James Bond film, *On Her Majesty's Secret Service,* perches high above the town, on the Schilthorn Peak.

There were no other guests at breakfast. At first I thought it was because I came down so early, but I was not just the only guest in the hotel; I was the only person in the building last night. Tourist season is over, and ski season is a month away. The owners don't live in the hotel; they left after they closed the restaurant on the ground floor.

Imagine riding a train like the *Panoramic Express*, and being able to claim mileage for it. The scenery was great from the beginning. Chalets were layered on the hillsides where cows with bells around their necks grazed. The alpine summits were trimmed with snow. From the window of the train I was seeing what Swiss postcards are made of.

My glass-domed carriage was decorated in the Belle Époque style. The train swayed so steadily that I would have been lulled to sleep if the scenery hadn't been so extraordinary.

While the train sat on a siding, waiting for our counterpart traveling in the opposite direction to pass, we were tipped slightly sideways. I could see the engine and the other carriages from the bar car. Back in motion again, the curves changed directions; I saw the end of the train. Lakes, gorges, and picture-perfect villages appeared by my window in quick succession.

One of the crew signed my document and volunteered to take it to a carriage where several members of the crew were gathered. Thanks to her, I ended up with four signatures.

We passed through an area of high stone walls with tiny waterfalls trickling down. Moss was growing out of the cracks in the stones. From the other side of the train I watched creeks running through gorges. Trees ablaze with autumn foliage grew amidst majestic evergreens. I saw a few small villages, but only one person, an old man waving at the train. Purple flowers were climbing up the hill toward him, contrasting with the snow-topped mountains in the background.

I detrained in Montreux on Lake Geneva *(Genfersee)*. *Chateau De Chillon* (Chillon Castle) rises up from the edge of the lake, on a huge jagged rock. One can see it from the train windows. I went to Basle over a new route. The first conductor I asked to sign said, "No problem," but when I asked a second conductor, he declined. He was my first refusal in Switzerland. He was rude about it too, *"Mais, Non!"* But, no!

Going back to Interlaken by another route gave me a few extra miles, but the train only took me as far as Giswil, due to track work: I took a bus to Meiringen. We traveled on mountain roads with hairpin curves. I missed a few rail miles, but I saw some great scenery (when I could bear to look). Night descends early in the mountains in late autumn; the darkness made the ride even more alarming. We passed other buses around sharp curves and along unfenced sections of the road. The deep gorges appeared to be bottomless.

When we made it safely to Meiringen I took a train to Interlaken, returning to my hotel for the night. No one had checked in; I was alone in the building again.

I left my satchel in the baggage department at the station; I'll pick it up in a few days. My backpack is all I need. Today I rode the *Glacier Express*. As we ascended towards Andermatt I had a fleeting glimpse of the Rhone Glacier, barely tinged with palest green, before the train slipped into the Furka Tunnel. According to my brochure, it is the world's longest narrow-gauge tunnel.

By the time we got to Disentis the train had climbed to almost 6,000 feet. We moved through the Rhine Gorge where massive white cliffs had formed as the river forced its way through. There is a stretch on the Rhine in Germany that is also known as the "Rhine Gorge." The train followed the river for a long time. Numerous castles and fortresses dot the hills. It was only six o'clock in the evening when I arrived in Saint Moritz, but I stopped for the night.

Planning a quick getaway, I went down to breakfast early, but I had to wait for the manager to arrive before I could pay my bill. By the time the office opened I had missed my train. I was no longer in a hurry; I walked back to the station and caught the 11:00 a.m. train to Landquart, transferring three times before arriving in Schaffhausen, on the Swiss/German border.

I checked into a hotel near the train station, in the pedestrian zone. The young barmaid, who was also the hotel receptionist, asked me to pay in advance, as she would lock up and go home at midnight. I knew what that meant; I would end up as the only guest in the hotel that stayed the entire night. All the stores would close; the squares and alleyways of the pedestrian zone would be deserted. I would be alone in the hotel and in the neighborhood. There would be no breakfast without an employee on the premises. But, time to stop pampering myself. I paid for my room and started up the steep concrete stairs to the third floor. I paused, asking in German, "What about the key to the outside door? Where shall I leave it after I unlock the door in the morning?" The receptionist pointed to a shelf behind a desk.

My room was on the third floor; the WC and the shower were down the hall. It was kind of spooky up there; I hoped I wouldn't have to make a trip to the WC in the middle of the night. I hurried to take a shower before everyone left and I would be the sole occupant. The hotel was still under construction; it smelled of fresh mortar. It was more like an office building than a hotel.

I heard voices in the hall just after midnight. I peeked out, and saw a man and a woman enter the room next to mine. I was relieved; I wasn't the only guest. An hour later, I heard laughter and talking. They went downstairs and out the door. I was alone again and hoping they had locked the outside door.

Waking before daylight, I grabbed my gear and started down the steps. The lights in the hall were not working, and it was pitch-black. My tiny flashlight tried, but didn't help much. It didn't help at all after I dropped it, and it bounced down the stairs. When I got down to the second landing of the second floor I felt something slide up the back of my neck. I just knew it was an arm. Probably hooked to a mugger. Or worse! I stood so still I could hear the silence. The hair on the back of my neck stood up against the "arm." In the darkness, I couldn't see to run down the steep steps. When I couldn't stand the suspense any longer I slowly reached back. My automatic umbrella had eased up from my backpack, and was against my neck. There was no mugger; I was still alone in the building. I was ashamed of myself, but took no chances; I hurried down and outside to the pedestrian zone. I didn't replace the key, either; I unlocked the door and threw the key toward the desk. It was still dark as I entered the pedestrian zone, but delivery trucks and storekeepers were already starting their day. I bought a fresh-baked hot roll from the baker to eat on my way back to the station.

I was on a train by 6:45 a.m., traveling over Winterthur back to Interlaken to secure a room for the night, before racking up a few more miles.

In Interlaken I checked into another hotel near the train station, stowed my pack and caught the next train to Bern. I spent the day riding one train after the other, to Palezieux, Kerzers, and Avenches, returning over a different route for extra mileage, barely making the last connections back to Interlaken.

The owners of the hotel had gone home. I had the feeling that I was the only guest here, too. The hall windows on my floor were wide open and a cold wind was blowing the curtains into the hall. I would have shut the windows but I wasn't sure if I would be keeping an undesirable out, or keeping one in. There is a WC on my floor, but the shower is one floor down. I would wait until morning to shower; I wanted to hurry to my room and lock the door behind me, because the owners leave the door leading to the alley unlocked all night rather than give each guest an outside door key. My room was a dorm with eight cots. Why hadn't they given me a single room? I had to pass through a separate little room to get to mine, giving me one more reason to imagine things. It would be OK if I wasn't alone in the building, the windows weren't open, and the back door wasn't unlocked. Anyway, the price is right.

I booked the room for another night, leaving everything except my documents, and hurried to begin my rail day. Five trains later I was in Lausanne, approaching it from a new route that was absolutely breathtaking. At Villeneuve I could see Lake Geneva below. Homes were built high on the hills. At Saint Saffron I saw old stone walls and a castle.

From Montreux, four more trains and I was back in Interlaken for another lonely night. I was right; I was the only guest. Where were all the tourists I sometimes try to avoid?

At three o'clock in the morning I was awakened by a loud noise from the next room. Something struck the wall with a force that caused the porcelain soap dish to spring off the wall in my room, and smash into the sink. I knew a burglar wouldn't make so much noise; it must be one of the tourists I had wished for. Then I heard a small child crying, and all was clear. I went back to sleep.

The next morning when I went down to breakfast there were three place settings at one of the tables. A young American couple working in Paris had driven down for a holiday with their two-year-old daughter. They had been sent a room key in the mail, and told of the open door leading to the alley in case the owners were not there when they arrived. The Americans had arrived at three o'clock in the morning. They were the "noise."

Today I had no set plan; I caught the first train I saw. It was going to Biel/Bienne. The conductor was very rude. When I asked for his signature, he said, "No! Certainly not!" I politely explained my need for his signature on my document, but he said, "You cannot send anything to London! Is it so bad that I will not sign?" After he walked away I wrote him a note, in German, letting him know that I was not just a tourist who wanted a signature for a journal or a memento of the trip, and that I was serious about breaking the record. At the end of the note I wrote, 'Is it too much to ask for a signature? Even so, you didn't need to be so rude to an old lady.'

When he passed by again, I gave him the note. In a few minutes he came back, reached for my document and stamped it. I thanked him, but he said nothing. He walked away; I didn't see him again.

From Biel/Bienne I took a train to Le Locle, via La Chaux de Fonds, passing through delightful Swiss villages that I had never been through before. The conductor was so different from the grouch on the last train. He signed my document and wished me well. When the train ended in Le Locle the conductor almost sang his announcement, "*Alle, alle, all sind frei!*" He was telling all the passengers to leave the train. "All, all, all are free." The *Alle* sounded like *Ole*. For more than fifty years I had thought the singsong words we yelled out to call the other children in from a game of hide-and-seek were of Swedish origin. We pronounced them "Ole, Ole, Olsen free!" Hearing the Swiss conductor today, I recognized the words as being German, spoken in "Schweitzer Deutsch," the Swiss-German language of the German-speaking section of Switzerland. The only difference in the childhood version was that we said "free" instead of "fry," as the Germans and Swiss pronounce *frei*. Now, I no longer have to wonder who Ole Olsen was.

I waited an hour for a train to Neuchatel, where I caught a "TEE" *(Trans-Europe Express)* to Frasne, across the French border.

37

Remembering the TEEs' from the good old days of Eurailing, I was glad to ride one again. Some of them have been made into tourist trains. Only a few make regular runs. In Frasne I found I could take a bus back across the border to Fleurier, and return to Neuchatel over a different route, by train.

I had a two-hour wait for the bus; I decided to have lunch in Frasne, but I had forgotten that the stores and even most of the restaurants close between noon and 2:00 p.m. in some European towns. The owners and employees usually go home for lunch. I saw a sign that said *Boulangerie* 20 *metres*, but the little bakery was closed. It looked like part of an old brick castle with its arched, iron door with a huge door pull. The foundation of the building was slanted; it was on a narrow alleyway of cobblestones that snaked downhill.

There were only a few other passengers on the bus to Fleurier. When we stopped at the French/Swiss border we got off the bus to show our passports. From my wide picture window I watched the landscape change from green meadows to thick forests, to rocky cliffs. From Neuchatel I traveled on to Zurich, and headed back to Germany, making new mileage around the *Bodensee* (Lake Constance). I am now traveling on my three-month EurailPass. Arriving in Frankfurt after midnight, I went on to the North Sea area. Crossing the narrow rail bridge to Westerland, on Sylt, one of the North Frisian Islands was quite an experience. After a few short routes, I was on an overnighter toward BK.

Chapter 4
To The Adriatic

I spent the next few days traveling through new routes in Germany, on both sides of the Rhine, then heading slightly northwest. In Rheydt, a city near the border with the Netherlands, I saw a crowd of people watching a demonstration march. There were cries of "A-dolf Hit-ler! A-dolf Hit-ler!" I thought the marchers were Neo-Nazis, but one of the onlookers said it was a demonstration against the Neo-Nazis (the ones interrupting with the Hitler cries). Several police vans followed slowly behind the demonstrators. To show support, I joined the march. I didn't carry a sign or say anything, because I am an outsider. The demonstrators stopped at a plaza near the bus station, and a man gave a long speech. Agitators were shaking their fists and trying to drown out the words of the speaker by yelling their Nazi slogans: *"Auslanders Rausch! Rausch vom Deutschland!"* They were demanding that foreigners leave Germany. After each slogan someone would repeat the words "Adolf Hitler! *Sieg! Heil!"*

On my way back to the station I was talking with three young black men from Africa. They told me there hadn't been much trouble with the radical groups in Rheydt until lately. Hearing the Hitler cries again, I looked behind us. Two of the agitators were running toward us. I said, "Hurry, they're after us!" We ran up the steps and to the platform. The agitators passed us. They were just running for their train.

I didn't wake up as early as I had planned; perhaps my body knew I needed the rest. Later in the afternoon I left on a local train, changing to EC # 19, the *Andreas Hofer* to Munich. Arrival was at 7:00 p.m., which gave me four hours to spend before my next train. I knew where to get potato pancakes with applesauce in Munich, complete with *Blasmusik* (the brass band sound). The *Mathaser Bier Stadt* (Mathaser Beer City) is only two blocks from the station. My luggage was safely stored in a locker. I hurried past the "scaries" hanging around the station, and on to an evening's entertainment that had been "forced" on me by my hunger and the train schedule.

The *Mathaser* is huge. It has the Guinness Record for the largest beer-selling establishment in the world. There is a beer garden, and a restaurant with tables made of beer barrels. The main hall is always crowded, but not as touristy as the famous Hofbrau Haus is. Whenever I go to a beer hall I look for a family, a couple, or other women to sit with. I am always concerned that someone will think I am a prostitute if I come in and sit alone (youth is not a prerequisite for being a prostitute in Europe). I went to a table near the stage, and asked two German women if I could join them. Of course, the answer was *"Ja, bitte."* Unless a person is behaving in a dangerous or obscene manner, he or she is never refused a chair. The two women and I had a conversation in German while I was waiting for my food.

When the band played "Rosamunde" (The Beer Barrel Polka) some of the patrons got up and started dancing, but soon a bouncer urged them to sit down. Dancing is not allowed. The song was originally titled "Skoda Lasky" and was written by a Czech nationalist. It means "Lost Love," and was such a hit, that other countries embraced it, giving it different titles and lyrics.

Just after I finished my potato pancakes, and was ready to start on my apple strudel, two men came over. They knew both of the women, and soon one woman was sitting on the German man's lap. Well, that was OK, but then, the other man, who was Turkish, said in German, "I think I'll take the new one." I wondered, new what? He motioned for me to sit on his lap. Uh oh! He meant me. The other two women were 'Ladies of the Evening', and I was the "new one." I deserted my dessert.

I boarded a Direct Express thirty minutes before departure time. Tomorrow my through carriage would have me in Venice. Alone in the compartment, I stretched out and slept. I woke just before the Italian border, and after customs check, went back to sleep.

When we stopped in Vicenza the next day I saw some young Italian soldiers dressed in camouflage, on a train marked TRIESTE. I leaned out the window and asked if I could take their picture. They smiled and waved; I took that as a "yes."

Just before we pulled into Santa Lucia Station in Venice, I couldn't resist singing a song I still remember from the third grade, "Saa-aahn-ta-ah Lu-uu-chee-ah, Santa Lucia!" It was not completely insane; I was alone in the compartment.

In Santa Lucia station I had time for a shower and a vaporetti (waterbus) ride around the Grand Canal before the 12:20 p.m. train left for Trieste.

Venice always looks flooded, but now it really is. They have had a lot of rain and the water is up to the level of the walkways. The Piazza San Marcos is wet with the rising waters; the Basilica di San Marco seems to be floating. Venice is different. Rather than feeling like I have stepped into a storybook, I feel like I am in a sixteenth-century painting. Venice has 118 islands, with 150 canals separating them. More than 400 bridges cross between the islands.

Workers were gathering outside the station, threatening a strike against the Italian Railways. A train to Trieste was ready to leave. I boarded.

From the harbor in Trieste I saw so many military ships in formation that I thought perhaps they were on alert. Trieste was made a free territory in World War II, but Italy and Yugoslavia were soon disputing ownership. Eventually, Italy won out. I was close to Slovenia, part of the former Yugoslavia, but I wanted to approach it from Austria, gaining more mileage.

At Carnia I had to take a bus through the mountains to Tarvisio for a train to the Austrian border. It was a hair-raising, three-hour ride, but the scenery was worth it. The bus toiled up winding mountain roads, and eased (still too fast, I thought) downhill. Sometimes we were precariously close to the escarpment.

Although the bus was crowded I managed to have a double seat to myself. Hearing odd noises from the seat behind me, I looked back and saw that something or someone was under a blanket or a coat. It took me a minute or two to realize there were two persons under the cover, and they weren't sleeping. I would have · changed seats if there were any empty. The other passengers ignored them; I seemed to be the only one who was embarrassed. When we came to a little village on the edge of a cliff the twosome threw off the cover, adjusted their clothing and got off the bus. They were only about fourteen years old and they had their schoolbooks with them.

It was almost eight o'clock in the evening when we got to Tarvisio. I caught a train to the border immediately. In ten minutes I was in Arnoldstein, Austria. The conductor wouldn't sign my document. He said, "Why should I?" He didn't find it humorous when I retorted, "Why shouldn't you?" It was only ten kilometers and my passport was stamped at the border, so I could prove I was on the train anyway. After a short wait I went on to Villach and checked into a hotel near the train station.

Breakfast was a huge buffet with plenty of choices. I had more food than I have had at one sitting in a long time. Everything would have been perfect if the receptionist hadn't accused me of taking something from the mini-bar in my room and not reporting it. As I was checking out, she asked if I had used the mini-bar, and I said I hadn't.

"Just wait here, and we'll see if you did or not." When she came back she said a "Pago" was missing. "The maid always puts two of everything in the mini-bars."

"Either the maid can't count, or she ran out of Pagos before she got to my room, whatever a Pago is." She tried to charge me anyway, so I told her to call the maid. I could have paid the paltry sum and let it go at that, but it was the principle of it, after all. She rang the maid, who told her that she had run out of Pagos and had forgotten to replace it. I won, but by a narrow margin; the receptionist didn't apologize. Then, rather than feeling guilty that I had eaten so much breakfast, I wished I had taken enough food from the buffet for a picnic lunch.

I headed for Spielfeld-Strasse at the border of Austria and Slovenia, leaving Villach on train # 1734. The conductor showed me how to spot the train number on the stamp he used on my document. There wasn't always time to check the train number on the schedule in the station, and sometimes a number wasn't listed. I was close to Slovenia from Villach, and even closer from Trieste, but I wanted to take another route in Austria, over the town of Bruck an der Mur (Bridge on the Mur River) to Graz, then back towards Slovenia and Croatia.

Arrival in Spielfeld-Strasse was at midday. I spoke with the Slovenian customs officials, explaining that I had no visa or train ticket, but I would like to travel through Slovenia, and into Croatia, and back. I would come out of Slovenia through another border with Austria. The two men who spoke with me were very polite and cooperative, even offering to ride the train across the border with me to translate. A train would be leaving in two hours; I was to let them know if I wanted to be on it.

As I walked around looking for a restaurant, people stared at me. I felt as though I were wearing my "Typical Tourist" T-shirt. There was a café in the station, but it was so smoky I didn't want to eat there. It was interesting though; one could only enter it from the station. The street entrance to it had been closed off, because of the Slovenian border. To patronize the café, customers have to go through customs on the lower level of the station if coming from the town, or approach it after alighting from a train on the platform. I didn't find another restaurant, and the stores were closed for the noon break.

I suddenly felt tired (I was fighting a cold) and slightly uneasy, so I didn't go into Slovenia. I went back to Vienna over another route, planning to travel back into Italy on a night train.

When I got to Vienna my anxiety increased. Thinking that perhaps there had been a message from my family in Arkansas, I decided to take an overnighter to Frankfurt, and go on to BK. I went into the market in the station to buy a snack for the train. Now I know what a "Pago" is. There were rows of them in the cooler. It is a fruit-based soda.

On my overnighter I was in a compartment alone. In the middle of the night I had to use the WC. I came back to the compartment, and was almost asleep again when I sensed someone near me. A swarthy man wearing glasses was leaning over me, reaching for my travel purse that was strapped across my shoulder. I rolled off onto the floor, surprising him and almost knocking him down as my body landed on his feet. He ran out of the compartment. My valuables are well hidden. I carry only my glasses, comb and a little money in the travel purse, but from now on I will put it in my satchel on night trains, removing the temptation. I went out into the corridor to see if I could find a conductor; I saw only the thief, two compartments down. He was alone. I didn't see any other passengers or conductors. I was afraid to go back to sleep, so I stayed in the corridor, near the door. He got off the train an hour before my transfer point.

As soon as I reached my base I called home. Everything was OK there, but the next day I heard the news that NATO war planes had bombed a Serbian-controlled base in Croatia while I was on my way back to BK. The ships I had seen in Trieste were NATO warships; I suppose the soldiers I had photographed on their way to Trieste were with NATO also. The air raid was the worst since World War II. I was glad I was no longer in the Adriatic area, particularly Croatia or Slovenia.

The Bridge Houses in Bad Kreuznach

Chapter 5
The Long Way to Spain

Today is Thanksgiving Day back home, and I am alone, a world away. I wondered where and what I would eat to celebrate. My train day began early; I was in Koblenz by 10:00 a.m., and heading into the Westerwald area, east of the Rhine, twenty minutes later.

Taking a succession of trains, I returned to Frankfurt by a new route, and without delay continued on to Amsterdam by two InterCity trains. I was able to get my documents signed up until the second InterCity, the *Rembrandt*. One conductor agreed to sign, but didn't come back, so just before time for a crew change, I went to the conductors' compartment. There were four of them sitting together, talking and laughing. Confronting the conductor that had agreed to sign, I asked in German for his signature.

"Ask my *Hollander Kolleagen* to sign when they board."

"Excuse me, but I need a signature for the kilometers through Germany, to prove I was on the train."

"Yes, she needs to prove to her husband where she has been!" Laughter ensued, and I returned to my seat, determined to quell my frustration.

There had been no time between trains to eat lunch and it was about time for dinner. In the restaurant car I thought about the pies my daughter-in-law, Crissy would be baking for the Thanksgiving Day feast. Apple, cherry, and pecan made with nuts from the huge tree in their yard. I settled for a small piece of biscuit-like cake, prepackaged in cellophane. But there was no need to feel sorry for myself. After all, it was not Thanksgiving Day in Europe, and I was on a train, about to cross yet another international border, not sure where I would end up, or where I would spend the night. For that, and for many other things, I was truly thankful.

When we stopped just before the Netherlands border, I looked out a corridor window and watched the fearless four as they stepped off the train and sauntered down the platform. And I, the Ugly American, called after them, "If your mothers ever come to America, I hope they will be treated with more respect than you have given me!" The phrase (with modification) was to be repeated often throughout my journeys.

The Dutch conductor was congenial, but misunderstood me and wrote only the route on my document. When I tried to explain further, he drew arrows from each town toward the top of my document. I stopped while my document was still comprehensible; I smiled and thanked him. "Been there, done that," but can't prove it.

It was 10:00 p.m. when I arrived in Amsterdam. An overnighter to Paris was ready to board. I had room to lie down and sleep, but I woke up every couple of hours to secure another signature. The conductor who signed in Aulnoye, France misunderstood my request and wrote on my document, "One person is on the train to Paris." Perhaps he figured I needed to prove to my husband that I was not traveling on the train with a companion? Just kidding. Or, perhaps I was the only person on the train? That hadn't happened yet, although there were several times I was the only passenger in a carriage and many times alone in a compartment.

At dawn, I arrived in Paris Gare du Nord, the North Station. Nine minutes later I stepped aboard a train to Calais on the coast. From Calais, I took several trains via Lille (France), Tournai and Mons (Belgium) back into Germany. The short day trip I had started out on became a series of trips on a series of trains. Nineteen trains in thirty-eight hours, traveling 1,924 kilometers but having only 1,403 signed for.

By 10:30 p.m. the next night I was in Lyon-Part Dieu Station in France, waiting for a train to Port Bou, Spain. In the waiting area a pretty young blonde sat next to me on a long bench. We introduced ourselves; she was Geri, from Ohio, studying at a university in Paris. She asked how I had known she was an American, as she is often mistaken for a German. Being truthful about it, I told her I had thought she was French or German at first, thinking, "Boy, she sure is trying to look like an American with those running shoes and Levis." She laughed and showed me her Nike socks. Another young woman, an Australian, joined us. Sandra said she was just "going about" Europe for a month and was heading for Spain to "see a cousin I have never met. We are going all over the country on his motorcycle."

When we reached Port Bou at 5:40 a.m. we went through customs inside the terminal. I had left my umbrella on the train. In the night there were some questionable characters peering into my compartment, so I kept my umbrella beside me in case I needed a weapon, which I didn't. In my rush to detrain, I forgot my umbrella.

EuroCity # 477 would have us in Barcelona in three hours. I sat in second class to be with Geri and Sandra (they had Eurail YouthPasses, valid in second class). In Barcelona I stored my things in a locker; I would have a long wait before my train to Valencia. Geri suggested we go to a couple of museums, but I felt I might slow them down a little. I was experiencing rail lag, which at first made me feel old, but then, on second thought, the young ones weren't fresh off a nineteen-train marathon, as I was.

I traveled to Valencia on a "Talgo" tilting train, built to glide smoothly around sharp curves, while keeping up its speed. In Valencia I switched to an InterCity to Madrid.

It was 10:30 p.m. when the train pulled into Madrid's Atocha Station. I took a room at the Hotel Mediodia.

I checked out early, changed money again, and went back to Barcelona over a different route, arriving at six o'clock in the evening. I stored my things and took a bus to the harbor.

When it became too dark for sightseeing I strolled along one of the main shopping districts. Businesses were open late; the streets and stores were crowded. I went into several restaurants and showed a veggie note I had written (the words gleaned from my phrase book). I got some odd looks, but no food.

As I walked back toward the station, I saw a bar with a food counter. When I held up my note the man behind the counter shook his head and shrugged his shoulders (I get a lot of that). I went around the corner and looked through the window of a restaurant. There were no customers, but the tables were covered with white tablecloths, and set with wineglasses and candles. I decided to go in, even if all I could get was a salad; I needed to feel like a normal tourist for a change, eating a sit-down meal in a sit-down restaurant. I went in and sat down. Instead of showing my note, I took a chance and asked in English if they served meatless pasta. Although I seem to have a lot of difficulty in Spain finding hot food, this time I was in luck. The young man spoke English. "I can cook a special pasta for you, with a cream and cognac sauce." I wasn't ready for that on an empty stomach, so I asked if he had canned tomatoes. He did, and I said that would do for a sauce. When I ordered mineral water, he started to take away the stemmed wineglass, leaving the water glass. I said, "Please, I want to drink my water from the wineglass." It was perhaps a foolish thing, but I had been drinking from a bottle or a carton repeatedly and I just wanted a change.

When I started to eat the spaghetti my stomach began growling. Of late, it wasn't accustomed to a real meal. I thought it would cease after I had eaten a little, but it didn't. It kept growling and I kept feeding it, while trying to retain my decorum.

When I paid the bill the waiter told me I could go out the other door. I went through a narrow hall, up two steps and I was in the bar where I had displayed the veggie note. They were the same establishment, but the bar faced one street and the restaurant another.

Back at the station, while wondering where to go next, a man approached me, and spoke to me in English. He said he had a nice room for rent, right across the street. I don't often book a room that way, but it is an accepted practice and many Eurailers take advantage of the low price and the convenience. Sometimes it works out well, but it can be disastrous. It *was,* almost. When we got to the huge, thick wooden door of the entrance to the apartment building, the man unlocked it and told me there was no extra key. I would have to stay in the room all night once I checked in. I hadn't intended to go out again so I agreed. Usually I insist on having a key for the outside door in case of an emergency. I just wasn't thinking. The building was dank and timeworn; the stairs creaked as we went up the two flights to his apartment.

The lady of the house nodded to me as we came through the door. I showed my passport (normal procedure) and paid for my room. It was tiny and musty. The bed was a narrow cot, but the sheets were clean. When I asked about the shower I was told to wait until morning for hot water. A man, about thirty years old peeked out from a half-closed door. I asked if there were other guests, and the answer was negative. The man must have been a relative.

The transom above my door wouldn't stay closed. I tried to hook it with a wire hanger, but when I stood on a chair to do so, my foot fell through the worn, caned chair seat, causing me to fall against the wall. The man who rented me the room knocked on the door to see if I was OK. He also said the family would like to get some sleep. I opened the drapes to let a little light in from the street; there was no window. It wasn't the first time I stayed in rooms where the window had been closed in, but this was wallpaper over drywall. Perhaps there had never been a window. The whole apartment could be in the center of the building. Claustrophobia began to gnaw at me.

When I went to the WC down the hall, I passed the kitchen (converted from a small closet). There were mounds and mounds of dirty, greasy pots and dishes, some with meat and gravy spilling over the drainboard and onto the floor. Roaches were crawling everywhere, and the odor was horrible. There were no windows in the WC or the kitchen. By then it was too late to find another room or catch a train. I hurried back to my bed and longed for morning, glad that breakfast was not included.

Dawn arrived, none too soon for me; I headed for the shower. The door of the bathroom was ajar. I pushed it open and found the lady of the house standing in the tub with her shoes on. There was no water in the tub. She was wearing the same clothes she had been wearing the night before, complete with the soiled apron. Then she began making strange guttural sounds and frightening gestures to me. I rushed to my room, packed up and hurried down the stairs. The outside door was still locked; none of the tenants had gone out of the building yet. Just as I decided to brave it and go back up and ask for someone to let me out, a woman came out of another apartment. I followed her down and made my exit. It was time to make tracks.

I traveled for several days through Spain. The scenery along the Atlantic Coast is breathtaking, especially around Vigo. After we passed Villagarcia the train veered inland to Santiago De Compostela, the last stop on the famous pilgrim's walk, the "Way of Saint James." Another name for it is "The Route to Santiago," the English interpretation of the Spanish name of *"El Camino de Santiago."* The route begins in the Pyrenees Mountains (a range between Spain and France) at the town of Roncesvalles (Roncevaux, in French) in Northern Spain, five miles from the French border and near the Roncesvalles Pass. Pilgrims must arrive in Santiago on foot, by bicycle or on horseback in order to receive the official scroll attesting to their accomplishment.

When the train neared Santiago it was raining lightly. Only a little patch of blue was visible through the gray sky. I saw the cathedral from my window. The remains of Saint James are supposedly buried in the cathedral, beneath a statue of him.

The scenery from Santiago to the port city of Coruna, at the northwestern edge of Spain, on the Atlantic is spectacular. My train climbed through wooded mountain passes until it reached the coast. Coruna has several names, La Coruna, La Corunna and the ancient Roman name of Brigantium. From Coruna I took a Talgo train to Madrid, then an overnight train to Malaga.

Arrival in Malaga, on the Costa del Sol was in the early morning. The sky over the Mediterranean was something to behold. Periwinkle blue, streaked with several shades of rose touched the gray-blue horizon. It's only a short distance from Malaga to the Strait of Gibraltar, blending the Atlantic with the Mediterranean, and Europe with North Africa. I thought of taking a ship to Morocco, but ... it would have to be more trains.

On a regional train to Seville, the scenes from my window were mostly of orange groves and olive trees that tempted my vegetarian palate. In small villages, pack donkeys were led by their masters, some to work in the fields, others to haul wood or produce.

Suddenly I had a craving for olives, but there was no restaurant car on the train (not that the waiter would sell me a serving of olives). Searching my nearly empty feedbag, I found only a package of potato chips and a few plastic packets of strawberry jam. I spread jam on some of the chips and created a new kind of sandwich. I was no longer hungry, but the more olive trees we passed, the more I craved olives.

On arrival in Seville I bought a jar of green olives and a loaf of bread. I walked along the streets and plazas, enjoying my ambulatory lunch. Some of the churches are so grandly embellished that they look like palaces. Seville may have more churches than any other city in Europe, or so it seemed to me.

I had a sudden urge to take a quick trip to the border of Portugal; I could gain a few more miles, and finish my sightseeing in Seville later. The overnighter to Madrid wouldn't leave until 11:45 p.m.; I could be back in Seville with plenty of time to spare. I took a local to Huelva, less than an hour away.

As soon as I arrived at the station I checked on the buses into Portugal from Huelva. The trains don't run into Portugal on this route. I also checked the trains going to Madrid from Seville. The woman at the information window quoted me a reservation fee and supplement for an "AVE" train *(Alta Velocidad Espanola)*, Spain's high-speed wonder. When I disagreed with the high price of the supplement, she neglected to explain that the train in question was a special overnighter without regular seating. It was one of the deluxe new "Hotel Trains." I had been fleeced many times by unscrupulous clerks, so I was suspicious, and became the Ugly American once again. I went into the office of one of the administrators and complained. When he went to the woman at the information window to clarify the situation, she told him my EurailPass had expired! I showed him my pass, and he said he couldn't imagine why she had said that. He did tell me about the special train, and I admitted I was wrong. I went back to apologize to the woman, but first I asked her why she said my pass had expired. She answered smugly, "Your EurailPass has expired because I have canceled it!"

"You are not big enough to cancel my EurailPass!" The Ugly American retorted, without offering the intended apology.

Returning to Seville on the next train, I still had the evening ahead of me. I thought briefly of dinner and Flamenco entertainment, but I was wearing jeans, running shoes, and had spilled olive juice on my jacket. I opted for more strolling around town. When I became tired, I caught a bus, jumping off whenever I saw anything of interest.

I stopped to see the Cathedral of Santa Maria de la Sede and was amazed at its size. But, after all, it is listed in the *Guinness Book of World Records* as the cathedral with the largest area, 414 feet long, 271 feet wide and 100 feet high (to the vault of the nave). There are eighty chapels within its grand interior.

The cathedral's 295-foot Giralda bell tower was part of a Moorish mosque until the thirteenth century, and is the only remaining part (other than the "Patio of Oranges"). The cathedral was built over a remnant of the mosque. Seville was once the center of a Moorish Kingdom. Its Arabic name was *Isbiliah*. The Romans called it *Romula Augusta.*

While I was standing outside, reading a brochure I had picked up in the tourist office, a tall, middle-aged Spanish gentleman (I knew he was a gentleman, he was wearing an ascot) walked up to me. He asked in fluent English if I was an American, and if I liked the cathedral.

"Yes, I am an American tourist. Your cathedral is magnificent."

"We have many beautiful places in Seville. May I show you some of them? If you are alone in my city."

"I am alone, but I will be catching a train soon. I thank you for the offer."

"My name is Michelobe. In my country it is also the name of a fine champagne. Could we go dancing? I know many places."

"No, I have only blue jeans with me, and I must leave tonight. My name is Mona, and in my country Michelobe is the name of a fine beer."

"But I will buy you a wonderful dancing dress!" It was time to end the encounter.

"I am married, and not interested. I must hurry to the station now. Good-bye." I looked back to see if he was following me, but he was just standing there, adjusting his ascot.

My train to Madrid was mostly over new territory; I could sleep while making mileage. I was hungry, but a visit to the snack bar only netted me another package of potato chips. The sandwiches were all made with meat.

I found an empty compartment, but was soon joined by a young man and a young woman. They were not speaking Castilian or Catalan. It took awhile for me to realize I was hearing Euskara, the language of the Basques. The man wasn't dressed like any of the Basque men I had seen. He was wearing striped jeans, a Hawaiian-print shirt, and a baseball cap (turned backward) instead of the traditional beret. The removal of his cap revealed hair cut so short, it almost wasn't there. He had a gold earring dangling from one ear. The woman was wearing a long dress the same shade of rust-brown as her shoulder-length hair. With just three of us we could pull the seats out to sleep, but we didn't. The man sat up all night; we left the seats in a sitting position. At first he was watching me, as if he suspected me of planning to steal his luggage, but I had all I wanted to carry. Then, he stared out the door into the corridor. Finally, I dozed off for an hour or so.

When we arrived in Madrid, I thought I knew why the man was acting so strangely. His face, or one remarkably like it, was on a wanted poster in the station. The man in the picture had long hair and a goatee, but there was no disguising the unique chin and jaw line. If he was the man on the poster, and I was almost positive he was, he had done a good job of changing his appearance. I read the poster; the man was considered a terrorist. Anyone seeing him was to report to the local police or Interpol. I was sure he wouldn't be hanging around the station if he was wanted, and if I reported it, they would just detain me. Anyway, I may end up on another train with him, and if he suspected that I reported him he may harm me. I caught an InterCity train from Madrid to the border of France. There was nothing hot for me to eat in the restaurant; I had another package of chips and a coffee in the snack bar.

When I detrained in Hendaye, just over the French border, I checked the schedule. The TGV to Paris would be leaving soon, but reservations were mandatory, and the fee was eighteen French Francs. I needed to change money, but there was a note posted on the counter, "Back in fifteen minutes."

It was almost time for the train and the counter was still unmanned, so I went to a ticket window and explained my predicament. The clerk suggested I talk to the conductor. I did, and he said I didn't have to pay; I could just get on the train.

In a few minutes he came to my seat, stroked his fuzzy black beard, and said I would have to pay a penalty equal to ninety French Francs. That was the penalty for not having a ticket. I had only neglected to pay for a reservation. He asked me how many Spanish Pesetas I had. Watching as I counted out 4,000 Pesetas, he collected 3,395 from me, and refused to give me a receipt. The Pesetas were worth more than ninety Francs. They were equal to twenty-seven American dollars. I showed him a note I had written in French requesting a signature, but he wouldn't sign. Over 800 unaccredited kilometers!

In the snack bar I met a young French woman who spoke English. I had a ten-Franc coin and a couple of lesser ones, enough to buy a soda. When the bearded %&#@&%#$^ came in I recruited the young woman to act as an interpreter. I wanted him to understand that I should have been charged only an extra eighteen Francs as a penalty, not ninety. He said the penalty was charged because I had not purchased the reservation slip in the train station. But the penalty for that is only double, which would be a total of thirty-six Francs. Another conductor overheard and questioned him. Somehow he made it sound right, until I complained that he had also refused me a reservation slip. When the other conductor told him to write me a receipt and a reservation slip, he said something in French, and walked out without giving me either.

I had asked in one of the Eurail Aid Offices why I was charged twice the price for the reservation fee most of the time in Spain, even when I made an advance purchase. The answer was that some of the personnel charged more because they could get away with it. But this was France! I wasn't sure if the conductor was Spanish or French.

To top it off, the waiter refused my ten-Franc coin, pointing out that it was one of the obsolete coins. The banks will exchange them, but merchants don't want to bother with them. He let me pay in dollars, and gave me one of the obsolete ten-Franc coins in my change. Mischievously, I wrote out a receipt for the waiter to sign. It said, in English, "I gave this tourist an old ten-Franc piece, to cheat her and to fool her." I had the cooperation of the English-speaking woman to help me fool him. She told him it was a receipt for my business deductions. It worked. He signed and I felt a little better. Later I threw the receipt away; it was only for a little one-upmanship on my part.

In Paris I had to hurry to Gare de l'Est for overnight connections back to base. I sat in a parlor carriage in a single seat nearest the door. It was cold, so I used my jacket as a cover, putting it on backward to protect and conceal my "neck safe" (a thin pouch worn around the neck), where I carried my valuables. My jacket was multicolored. Don't try the system with a white jacket; it will look like you're in a straight jacket. I fell fast asleep. A few hours later the conductor woke me up. He wanted to show me a more comfortable seat in another carriage. I wondered what he thought about my backward jacket. We went to an empty carriage and I sat in a double seat, facing a double seat, and stretched out.

In the early morning, I woke just in time to catch my next train. I had been sleeping on trains for more nights than I care to remember. When I arrived in BK I took a long nap. Dirk and I went jogging in the evening. Both of us were wearing running shoes with lights that blink on and off as we run. In the pedestrian zone we stopped outside of a bar, and danced to the blaring music, our lights keeping time with our steps, if not the music. Dirk thinks I'm *"Klug,"* a cross between clever and cool.

Chapter 6
Happy Holidays

It was raining in BK as I walked to the station. I stood under the shelter on Platform 2, but it was hard to find a dry spot; the roof was leaking.

My train was one of the old "Silver Fish," so named because its shiny exterior resembles the fins of a fish. I was on my way to visit the Christmas Market in St. Goar. In German cities and towns the Christmas Markets begin right after Advent, which begins four Sundays before Christmas. Some markets begin in November, and some as late as the middle of December.

The Rhine and the mountains above it were gray. A light misty rain and the assorted grays of the sky gave the scene from my window a neutral effect. Castles loomed over the river; some of them were gray also. It was like watching an old black-and-white movie from my plush orange seat, on my silver train.

The *"Christkindl"* market stretches down the pedestrian zone toward the giant cuckoo clock that protrudes over the sidewalk from the outside wall of a shop. It is reputed to be the largest hanging cuckoo clock in the world. There is a much larger cuckoo clock in Wiesbaden, Germany, but it is a standing clock. Castle Rheinfels towers above the winding streets of the town. The children's carousel (set up for the special market) is painted with pictures of fairy-tale characters and castles. Life-size castles on the hills seemed to be part of the fairy tales.

The drizzling rain became a downpour. Since I had left my umbrella on the train to Port Bou, I took my umbrella hat from my backpack and placed it on my head. It is multicolored, and looks just like a tiny umbrella. Everyone I met laughed, and I would explain, in German, that in America it is normal to wear such a hat to shield one from the sun or the rain.

At one booth, the cook was preparing Belgian waffles and potato pancakes. There was no shelter for the customers. My umbrella hat helped only a little, but I managed to eat three potato pancakes before the pounding rain made them too soggy.

I had a photo taken beside three donkeys with large umbrellas on their backs. We made quite a picture; I could caption it "Four Jackasses with Umbrellas."

My shoes were waterlogged and my jacket was wet. I don't need a cold; I'll be traveling again tomorrow. Reluctantly, I returned to base and had everything ready for the morrow before turning in for the night.

I woke early, intending to stop in Frankfurt at the American

Express before beginning my next journey. At breakfast Rosi told me she wanted to go to Frankfurt with me and see the Christmas Market. I agreed, but said I couldn't stay long, as I was ready to travel again.

We strolled along the *Zeil;* a long pedestrian zone lined with department stores, clothing stores, and gift shops. The Christmas Market covered the length of the *Zeil* and beyond. Vendors offered gifts and decorations from all over the world, as well as local handicrafts. Pretzels were baking in portable ovens. There was a table of Christmas candles and a long counter filled with gingerbread baked in various shapes and sizes. Marzipan candies were offered in assortments of Santas, fruits, pigs, bears, chimney sweeps and ladybugs. The proportion of sugar versus almonds used in the making of the marzipan has been kept secret through the years. Only the bakers know for sure. By the taste of marzipan, I would guess the proportions to be about equal.

The booths were adorned with greenery and berries. Aromas of roasting chestnuts and gingerbread fused with those of perfumed oils and exotic spices.

We watched a Ukrainian dance troupe, twirling in full costume, and listened to the music of a rock band, Gypsy violinists, and an organ grinder, complete with a monkey that collected money in a tin cup. The time was slipping away, but when I said I must go, Rosi said, "Oh, you can catch a train tomorrow. I am hungry. Let's have lunch. And I want to shop for a nutcracker for Herb." Well, what could I say; my husband wanted an authentic German nutcracker, and I was hungry too. After lunch we shopped some more. Rosi bought a blue-uniformed "Prussian Emperor" nutcracker for Herb's Christmas present and two silken angels for me. I had missed my train for sure; I would wait until tomorrow.

Our friend Erich was standing at the top of the stairs when we arrived at Rosi's apartment.

"Mona! You are here! You didn't go!"

"No, we stayed too long in Frankfurt, so I missed the train." He paused. I waited for an explanation.

"It was on TV! Your train crashed outside of Mannheim. Some passengers were killed!"

I was visibly shaken; Rosi's insistence that we stay longer at the Christmas Market had spared me a train wreck, if not my life. Later we heard the news that a doctor from Bad Kreuznach had volunteered to go to the crash site with a rescue crew. The helicopter he was flying in crashed at the scene of the train wreck. He was killed. The death toll was twelve from among the passengers and crew that were on board the train. It was time to contemplate fate and revise my traveling strategy.

Rosi and I spent the evening reminiscing about past Christmas holidays. She told of Christmas in BK and I regaled her with stories of mine in Washington, D.C. I told her about the Christmas that my husband and I had spent in BK so long ago. The Christmas Market was held on Mannheimerstrasse then (the pedestrian zone took over much later). There were only a few tables lining the sidewalk, and only the handmade items were from Germany. The decorations and bulbs had been imported from Czechoslovakia and Poland. Rosi was only six years old at the time. She told me that the American soldiers always said, "Hi" to her when she and her mother passed them on the street, and sometimes they would give her candy or chewing gum, which she pronounced "shevy goom." Rosi said the soldiers all seemed to be wearing the same after-shave, "Old Spice." I said that perhaps Herb had passed her on the street, and had said, "Hi" to a little German girl. He also wore Old Spice. He still does.

I showed her some old photos I had brought. One was of Herb and me in 1953 with Sankt Nikolaus. Then, I handed her a picture of the *Heilige Kreuz* (Holy Cross) church that stands near the train station. Rosi stared at the picture for a moment or two before tears trickled down her cheeks. It was more than nostalgia.

"Rosi, what is it?"

"The church steeple! It is not the same today. I remember now. I was walking with my mother when the cranes were there, putting up the new one. I have never thought about that day, not in all of these years. But now, I have a new-old memory of my mother."

Her mother had passed away when Rosi was only twelve years old. She moved in with her aunt and uncle, a childless couple. I gave her the picture of the church with the old steeple. Rosi remained pensive for a moment, and then...

"Mona, did you have panny lovers when you were young in BK?"

I couldn't imagine what she meant.

"Have what?"

"Panny lovers, the brown shoes all American women wore then. All the army wives had them."

"Penny loafers! Of course I had those shoes, didn't you?"

"No, there was nowhere for Germans to buy them. They were something that only Americans had. All of my life I have wanted a pair of panny lovers."

"You never told me! I will call Herb, and see if he can find a pair. I haven't seen them in the stores for a long time, but he can try." I called Herb; perhaps Rosi will have a special gift.

The next few days were spent traversing Germany, Holland, Belgium and Luxembourg. In Luxembourg City I took a bus to the American Cemetery. I walked along the rows of graves, marked by crosses or Stars of David. General Patton is buried there too. The American Flag flies above the cemetery; the hallowed ground belongs to our people.

On the return trip to Germany, I went down through France, ending up in Strasbourg just after midnight, which meant sitting in the station the rest of the night with the winos. My train back to Germany wouldn't leave until 4:00 a.m.

Out of the seven people in the upstairs waiting room (on Platform 1) I was the only one who was neither a wino nor a homeless person. I knew, because the station police kept coming in and chasing out those without a train ticket, and I was the only one who had one. When the police left, the winos would return. I had to open the door from the inside for them; the huge wooden door locked automatically when shut.

Some of the men started a fracas and the police ran them all out again. After some of them came back in, still bickering, I went out to the platform to wait for my train. It was cold outside; I tried to get back into the waiting room, but the winos wouldn't open the door for me. I remained on the platform shivering until my train arrived.

I couldn't risk taking another long journey in case of delays; my husband would arrive in a few days to join me for the Christmas holidays. Traveling over new territory, I took day trips from my base; combining sightseeing and Christmas Market visits with accredited mileage. On a train between Wurzburg and Steinach, three little blonde girls in my compartment began singing "*Stille Nacht*" (Silent Night). Their parents were surprised when I joined in.

Stille Nacht, Heilige Nacht
Alles schlaft, einsam wacht.
Nur das traute hoch Heilige Paar
Holder Knabe, im lockigem Haar
Schlaf in himmlicher Ruh
Schlaf in himmlicher Ruh! (All nouns are capitalized in German.)

Then I sang it for them in English. Our lyrics are much prettier than the original ones in German, which translate more or less to:
Silent Night, Holy Night, all sleep, one wakes.
Only the wedded high Holy Pair, holding a boy with curly hair.
Sleep in heavenly rest. Sleep in heavenly rest.

From Steinach, I went to Rothenburg ob der Tauber, the famous well-preserved medieval village. Its name means "Red Castle above the Tauber River." I walked the length of the old town walls for views of the town and the river, and for the feeling of being transported back into medieval times.

Dirk made me a small cardboard Christmas tree to carry in my mileage notebook. On board trains I sat it up on the foldaway table, leaning it against the window. I had a portable Christmas tree, complete with drawings of a garland and bulbs, painted in bright colors.

It was late when I returned to BK. A display of long silver-colored metallic ribbons had been fastened to each branch of a tree outside the Holy Cross Church across from the station. High-intensity lights had been placed above the tree. As the wind blew the ribbons around, the light beams moved along the silvery ribbons, reflecting back and forth across the church, the sky and the tree. The effect was ethereal.

On December 22nd I met Herb at the airport in Frankfurt. We went directly to Bad Kreuznach. Now that Herb was with me, it was even more like old times. I knew where he would want to go first. We went over the *"Kuhberg"* (Cow Mountain) and down on the other side to Bad Munster am Stein, a neighboring spa town. Its proper name is "Bad Munster am Stein-Ebernburg," since it has combined with the small town of Ebernburg. The name means "Baths at the Cathedral on the Stone/Castle of the Wild Boars."

We took sandwiches, chocolate bars and cans of cola for a picnic on the castle grounds at `Ebernburg,' the Wild Boar's Castle. The castle, high on the crest of a hill, seems foreboding from the outside, but it is now the home of an adult school, and a restaurant.

On Christmas Eve we went to a party at the home of Denise, the married daughter of Rosi. She and her husband Stefan had cooked up a feast, including Raclette, a Swiss specialty of melted cheese, served with boiled potatoes and pickles.

After dinner, Dirk and Sascha (Denise's one-year-old boy) opened their presents. Then it was our turn. Herb was happy about the nutcracker from Rosi. We also received gifts from Denise and Stefan and our friend Erich. In addition to the two silken angels purchased at the Christmas Market in Frankfurt, Rosi and Denise had bought brother and sister porcelain dolls for me.

When everyone had opened gifts Herb had brought from America, he brought out one more. It was for Rosi. With all eyes on her, she opened it, and found a pair of "American panny lovers." Herb had put a shiny new penny in the slot on the toe of each shoe, just the way I had done in my youth. She couldn't speak at first. The tears flowed down her cheeks. Then she said, "Panny lovers. I have real American panny lovers."

She held them in her lap the rest of the evening. Herb had searched in shoe stores and department stores in several towns near our home to find them.

Herb and I took a train to Saint Goar on Christmas morning. Our son, Tim and his family had sent a cash gift for us to spend a night in a castle on the Rhine. The Castle Rheinfels was booked solid, so we stayed in an old half-timbered hotel that looks just like a small castle. We had a wonderful view of the Rhine.

All too soon it was time to head for Switzerland. Herb was flying home from Zurich on the first of January, and had booked a couple of nights there in a hotel for us. Most of the miles we traveled together were repeat miles for me, therefore unaccredited.

After checking into the Hotel Montana, we caught a train to Chur (Coire). The *Chur-Arosa Bahn* leaves from in front of the station, where it sometimes blocks the way of pedestrians crossing the street. I have seen some of them use the train as a pass-through. The little red train travels through town, as if it were only a streetcar.

We climbed higher and higher, into deep woods with creeks that became fringed with ice as we chugged even higher. We saw deer drinking from the creeks. Snow decorated the evergreens with fat fluffy blobs like huge cotton balls. Before we reached the ski resort of Arosa (at the top of the mountain) large snowflakes began to fall. The trip only takes an hour each way, but what an hour. It was like riding through a series of sparkling Christmas cards.

There were crowds of people in Arosa. Everyone seemed to be riding a sled or skiing. Most of the houses and hotels were chalets. The larger hotels were multi-storied chalets. We had hot chocolate in a small teashop (a chalet) before catching the train back down the mountain to Chur.

It was dark on the way back, but the moon was full and shining brightly on the snow. When we had been descending for about fifteen minutes I saw a wolf standing in a clearing not far from the train tracks. His head was thrown back; he was either howling or sniffing the air. Just a couple of minutes later I saw a small buck at the edge of the woods. I hope the wolf didn't find him.

It's New Years Eve, and Herb must leave tomorrow. There are several bridges over the Limmat River in Zurich, and tonight there will be dancing on one of them, the night culminating with fireworks over the bridges and the river.

The dance area was so crowded we couldn't get near it, but everyone was dancing or swaying to the music, wherever they were. At five minutes before midnight the church bells began ringing the old year out, and the new one in.

Herb couldn't spend all of New Year's Day with me; breakfast was our celebration. Then we went to the airport in Zurich; it was time to say *auf wiedersehen*. We hugged each other, and he walked through the gate to his plane. I waved as long as I could see him and then went to catch another train. According to a newspaper I picked up on the train, the State Department had issued a warning to Americans in Germany. There were unconfirmed reports of terrorist threats against American military and civilians.

Optimistic, I went to Bad Godesburg to arrange for travel to Russia. At the Embassy of the Russian Federation, I sat down to wait for a representative of the visa department. I had expected a long wait; there were many people ahead of me, but in less than ten minutes a woman in her mid-thirties, carrying a sheaf of papers approached me. When I gave her my proposed itinerary, she was amazed.

"Madam, you may not go everywhere you want to go in Russia! There are rules. You may be able to do this (we were speaking German), but you must buy vouchers for every day you spend in Russia. We do not book your journey here. You must go to an approved agent, book your complete journey, and then we will give you a visa." That sounded reasonable, the rule also applies when booking a Russian trip from the United States. She suggested an agent in nearby Haan, gave me a visa application to return by mail, wished me luck, and said good-bye. The visa regulations filled three pages (in English), with many lines and words typed in bold and underlined. Scanning the nine rules and long paragraphs of instructions, I was stunned when I read "MULTIPLE VISAS (for more than one entry and exit from the Russian Federation) can be granted only to persons traveling on business purposes." Could breaking a world record be considered business? I wondered. It certainly is work! Reading further, I was even more discouraged. "Business trips require an invitation from a business partner or firm. An invitation is considered to be invalid unless sealed and signed by the president of the inviting partner-organization." Another of my plans had gone awry. On the train to Haan I tried to devise plan-B. The office of the agent in Haan was over three kilometers from the train station. Asking directions of several people brought the same response. "It is too far. It is on the mountain. Take a taxi." I walked (uphill all the way), only to find the office was in a private apartment, and no one answered the door. Back at the station I called the travel agent and was assured he could book me on all the train routes in Russia and beyond, but I envisioned only a little ray of hope.

Two days later I received a letter from the visa department of the Embassy of the Russian Federation, informing me that they would be unable to issue my visa without a German work permit or a document proving German Citizenship. Perhaps the representative thought I was living in Germany, since I speak German, and I gave my address in Bad Kreuznach.

Chapter 7
Snowstorms and Floods

It was 10:15 p.m. when I boarded # 223, the *Donau Kurier* (Danube Courier) to Budapest. The compartments in the seating carriages were quickly filling up with passengers. It's easy to spot the overnight travelers; they clutter the seats around them with their backpacks, food bags and jackets to discourage others from "intruding." They create their own little world, a space to stretch out for the long night. The commuters just pile into any compartment. An overnighter myself, I hurried into an empty compartment and took a seat by the window.

A young man with dark slicked-back hair paused in the doorway before entering the compartment. After hoisting a large black suitcase onto the overhead rack opposite me, he spoke to me in German.

"I am from Algeria. Are you German?"

"No, I am an American tourist." He didn't take his long, brown leather coat off; he pushed one sleeve up a little and showed me an identification bracelet engraved with "Fodil."

"I am Fodil. I am tired. Can we do the seats?"

The conductor had made his rounds, so I agreed. Since there were only two of us, we raised the arms between the seats and each of us had a private "sofa-bed" with plenty of floor space separating them.

Within five minutes Fodil tried to fit himself onto my bed with me. I pushed him away, chastising him, and reminding him that I could be his grandmother.

All was calm for a few minutes, then he tried it again. He was still wearing his long coat, and threw the skirt of it across me. I shoved him onto the floor, calling him a jackass and a few other things. The conductor had gone into the sleeping car, so I left all of my gear except my backpack (my mileage documents were in it) and searched for another compartment. I couldn't pass through to the rest of the train, because the sleeping carriages that separated it were locked.

I found one empty seat in a compartment in my carriage. Several young American soldiers, who were in various stages of sleep (and intoxication), occupied the compartment, but they were preferable over my last seatmate. After explaining my problem to them, I was welcomed to the compartment with cheers and offers of beer and wine. I declined the drinks, and leaned back to rest. The soldier next to me kept dozing off, his head falling against my shoulder. He had placed his nearly full bottle of beer between his legs and it kept spilling onto the seat and down one leg. When the train began to speed up and shake, I reached for the beer bottle (still between his legs), thinking I would set it on the floor. The soldier woke up and grinned at me; he thought I was trying to get fresh. Embarrassed, I went back to the other compartment to see if Fodil, the creep had gone. He was rifling my suitcase! I was furious. He was a thief too. Without fear of the outcome, I starting kicking him in the shins and pummeling his arms and shoulders. He could have hurt me, but I think he was shocked; he just tried to hold me at arm's length. Anyway, it wouldn't look too good if someone came by and saw him beating up an old lady. Never mind that the old lady had hit him first. He cursed me in German, and scolded me in what sounded like Arabic. I called him a name that was pretty close to cursing, then went back and stood out in the corridor near the compartment of the soldiers (in case I needed protection) with my satchel and my backpack, hoping a conductor would come by, but I saw no one. I thought of kicking Fodil some more, but I didn't want to press my luck.

The Algerian got off the train at 4:30 in the morning, at the last stop in Germany, before the train crossed the Austrian border. I went back to my original compartment, but didn't sleep.

The train ended in Budapest, at noon. It had been a long night; I was ready for breakfast. I exchanged a few dollars for Hungarian Forints and bought a croissant and a cup of coffee. Croissants supposedly originated in Budapest in the year 1686. French bakers, up early to begin their baking, heard the Ottoman Turks digging underground passages in order to surprise the sleeping citizens, thus besieging the city. French bakers sounded the alarm and saved the city. They were given the honor of creating a special commemorative pastry. The Turkish flag, with its crescent emblem inspired the bakers to produce a crescent (croissant) roll. True or not, I enjoyed having a croissant in the city where it was said to originate. It was like drinking Rhine wine on the Rhine, or hearing the "Blue Danube Waltz" while relaxing on a ship on the Danube.

My plan didn't include staying in Budapest at this time; I would pass through it again on my way to the Balkans, after the problems in Bosnia are solved. A train was leaving for Szombathely (Steinamanger), Hungary. It was only a four-hour journey. I needed a short trip, and a rest.

After walking for several hours in Szombathely, I checked into a hotel. My room was on one of the higher floors, where everything seemed to be in a state of unfinished renovation. I had to step over planks of wood and assorted tools to reach the door to my room.

I walked the several kilometers back to the station, picked up my luggage and caught a train toward the alpine area of Germany. Today I planned to go to Garmisch-Partenkirchen and take the cogwheel train and a cable car up to the *Zugspitze,* the highest (9,721 feet above sea level) peak of the Bavarian Alps. Then I could go down the other side of the mountain to Austria on the Austrian *Zugspitzebahn,* and take a train over the Brenner Pass to Italy over a new route.

But, the weather outlook wasn't too good for the alpine area; I didn't go up to the *Zugspitze.* When I got to Garmisch-Partenkirchen I stayed on the train, continuing toward the Italian Alps via Innsbruck, taking a chance on getting through the mountain passes.

The road signs and the station signs were completely covered with snow; I couldn't tell where we were. As the train moved along the tracks it made its own little snowstorm, scattering snow everywhere.

The train stopped in Mittenwald; the tracks were impassable because of deep snow. More storms had left the alpine passes blocked. Everyone got off the train and went into the station to hear the weather broadcast. It wasn't good news. An hour later we learned that the train would not be going any farther. We had a choice of staying in Mittenwald or going back toward Munich. If I had been sure I would only be stranded for one night, I would have stayed. Everything was blanketed with deep, sparkling snow.

It was impossible to tell where the platform ended and the tracks began. I asked a woman to take a picture of me, but I misjudged as I stepped back for a better background view, and fell down through a snowdrift onto the tracks below. It took some doing to climb up from the tracks onto the platform. I kept slipping and sliding; I was glad the trains weren't moving.

A clerk in the station stamped my document and wrote, *"Strecke gesperrt zwischen Mittenwald und Innsbruck"* (the section of tracks between Mittenwald and Innsbruck are impassable). I bought a newspaper outside the station. Workers were stranded on top of the *Zugspitze.* There had been severe snowstorms and neither the train nor the cable car could make it down the mountain. If I had followed my original plan, I would have been stranded up there too.

Some of the Mittenwald residents, expecting to be snowbound, were pulling sleds loaded with supplies. I asked for a ride on the snowplow, but the answer was no.

When a train was ready to go to Munich, I boarded. Secretly, I had always wanted to be snowbound, but I needed mileage.

The snow draped itself over the evergreen trees like bridal veils. Chalets looked like Christmas gingerbread houses, frosted with icings of snow. Cross-country skiing was now possible from town to town. People were walking on skis a few feet from the railroad tracks.

The train slowly made its way to Munich. News wasn't good there either. According to my paper, the buses were delayed and there had been several accidents in the area. Streets in Munich were iced over, adding to the danger. Upper and Lower Bavaria were covered in snow and ice; there was no way for me to get over the Alps to continue on my way down south. Eight mountain passes were closed, including the Brenner Pass that I had planned to go through. I heard one report of an avalanche, and several areas were under alert.

Based in Munich, I took day trips on different routes around Munich. Although my hotel in Munich is on a street that is famous for nighttime "action," it is a respectable, family-run establishment. It is inexpensive, and conveniently close to the train station. However, whenever I ventured out at night, one or more men accosted me, looking for "action." My reactions ranged from shock to humor, depending on who was asking. When a young American soldier (in uniform) loudly and lewdly propositioned me from the window of a taxi one night, I gave him Hell. My response to a young man in his twenties, who approached me in broad daylight, was to laugh in his face. Didn't he know it had taken many years to acquire these wrinkles?

More than once in the few days I spent in Munich, I slipped and fell on the icy streets and streetcar tracks, sometimes barely picking myself up before a vehicle could run me over.

When the storms were over I took an overnighter from Munich to Italy. The carriages with seating compartments were all second class. It is a setup I have been seeing a lot lately, just another way of saving money for the railroads I suppose, but it deeply affects first-class rail pass users. I would rather they save money by not having so many fancy new trains with uniformed hosts to greet the passengers on the platform, as I have seen in some European countries.

The train wasn't crowded. I found an empty compartment, but if it had been tourist season, I may not even have had a seat if there were only second-class carriages. I don't expect guaranteed sleeping space unless I rent a couchette or sleeper, but there really should be at least one first-class carriage on overnighters for passengers who have paid the first-class price.

Snow was still piled up beside the tracks all through the alpine area, and more snow was coming down in large flakes. The top layer of snow glimmered from the light of the moon; it was like gliding through a winter wonderland.

When we stopped in Kufstein, at the Austrian border, I could see the twelfth-century fortress from the window of the train. Jumping off the train to make a snowball, I was almost left behind on the platform in my sock feet. I hadn't taken the time to put my shoes on. Jumping back on the train was a little more difficult; it was slowly pulling away. I dropped my snowball.

The curtains on the outside window and on the door had been removed. Anyone passing by the corridor could see that I was alone. I had seen a couple of people I thought I should be wary of, but my door squeaked loudly when I slid it open; I would hear if someone tried to enter the compartment. Some compartments have locks on the doors, but mine was not one of them.

It was cold, so I covered with my Mylar emergency blanket. I always carry several on trips. They are lightweight, but the special material keeps the body heat in. The only problem is that once I open one and unfold it, I can never fold it back to its original tiny size. I always end up with a big, wrinkled, silvery object that barely fits in my backpack.

At the Italian border, the German shepherd dog startled me. The border guard slid the compartment door open, allowing the dog to enter first. I must have been sleeping soundly; I didn't hear him open my squeaking door, after all. The dog that entered my compartment obviously had never encountered a Mylar blanket before. He stuck his head under it, moving it from side to side against my feet. I screamed and threw the blanket off. It landed across the dog, and he thrashed around in it. The guard came in quickly, turned the light on, and said something to the dog as he took the blanket off. Somehow, the guard knew I was an American. He said in English, "It's OK! He won't hurt you." I was glad I hadn't remained facing the window, or my head, instead of my feet would have been by the door when the dog came in.

The next day I detrained in Bologna. A local train to Ancona was ready to board. From Ancona I traveled along the Adriatic Coast to Brindisi, where I had a four-hour wait for a train around the "toe and heel" of Italy's boot.

In Brindisi, I found an Italian restaurant not far from the station. The owners and several family members were sitting at a large round table drinking wine, but I was the only customer. A white cat wearing a rhinestone collar was sitting on the lap of one of the women.

About halfway through my meal the woman asked if I'd like to see the cat do a trick. Choosing not to appear snobbish, I said I would, although I don't condone the European practice of allowing pets in restaurants. The cat jumped up on the table and began to dance on his hind legs. On cue, he would stop, sit down, and when cued further, he would dance again. At first I was so surprised that I didn't say anything, but when I remembered that it had been a long time since I had entertainment with my dinner, I applauded loudly, and said, "Bravo!" The cat was rewarded with a bite of meat, and I was rewarded (for my enthusiastic applause) with a bottle of cola. As I was leaving, an Irish setter came ambling out of the kitchen. I said good-bye to the family and walked to the station, perhaps missing a doggy trick.

In the waiting room I sat next to a man and a woman who were speaking in a language I had never heard before. They seemed sad, and a little bewildered. I asked them where they were from, first in English, and then in German. The man spoke a little German. He said they were refugees from Albania. They had just come over on a boat and were only able to bring one small bag each. Not sure where they would go, they were just sitting in the station. The woman was wearing blue-plaid house slippers. I asked the man if she had injured her foot, and he said she had no shoes. Her feet looked to be about the same size as mine. I had only the shoes I was wearing, but I gave her my fleece-lined rubber boots, and she put them on immediately. She had tears in her eyes, so I said good-bye and went out to the platform to wait for my train. I didn't want them to see *my* tears.

I had a first-class compartment to myself. It was only the second overnighter on this segment, so I wasn't very tired. I hadn't seen any suspicious characters on this train, but I had another safety feature tonight. The door was broken. Whenever I slid it open it fell into the compartment. If a thief came in he would fall in. The conductor might fall in.

As the train swayed and shook, the door flopped in and out of the compartment. In preparation for the conductor's entrance, I opened the door as far as it could go without it falling forward. At first he refused to sign, and when I showed him a note about my Guinness Record he was quick to retort, "You are no the Guinness Book! I know what is Guinness Book! Is book on my coffee table in my home. Guinness Book is write long time!" He thought I was claiming to write the *Guinness Book of World Records.* There must be a flaw or two in my self-scribed note in Italian. I tried to explain (in a mixture of English, French and Italian) that I was breaking a record and needed his signature. Then I added *"E importate, E urgente!"* to my note. It wasn't easy, but he finally understood (I thought), and signed. But, when his shift was over (on arrival in Taranto) he stopped by the compartment and told me that he would take a train back to Brindisi, where he lives, and wanted me to stop by the next time I was in town and go out for coffee. He would bring his Guinness Book and I could show him my name. Without an interpreter, there was no way to make him fully understand that I had not yet broken the record and I am not in the current book.

We followed the sea for a long time after we left Taranto. The blackness of the sea was striped golden by the lights on the shore, and the black sky above it was sprinkled with golden stars. Taranto is the end of the "heel," and is at the northeastern point of the Gulf of Taranto, part of the Ionian Sea. I managed to sleep through the noise of the flopping door.

The train skirts the coastline, a wondrous sight in the early dawn. At Reggio di Calabria we passed alongside the Strait of Messina to Villa San Giovanni where I changed to an InterCity just in time for a continental breakfast in the restaurant car. An American man was complaining to his wife about the hard biscuits they had been served. He was going to tell his travel agent when they returned home. I wondered what the agent could do about it? Refund them the price of the breakfast? They evidently didn't know that the bread wasn't stale. The Italians are only trying to share with tourists the biscuit-like bread they prefer for breakfast. One needs only to ask for soft bread if preferred; the Italians are famous for their delicious breads. The train was still going along the coast, but we were now gliding by the Tyrrhenian Sea.

The overnight train to Frankfurt was canceled; I caught an InterCity to Milan. Because of the cancellation of the other train, the IC was extremely crowded. I walked back and forth through the carriages several times but couldn't find a seat. Some passengers in first class were actually blocking the doorways of compartments to keep others out while they waited for friends to board. I stood in the corridor for five hours, but I had been sitting on trains so much, I didn't mind. But I *did* mind all the business people who left their seats to stand in the corridors, talking on their cellular phones, making it difficult for others to board the train or walk down the corridors to find a seat.

My overnighter to Mainz (I was going back to BK) from Milan traveled over a repeat route, but I wouldn't have accumulated miles if I had slept in a hotel either.

It had been raining for several days in BK before I left, and it was raining when I returned. I would have to leave again after a night's sleep; the river was expected to overflow and the trains could be delayed or canceled. Some of the tracks near BK were already closed off.

My timing was off; the Nahe exceeded its banks in the night. I awakened to a world of brown, flooded streets. But, unlike Venice, it didn't resemble a sixteenth-century painting; it looked like the aftermath of a disaster. Cellars were filled with water, which flowed back out into the streets, carrying clothing and household items with it.

Dirk and I went down to the old stone bridge. The rushing waters were jumping the sandbag barriers. We went to the pedestrian zone, only to find the water so deep that several people were paddling boats up and down the middle of it. One man was floating along in a large plastic swimming pool (imprinted with cartoon characters). Much to the delight of the crowd, it tipped over every few feet. Most of the stores in the pedestrian zone were closed, but a few of the more adventuresome owners had placed homemade steps in front of their stores, enticing customers with signs that read "*Hochwasser Angebote*" (high-water bargains).

Newspaper reporters were taking pictures of the mess. We tried to plant ourselves in the scene, but we were passed over for shots of a flooded basement, and a boy on a bicycle, riding through the deep water. Dirk wanted to stay longer, but I needed to get out of BK while I could still get a train. Anyway, our boots were full of muddy water; it was time to go.

According to the news the Scandinavian countries were wracked with severe snowstorms and the waterways and seas had risen. The Rhine and the Mosel had overflowed and some of the train tracks were out of order. Cologne was fortified with 200,000 sandbags; the water level was the highest since 1926. The flooding in Bonn caused the US Embassy to close its doors. The Main River had overflowed, sending enough water onto the streets of Frankfurt to break a twenty-five year record. Eastern France was flooded, and 10,000 people were evacuated. Fifteen people died. Parts of Belgium and the Netherlands were flooded too. In the Nijmegen region of the Rhine, over 700,000 people had to leave their homes, because of the high waters. I didn't leave BK after all.

Chapter 8
The Arctic Circle: Winter

When the waters abated I headed for Norway. One local train and two fancy InterCity Expresses, and I was ready to take a EuroCity over the Fehmarn Belt to Denmark. In Puttgarden, Germany several carriages are shunted into a huge ferry for the crossing to Rodby, Denmark. I was in the cafeteria when we docked. There was a mad rush to find seats on the train on the lower deck. A young Australian man sat near me in a parlor carriage. We talked about our travel plans. He was going to Copenhagen to visit his girlfriend (also from Australia) before going back to England to begin his new job. A small cooking pot and a skillet dangled from his backpack.

"I carry a portable camp stove with me to cook inexpensive meals, sometimes while sitting on a curb, if I'm not near a park. I get some strange looks from people when I am cooking on the sidewalk."

I said, "Perhaps I should have brought a stove; I could have more hot meals. I get a lot of strange looks anyway, just for saying I'm a vegetarian."

When we got to Copenhagen our carriage stopped outside the station (we were near the end of the train). I looked up into a brightly-lit second floor window of an apartment building near the tracks. A tall dark-haired woman dressed in black was dancing with her back to the window. She was wearing a brief two-piece outfit. A black, feather boa was draped around her neck. Her wide-brimmed black hat was shifting from side to side as she danced. I was sure it was something the Australian had never seen before, so I said, "Quick, look up in that window!" The young man went over to look out the large window on the top half of the train door. He hurried back to his seat without a word or a glance in my direction. Four young Japanese tourists also looked out, and they laughed. I decided I had better take another look. Shielding my eyes from the bright light, I could see that the woman in the window was not alone. A man was facing her, and she wasn't dancing. They were either having sex, or pretending to. The whole scene was an advertisement for illicit sex. It was a house of ill repute. I was mortified. I didn't know if the man had joined her after I had first looked, or if I hadn't seen him because of the lights. The Australian had thought I was a neat old lady, traveling alone all through Europe. Now he must think I'm a dirty old lady.

When the train started up again and pulled all the way into the station, the Australian man stood at the door waiting to detrain. He murmured good-bye, and hurried out to the platform. The

Japanese tourists were going on to Norway, but didn't know which train to catch. I saw that our next train was ready to leave, so I told them to come with me. When we got to the right platform, and tried to board, the conductor said, "What is your seat number?"

"We didn't have time to reserve. We just arrived."

"Hurry, get on the very forward carriage!" She frowned as she spoke; the train was one that required a reservation.

In Helsingor, Denmark, several carriages of the train are shunted into a ferry for the crossing to Helsingborg, Sweden.

On arrival in Helsingor (still on the Danish side of the water) the conductor came to us and said we must walk to the ferry; our carriage was not one to be shunted onto it. Our forward car was no longer the first one. Somewhere along the line we had reversed and we were now last. It was sleeting when we stepped onto the platform for our walk to the ferry. The sleet was blowing sideways, stinging my face sharply, but it was exciting to walk through sleet to board the huge ferry among the vehicles and the train carriages.

We were assigned seats in another carriage. I left everything in the compartment except my backpack and went up on deck. The rough sea made it even more difficult to climb the wet stairs.

A train to Goteborg, Sweden was waiting when we arrived in Helsingborg, but with an arrival time of 4:25 a.m. in Goteborg there wouldn't be much sleep on the train.

Within fifteen minutes after arrival in Goteborg I was on a second-class train to Oslo, Norway. On every train in Scandinavia so far, I had secured signatures and stamps; the only problem was with the reservation requirements. I hardly ever had time in between trains to purchase a reservation. I couldn't purchase it in advance; I didn't always know where I would go next.

In Oslo, I had twenty minutes before my train to Trondheim, Norway, just enough time to stand in line for a reservation. Later I found that I didn't have to reserve; I had misunderstood *"Plassreservering mulig."* It means reservation possible, not reservation required.

Many waterways and waterfalls can be seen from the train. Evergreen trees line the tracks, and at some points spread out into a dense forest. Deep, powdery snow covered the landscape. Suddenly, the engineer brought the train to a screeching halt, narrowly missing the herd of reindeer grazing on the tracks. They scattered in several directions through the snowy fields and into the forest. Yet another wonder, from the window of a train.

Arrival in Trondheim was at 6:30 in the evening; I had five hours before my night train north to Bodo, the last town with uninterrupted train service on the western coastline of Norway. I was too tired to sightsee with a plan (it was dark anyway); I just wandered around the old city founded in the year 997. Trondheim is at the southern end of the Trondheimfjord. When my tiredness turned to exhaustion I went back to the train station and sat, and sat ....

It was eleven o'clock when the train to Bodo pulled away from the station. I was in a parlor carriage again; I wouldn't be able to stretch out to sleep. But, I was warm enough, my seat was comfortable, and I would be earning miles while sleeping. I slept, but only for an hour at a time; I was trying to spot the northern lights from my window. More than once I thought I caught a glimpse of them through a veil of snowflakes, but it could have been the glare of a snowblink, enhanced by the lights from the train.

I woke at 5:00 a.m. My neck was a little stiff from the way I had slept. The train pulled into Bodo four hours later. It was the first time I detrained above the Arctic Circle; it was a great feeling. I walked into town to find a bank. The Norwegian Sea is just outside the station. There were coastal ships all along the harbor. I looked out over the white horizon; it seemed like the end of the Earth. The deep snow made it difficult to walk, and more snow was beginning to fall. Not sure if I would go back to the station, or catch a ship, I took my gear with me. When I got to the door of the bank I slipped and fell back down the stairs and onto the grass. I was still holding the handle of my satchel, and as it hit the ground, it twisted my wrist a little. Because of the deep snow I wasn't hurt otherwise. I received two hundred and seventeen Norske Kroner (Norwegian Crowns) for fifty German Marks.

I decided to go back to Trondheim and catch another night train back to Oslo. Part of the way would be repeat mileage. But instead of going back over Roros I could go over Dombas and Dovre, gaining about four hundred kilometers. I could approach Sweden from a different direction without taking a bus or a ship.

The train back to Trondheim was a red NSB (Norges Statsbaner). I was in a first-class parlor carriage. My seat wouldn't lean back, but I managed to doze for an hour or two.

Large flakes of snow were falling again. From my window on the world I saw gorges that were so huge I was sure they were fjords. Things seemed surreal. We passed through tunnels and over bridges. At Bolna someone had built a large snowman beside the train tracks. Lakes were frozen, and then covered over with snow. I saw a cemetery surrounded by barbed wire. The graves were buried in snow. It was as if those who were interred there were buried twice, once with earth and again with snow.

In the evening when I was having coffee the train began to lurch. The rough stretch continued for about twenty kilometers, just long enough to goof up my coffee break.

By 5:00 p.m. it was so dark I could only see the whiteness of the snow from the window. It's winter, and daylight barely shows itself this far north.

From Trondheim I caught an overnighter. It was a rough night; I slept fitfully, sitting up. I was feeling bad; I always seem to have a cold or the flu lately.

The next morning in Oslo I caught InterNord train # 57 to Stockholm, another reserved-only train. I had a cheese sandwich, as a combination breakfast and lunch. Missing so many meals has paid off in weight loss, but I'm not sure of my health.

In Stockholm I took an InterCity to Hasselholm. I wanted to get back into Sweden by a longer route, through Northern Germany and across the Baltic Sea to Trelleborg (Sweden).

The conductor said I needed a reservation. He said all the first-class seats were taken, so I'd have to sit in second class. I assured him I didn't mind, and paid my thirty Swedish Kronor for the reservation. He refused to sign my document because I hadn't paid for the reservation in advance.

Later he came to me and said in English, "You tourists think you can get away without paying a reservation fee. When I visit my friend in Belgium, I pay for a reservation even though I work for the railroad."

I tried to defend myself; "The schedule in the station didn't mention a reservation. Most of the time when a tourist is traveling spontaneously with a rail pass, there is no time to stand in line and get a reservation. We know that we may be charged double if we board without one, but sometimes it can't be helped. Your schedules are not clear. If a train requires a reservation it should have an (R) listed beside it."

"You can go and get your free coffee because you have a first-class EurailPass, but you cannot change to a first-class seat even if one becomes available."

"No, thank you. I'll just punish myself by not having any coffee, free or not." I retorted. He became apologetic, offering to sign my document, but I said I would wait for another conductor.

At Hasselholm I changed to a local train to Helsingborg. Another refusal; it was exasperating. Oh well, it was only 78 kilometers; I have been refused on much longer runs.

The ferry to Helsingor, Denmark took only twenty-five minutes, but I had to wait for a train to Copenhagen, so I took a short trip to the town of Hillerod. It was a big mistake. The conductor wouldn't sign; I took a local train to another town a few kilometers away, thinking I could get a signature from another conductor on the way back to Helsingor. But, there were no more trains out, and there were no hotels open in the area.

A lot of people were gathering at the bus station. I found a man who spoke English and asked him where the buses were going.

He said one more bus would leave for Copenhagen and then there would be no more transportation out of town until morning. I stood waiting with the others until the bus came, about one o'clock in the morning. Counting as I boarded, I realized I didn't have enough Danish money; I stepped back off the bus. There was not another soul in sight. Everyone had boarded the bus. Then I panicked. Just as the bus pulled away I ran after it and banged on the door next to the conductor. She stopped. I boarded and showed her how much Danish money I had, and asked if it was enough to take me to a town where I could find a hotel or another bus or a train. All those options were negative, but she said I could ride to Copenhagen without paying; she didn't want me to be stranded. I thanked her and insisted she take my Danish and Swedish money.

When we arrived in Copenhagen the passengers exited the bus quickly and disappeared into the night, leaving me standing alone in the square. The bus pulled away immediately. I started walking towards the train station. Copenhagen is a big city; the train station should be open all night. A young man wearing a long, army overcoat and combat boots approached me. He asked me in English for money. I said I didn't have any Danish money. He said he would take any kind. I could tell he was on drugs so I walked away. He caught up with me and began grabbing at my face and pulling my hair, but I managed to break free (minus a few strands of hair) and run to the station (not easy with my gear). It was locked. Only one person was near the station, a young man. He said it had been open all night until a few years ago, but now it closes because of the increased crime in the area.

I couldn't find a hotel that was open in the immediate area. It began to rain. I had seen a bus shelter with a glass roof; I figured I could at least stay dry until I decided what to do, but I found it full of bicycles that had been stripped. There was no room to stand, much less hide. No taxis waited outside the station since there were no more trains leaving until morning. I couldn't call a taxi, because I had no Danish coins.

I walked back to the station, hoping to find someone who would give me a coin for the telephone, in exchange for another currency. There was only one person in sight, a young bearded man wearing an Aussie hat, and a black jacket adorned with many badges and shiny buttons. He asked me for money too. How did they know I spoke English? Was it obvious that only an American tourist could manage to get stranded in a dangerous area in the middle of the night? Is the European image of us true? They are so used to us doing unpredictable and crazy things, that we are always excused with, "Oh, it's OK, they're Americans!" I told him I had no money. He began screaming obscenities at me, following me as I walked away. I was too tired to run anymore; I turned around and told him to leave me alone. He shrieked all the louder. Two young girls came across the street and gave him some money and tried to soothe him. They said he was on drugs and he didn't know what he was doing. I asked the girls if there was a restaurant open nearby. One of them said that there may be one a block away. I headed in the direction she pointed; I hadn't had anything to eat since the cheese sandwich at ten o'clock yesterday morning.

The restaurant was closed, but there was an outside light and a bench. As I started to sit down to rest for a minute, a young man stepped out of the shadows. He was wearing a pink blanket cloaked around him, and over his head. Only his face was visible. I started walking away. He didn't ask me for money; he just followed me, chanting, but he soon tired of it and went back toward the restaurant.

I was getting desperate; I couldn't even find a policeman. How could so much happen in one night? Dejected, I started walking down a side street, hoping the "baddies" were all on the main street.

I saw a woman on a bicycle at a currency exchange machine and asked her to help me change my Austrian Schillings to Danish Kroner. It didn't work, so we tried Swiss Francs, but no go. I had a one-hundred-Mark bill, but I didn't want to take a chance on losing it in the machine.

She said I could go home with her; she walked her bicycle and put my satchel on the seat. I balanced it as we walked to her apartment. It was now 3:30 a.m. She explained that she had been partying with friends and needed cash for her early morning bus to work. Her roommate had gone away for the night; I could use the room. The woman was in her early twenties. Was I the only older person to be out late at night in Copenhagen? Everyone I had seen so far was very young.

She set an alarm clock for me; I planned to catch an early train out. I slept on a mattress on the floor, but it was really comfortable. Soon after I fell asleep the door to my room opened, and a man looked in, saw me, and quietly closed the door again. He (the roommate) had returned earlier than expected and hadn't known I was in his bed.

It was eight o'clock when I opened my eyes; I had slept through the alarm. I remembered taking my bra off in the night, but I didn't remember trying to put it back on. I must have been half-asleep; my bra was across my chest, on top of the sheet I was wrapped in. I hope it happened after the roommate had looked in. I left my benefactor (I didn't know her name) a note, thanking her, and hurried out to find the station.

EuroCity # 187, the *Karen Blixen* would take me into the ferry for the crossing to Germany. I was in a first-class compartment with plush, green seats that pull out to make beds. But, it was daylight, so I sat up anyway. I am beat. For four nights in succession I have slept either in a sitting, slumped, slouched or fetal position on six night trains and several ferries. In addition, I was on eight daytime trains. The only time I slept for more than two hours at a time was in Copenhagen at the apartment of the woman I met at the currency exchange machine. That was also the only time I slept lying down. I'm not complaining; I'm just making excuses for my exhaustion. It wouldn't be so bad if my rib cage and shoulder weren't hurting (from the Polish train incident).

Sleeping on a train without a sleeper for four nights in succession is easier than sleeping for four nights on an airplane. Not that I have ever been subjected to that. Over the past few days I have discovered there really is a "bone-weary." I am it. I had two hours to relax until we got to the ferry for the crossing to Germany.

When the ferry docked, my train was ready to board. I crossed Northern Germany and into the former East Germany to the harbor of Sassnitz, for another ferry crossing. Several carriages were shunted onto the ferry for the crossing to Trelleborg, Sweden. I was in a through carriage to Malmo, Sweden. This was new mileage for me, all the way.

From Malmo I caught a train to Stockholm, and then an overnighter, the *Nordpilen* (*Northern Arrow*), # 904. I was in a parlor carriage again, no stretching out, but there was a lever to tilt the plush gray-on-gray tattersall seat; I could lean back a little. The doorway leading to the next section of my carriage was too short; I had seen several men duck to pass through. But, I was in the land of trolls, wasn't I?

Not far out of Gavle we came to a little town with piles of snow everywhere. I could barely make out the outline of a white church against its background of white snow. With a mantle of snow, some of the huge two-story houses looked like whitewashed barns. Just out of town the scenery turned wild again, lakes and evergreen forests. Big snowflakes came floating down, spreading their fluff over the evergreens and the rocks beside the streams. It was fascinating to sit and watch the night fly by my window.

A game of Musical Chairs was going on among the passengers in my carriage, and I joined in. Although we all had reserved seats, when some of the passengers left the train we made a mad scramble to secure a better place. Better, meaning more space. After two changes, I finally got a double seat to myself, but one of them was broken. I slept in the fetal position, with my head next to

74

the window and my lower half lying uncomfortably on the broken seat. In the night, just the lower half of my body slid off onto the floor, twisting my back.

The engineer sounded the whistle often through the night. It was a comforting sound, a sound from the long-ago trains of childhood.

I woke with a sore back from my night on a broken seat. We crossed the Arctic Circle, the second crossing by train for me. I detrained in the ski resort of Riksgransen on the border with Norway. It was only forty kilometers farther to the end of the line at Narvik, Norway, but I might have missed the last return train. Unsure of accommodations in Narvik because it is ski season, I chose to catch the return train from Riksgransen (still in Sweden). There were ways I could interrupt the journey to Stockholm and cover some new territory.

The station at Riksgransen is made of corrugated, galvanized metal. It's a huge Quonset hut with a narrow platform for boarding and detraining. Trains use the Quonset as a tunnel.

Skiers were heading up to the slopes. Children were riding sleds, and a few people were riding snowmobiles. I saw people on snowshoes, pulling wooden sleds that resemble baby strollers.

The only building in sight was a hotel. I went into the hotel restaurant for lunch. I wasn't very hungry, so I wrapped my buttered rolls in a napkin, and took them with me. When I first arrived I had seen a man tie his two sled dogs outside the restaurant while he went snowmobile riding. I gave each of the dogs one of the rolls. When I spoke to them in English, one of them just wagged his tail, but the other one stood up on his hind legs and howled like a wolf. I had to hurry; I had spent the two-hour wait between trains in the restaurant.

Another night on the train, but I would change in Gavle to bypass Stockholm and gain a few documented miles. I had only two hours to wait in Gavle for a train to Goteborg, Sweden. There, I would catch a ferry to Frederikshavn, Denmark, going over a different route to Germany, adding new mileage and a change of scenery. The many reservation fees added up to a total of 150 Swedish Kronor so far. It is almost as expensive to ride in Sweden as it is in Spain. Even on half-empty trains one must reserve if it is listed as a reserved-only train in most of Europe. The final count for reservations was equal to over fifty dollars, just for one day and one night. But, I *did* take a lot of trains, and most required a reservation.

In Goteborg I had several hours before the ferry departure. The station has a special lounge for first-class passengers to rest in. I sat in a big, soft armchair and drank my free coffee and ate two of the help-yourself cookies; I stayed until they closed the room.

It was dark, and a light, wet snow was falling when I started my two-kilometer walk down to another section of the harbor to the ferry docks. After a few blocks the sidewalk disappeared; I walked on the edge of the road. Cars and trucks honked as they went by, alerting me to the danger. The snow turned to a slushy rain. I couldn't use my umbrella because of the wind, so my satchel and I were absorbing the rain. My documents and journal were safe; I carried them in my backpack, which was covered with a plastic bag. Semi trucks were coming out of every parking area, which was about every two or three blocks. One almost ran me down.

The Stena Line building is a huge complex with several floors. It was practically empty when I entered; I saw only the woman at the ticket window. I showed my EurailPass and she directed me to the big glassed-in waiting area. She said I could sleep anywhere I wanted to on the ferry; only truckers would be crossing, and they wouldn't sleep on board.

Trains are not shunted onto this ferry; passengers embark and disembark from the docks. I was glad; there would be no steep steps and long ramps to face. I would catch a train on the other side at the Frederikshavn Station.

There were no other passengers in the waiting area. I sat on one of the many wide, wooden benches. Live trees, planted in giant pots lined the room, giving it a tropical appearance.

The cafeteria and the restaurant on the mezzanine were closed. I was so hungry; I had only two pieces of bread for breakfast and two for lunch. So far, my dinner had been the coffee and cookies in the lounge in the train station.

I had a great view of the ship activity in the harbor; the glass extended across the length of the room. The benches faced the sea. I was afraid to doze off; I might have fallen into a deep sleep and missed the ferry.

When I heard noises from the cafeteria I went upstairs, but it was still closed. Two women were mopping the floors; I would have to wait until I boarded the ferry to eat. I had been thinking about food all day.

The cafeteria on the ferry didn't have anything hot I could eat; I bought a box of skim milk and a banana. Blue vinyl couches and chairs were all around. I claimed the longest couch I could find and stretched out for the first time in another four nights.

The good sleep was short-lived; we docked a couple of hours later. I was sleeping soundly; I didn't hear the announcement when we arrived. One of the crew woke me and rushed me off the ship. I was the last passenger to disembark. By the time I found the train station it had closed again and there was no one else in sight. Everyone had made the train except me. It was still dark. I stood for a time in the shadows of the building for protection against the elements and whatever or whomever I imagined lurked nearby. A man walked up to me and spoke in Swedish. When I didn't answer right away, he spoke English. "The train comes soon. I take it every day." He looked normal enough, although he stared at me, making me so uncomfortable that I walked away. I didn't get very far; I heard the train coming and hurried back to board. I would have boarded no matter where it was headed, but it happened to be going my way. Four more trains and I was in Hamburg's Altona Station. I took another train for the short ride to the main station for better connections to base. It was a repeat route for me, with no accredited mileage, but I had almost 4,000 miles of new track to my credit for the eight nights, ten days to Scandinavia and back. Intercity Express # 671 was waiting on the platform. It was good to be on an ICE train again. In first class, passengers have the option of being served a meal at their seats. The conductor brought me coffee and a sandwich. I relaxed, knowing that just two more trains and I would be home, just in time to go to bed.

Chapter 9
Trouble in Berlin

Today is a special day. There are *Fasching* (Mardi Gras) parades everywhere in Germany, and in much of Europe. Rosi and I walked just a block from her apartment to wait for the parade to begin in BK. It was raining, but that didn't stop the cheering crowd. The costumed riders on the floats were throwing candy, plastic toys and comic books to the spectators. After being hit in the head several times by pieces of hard candy and toys, I turned my umbrella upside down and caught a few pieces of candy and a comic book.

We walked across the street to the *Mainzer Rad* where they would be celebrating all day and most of the night. Food was served in gigantic portions; I had a salad and a bread dumpling (slightly larger than a baseball). Most of the revelers were eating grilled sausages that could probably make the *Guinness Book of World Records*. About nine choices of meat were on the menu. French fries were served on platters.

A live band composed of two of the owners played German folk songs, American oldies and a few marching songs. Yodeling got out of hand when some of us amateur yodelers joined in. They didn't play "Spanish Eyes," but I danced anyway.

I overslept, missing the trains I had planned to take to Berlin and back over two different lines. Although it was noon before I left, by 3:00 p.m. I was relaxing on my third train, an InterCity Express (ICE). From the window I watched the trees blowing gently in the wind. I felt rested and happy to be alive, and on a train.

I saw the snow from my window the moment it started. Big, fluffy flakes floated slowly to the ground, then a few kilometers farther, flakes fell faster and faster, dancing dizzily through the air. I didn't write in my journal; I just enjoyed nature's white wonder from my window on the world.

The ICE trains speed from Frankfurt to Berlin in five hours, an easy, comfortable trip. I could have caught a slow overnight train back to Frankfurt, but I was feeling good; I decided to extend the feeling by spending the night in Berlin.

I walked all over the area around the station, and up and down both sides of the famous boulevard, the *Kurfurstendam*. All of the hotels except the expensive ones were full. After walking down a few side streets I discovered the Hotel Bogota, just off the *Kurfurstendam*. It wasn't priced to suit my travel budget, but for Berlin, it wasn't expensive.

When I was looking for a hotel earlier, I had seen a homeless woman who was at least seventy-five years old sitting in an alleyway outside a fast-food restaurant. After my dinner I walked back and offered to buy her some food, but she said she had eaten scraps from the trashcan. I tried to give her money, but she said she always found enough to eat, and didn't need anything else. The woman was wearing a heavy coat and a hat, but no gloves. I gave her my green, waterproof mittens. She stuck one thumb up and said, "America number one! America good!" I smiled, and then hurried away; I was crying.

The next morning I passed the fast-food restaurant on my way to the station. The homeless woman was still there. She was wearing the mittens. I said, "Good Morning." She said, "America number one!"

I was back in BK in the late evening. I had a lot of bookwork to catch up on, and I hadn't had time to talk to Rosi lately. We stayed up late, watching television, talking and eating.

There are still several routes in and out of Berlin that I have not yet traveled. Berlin is like a huge hub of rail lines, each going out over different towns.

A local train, an *Eilzug* (semi-fast train), an InterRegio, two locals, and one EuroCity, and I was in Berlin just before 11:00 p.m. The changes were necessary to accumulate new mileage by taking some secondary lines. On the EuroCity the young conductor was very interested in my attempt to break the world record. She gave me her business card, and then went to her compartment and brought me her "InterCity" neck scarf. She wasn't wearing it, because she was on a EuroCity. I gave her a silk scarf from Italy, and a small stuffed lion. When I detrained, she ran down the platform, caught up with me and hugged me. It was a nice welcome to Berlin. It was late, and I was hungry, but first I needed to find a place to spend the night.

I planned to visit German friends in Berlin, and some that live in Ludwigsfelde, not far from Berlin, but I would wait until morning because I would be riding the Local trains (S-Bahns). They aren't safe at night; I only take them when I have to. For months the Neo-Nazi skinheads have been hassling foreigners on the streets and the local trains. One group threw a black man off a local train, breaking several of his bones. When an elderly German woman came to his aid, she was seriously hurt by one of the skinheads.

I had only my backpack for such a quick trip; it was easy walking down the *Kurfurstendam* toward the Hotel Bogota. Several young men and women were blocking the sidewalk outside a nightclub, talking and laughing. Taxis were lined up along the curb; I didn't want to go into the street around them, so I tried to pass between the group. I said, *"Entschuldigen, bitte"* (excuse me please). I didn't expect trouble from such a normal-looking group of people, but as soon as I spoke, with my accent, I got trouble. They wouldn't let me pass. One woman said, *"Auslander! Wir brauche kein Auslander in Deutschland! Deutschland ist fur Deutsch! Geh weg!"*

She had said, "Foreigner! We don't need foreigners in Germany! Germany is for Germans! Go away!" They were words I had seen on protest banners and written on walls by graffiti-mongers.

I tried to squeeze by without a reply, but they gathered around me. I didn't know what to expect, but I certainly didn't expect the sock in the eye that was delivered by the spokeswoman. Before I could think of what to do or say, she followed with another punch to the same eye. Someone behind me was beating my legs with a belt. I tried to fight back but one of the men held my arms down. *"Warte! Warte!"* (Wait! Wait!) I said quickly. When my arms were released I said (also in German), "If you really want to fight a lady older than your mother, then fight fair!" As I spoke, I slipped the spray canister of Mace from my pocket. I didn't fight fair. I maced them all, even spraying some into the air. The instructions warn against it; I could have breathed in some of it myself. Running to the first taxi in line, I said, *"Schnell! Bahnhof bitte!"* He drove me to the train station. My hasty departure was a far cry from my warm welcome on arrival.

The only overnight train I could get was over territory I had done previously, so I took a train all the way to Frankfurt. It would be without mileage credit, but I was out of danger. I went to the WC to check my eye; I was sure I would have a black eye by morning. I was still angry, but I worried about the ones I had maced, and hoped they had all recovered promptly. Perhaps it would have been different if I had thought fast enough to tell them I was an American tourist. The Germans resent the foreigners who work in Germany, taking jobs from Germans. Tourists bring money into the country. I'll have to remember to use that in the future; I should have said it tonight. Or, better yet, I should have said, *"Ich bin ein Berliner."*

I went on to base and slept for two hours. When I woke I showed Rosi my official railway scarf. She knew I had been trying to find out where I could buy one. But she was shocked when I told her what I had been through to get it (I do have a black eye). I am concerned about traveling around Great Britain with a black eye, but perhaps everyone will think I have been to a British rugby game. Since my Berlin trip was cut short, I had an extra day in BK before heading across to the British Continent. I made up my mind to make the best of it; I would do something special. I wanted to go up to the castle for a leisurely lunch. But, what about my black eye? Determined, I bought an eye patch and went up to the castle. I sat at a table by a glass wraparound window. It was wonderful to see the town and the river below from my private corner of the castle (although I could have seen more with two eyes). Perhaps some of the other patrons were wondering about my eye patch. "Who was that masked stranger?"

Chapter 10
Crossing to Great Britain

It took only four trains (with a short layover in Cologne) to get me to Oostende, Belgium for the ferry crossing over the English Channel. Only the miles from Liege to Oostende were accredited. Within twenty minutes of arrival in Oostende I boarded the ferry to Ramsgate, on the coast of England. A thirty-five percent discount is given on the fare to EurailPass holders.

On arrival in Ramsgate at 3:30 a.m., I had a wait of only an hour before catching a train to London's Charing Cross Station. I was tired, but not enough to warrant a hotel stopover. A train to Hastings was ready to leave; I made it just in time.

From Hastings I transferred to the *Capitol Express* back to London over a different route, arriving at the Victoria Station. I was playing a game of zigzag, going short distances from London and back to get the short lines over with while I was in the area. It was difficult to change trains so often, especially since I ended up in a different London station each time, taking the underground or buses between stations, and couldn't leave my luggage in a locker.

After another short trip I arrived in Paddington Station in London, took the tube, London's underground to Euston Station and caught the 10:00 p.m. overnighter to Aberdeen, Scotland. It was my seventh train since arrival in England. Counting from BK, I had taken a total of eleven trains, a ferry, a bus and several underground trains.

My overnighter was comfortable, but I was in a parlor carriage; there would be no stretching out to sleep. Distances are figured in miles in Great Britain and Ireland, making it easier for me to keep track.

Arrival in Aberdeen was in the early morning. I headed back to London on an InterCity via the same route as far as Edinburgh (Dunedin), and then a different route (East Coast) to London.

The *Northern Lights* is an InterCity 125, which refers to its speed of 125mph at some points on the route. In 1985 an InterCity 125 set the world speed record (for diesel traction), traveling at 144 mph.

The highlight of this beautiful rail journey is the crossing of the famous firth (estuary) of the River Forth, the "Firth of Forth" on the Forth Rail Bridge. Edinburgh Castle is visible from the train. Set high above the city on volcanic rock, it casts a giant shadow.

At London's Kings Cross Station I took a train to Brighton, arriving in the early evening. Then, I was really tired. I checked into a hotel across from the beach, with a view of the Royal Pier and immediately went to find a place to dine. It was raining hard, the drops were like pellets, and they hurt when they struck me as I jogged for a few blocks, on my way to a restaurant I had seen near the station. I was soaked; water was streaming from my hair. Somewhere along the line I had lost another umbrella. The restaurant was closed, but I found a little fast-food place that served pizza. It was an old building with linoleum floors, and wooden picnic tables and benches. I was reluctant to sit down because I was so wet, but the man behind the counter told me not to worry; he was just glad to have a customer in such weather. He played the jukebox for me, a Beatles medley.

The rain slacked up before I finished my dinner. I went back to the hotel and to a good night's sleep.

Despite my night of rest, I didn't get an early start on mileage the next morning. The breakfast room was a delight. I sat at a small table by a window with a view of the harbor and the pier. An embroidered doily was encased in the base of the lamp on my table, and there were fresh flowers in a tall vase. Ten male construction workers were sitting at a long table by the opposite wall. When I asked the waitress for something hot and vegetarian, she thought a minute, and then said, "What about beans on toast?" My surprise must have shown; she said she guessed I had never had beans on toast. When I confirmed the fact, she announced to the construction workers, "Lads, this lady has never had beans on toast!" They all looked at me (every last 'lad' of them) as though I had just landed on Earth.

I asked her what kind of beans she meant, and when she said canned beans, I thought of American canned "pork and beans," but she assured me that British canned beans are meatless. I told her that in America one had to ask for vegetarian canned beans to have them without meat.

"In Britain you have to ask for beans with meat if you want the meat," she replied. I couldn't help thinking how true the saying is; "The British are so civilized."

She poured me a cup of coffee, and said my beans would be up in a minute. They did come *up*, they were sent up from the kitchen on a dumbwaiter, still in the can. I was about to ask for a can opener, but the waitress opened them, heated them in a micro wave oven and served them to me with all the 'lads' looking on, waiting to see my reaction. They were delicious. I also had hot porridge (oatmeal) and sliced tomatoes.

The rain had ceased; I walked around the harbor and the town. Brighton was called "Brighthelmston" until mid-eighteenth century. George IV had his palace; the "Royal Pavilion" built toward the latter part of the eighteenth century. It was built in the style of palaces in India, but decorated inside in the Chinese style. Brighton has much more to delight the tourist, but for me, it will wait.

In Portsmouth for a change of trains, I had an hour of sightseeing time. The station is practically on the harbor. The HMS *Mary Rose,* the royal ship that sank in the year 1545 in battle (recovered from its watery grave in 1982) is on display, but my time was too short to tour the Shiphall and Exhibition. The HMS *Victory,* Admiral Nelson's flagship, sailed from Portsmouth in September of 1805, later winning the battle at Trafalgar. Three months later she sailed back to Portsmouth with the remains of Admiral Nelson. It is also on display, along with the iron-armored warship, HMS *Warrior.*

My next train took me to Cardiff, Wales. We traveled through a beautiful section to Swansea, passing green hills, river valleys and lovely old villages. My maternal Grandfather was Welsh, of the Pugh lineage.

I caught another train to Crewe, catching up with the overnighter from London to Aberdeen. Most of the miles were previously accredited, but I was saving time by heading north to some routes I need to do in Scotland.

From Aberdeen I went to Inverness and checked into a bed and breakfast, then spent the afternoon sightseeing. I had to see the "Flora MacDonald" statue. That is my mother's name, although my father had dropped the (a) before he married my mother, making us McDonalds. Now I claim both Mac and Mc, making for a very confusing signature. I'm glad I don't need to claim the original Gaelic spelling, MacDhomhnuill, as well. The MacDonald and MacDonnell spelling came into general use later, in the sixteenth century.

Marks and Spencer is a great place for victuals. I have never seen such an array of prepackaged pastries, candy, or cookies in one place. Fairy cakes! I finally discovered what the mysterious fairy cakes are that we hear mentioned on one of the English television comedies. The fairy cakes are like our American cupcakes, a light, (fairy-like) white cake with a variety of icings. I bought a six-pack with two each of chocolate, lemon and cherry icings; I will make use of the free coffee on trains for the next few days.

Leaving my luggage in a locker at the station, I carried only my documents, a change of clothing, a few first aid items, and toiletries in case I ended up stranded somewhere. I boarded the train to Thurso, which is at the very end of Britain's northernmost railway.

From my window on the world, lonely moors vied with

mountains for my attention. Skirting the Dornoch Firth, the train goes slightly inland to Lairg and Golspie, then follows the coast again, along the North Sea.

The train splits at Georgemas Junction, my section going northwest to Thurso, close to the Norwegian Sea, the other goes east, and slightly back towards the south, to Wick on the North Sea Coast.

In Thurso I had enough time before my return train for a scone and a cup of tea. The waitress asked if I'd like to try haggis, a famous Scottish dish. She said that many American tourists order it. After I told her I was a vegetarian, she laughed, and asked if I knew what haggis was. I said, "Yes, I do. It is made from the heart, liver and other yucky organs of a sheep or a calf. It is minced together with suet, onions and oatmeal, and then boiled inside the poor creature's stomach." I spoiled her fun. She said she usually tells Americans what it is after they have taken a few bites. Some tourists order it only because they have confused haggis with finnan haddie, which is a smoked haddock specialty.

I returned to Inverness (over a slightly different route) to retrieve my luggage, then a train to Stirling and another to Edinburgh, over new routes, gaining a few miles to my credit.

Edinburgh has several stations, but pulling into the Waverly Station at night is like entering a Disney-like movie setting. The beautiful old churches and buildings have an eerie blue-green glow, caused by the combination of the lights and the verdigris on the dream-like domes and rooftops. I caught the overnighter to London (just to sleep on the train), without new mileage.

On arrival in London I played my zigzag game again, taking seven different trains from London to Penzance via Salisbury and Exeter. From my train window I could see the beautiful cathedral at Salisbury, with its seemingly endless gray-white steeple. I saw a lighthouse at Plymouth, a reminder that the Pilgrims boarded the Mayflower in 1620, sailing from Plymouth to a new home in America. The towers of the cathedral at Truro were also visible from the train.

The old "Royal Albert Bridge" stretches for a half mile across the Tamar River. Crossing it was one of the many highlights I have experienced on my journey through Great Britain.

Near Penzance we passed the English "St. Michael's Mount," a former monastery. Not as imposing as France's *Mont St. Michel,* it is impressive enough, sitting on the edge of a crag, with the coastal waters just below it. Like the French one, access by land is only at low tide. I had always wanted to see it, if only to compare it with the one in France after which it had been patterned (and to brag that I had seen them both). France's Mont St. Michel takes its name from the Bishop of Avranches, St. Aubert, who claimed (in the eighth century) that Michael the Archangel bade him build an oratory on the granite isle.

The English St. Michael's Mount was named after a visit from St. Michael. There is a legend that the mount was once a part of *"Lyonnesse,"* an ancient kingdom, said to be part of Cornwall before sinking into the sea.

Arrival in the pirate town of Penzance, at Great Britain's southernmost rail station, was just after 5:00 p.m. I checked into the Trevelyan Private Hotel on Chapel Street, about a block from the harbor. It was easy to imagine that I had been transported back in time; the hotel was built around 1775 for a sea captain. After an hour or so of walking around, I went back to the hotel for the night. The whole town seems eerily quiet; it isn't tourist season.

I was tempted to remain longer after my host promised me that if I would stay, she would introduce me to a few of the locals who had seen a ghost or two. Perhaps I'll come back and meet them someday (the people *and* the ghosts), but today I had my record to think of.

I had about two hours to spend in Penzance before my first train of the day. According to the brochure I had picked up in the breakfast room, Penzance had been named for the ancient "Holy Site," where the Parish church now stands. The settlement was called *Pen Sans,* meaning the Holy Head. Chapel Street is home to many of the town's famous buildings. St. Mary's Vicarage dates from the eighteenth century; the house next to it was the home of the mother and the aunt of the Brontes', England's famous authors. St. Mary's Church (1835) replaces the chapel, which was torn down in 1822. The present structure of the Union Hotel dates from the seventeenth century. For one hundred years it prospered as a coach house inn. In earlier times it managed to acquire quite a history, including being set on fire by the Spanish in 1595.

I arrived in Stafford in the late evening after taking only three trains, and checked into the Albridge Hotel. Tomorrow will be a special day; I'll begin the search for my Brindley family roots. My paternal grandmother was born near Stafford.

I started my search at the station information office for directions to Stoke-on-Trent, a town near the ancestral home. From there I hoped to find the town where "Hope Farm" was, or had been. It was the birthplace of my grandmother. I wasn't sure if it was the name of a town (I couldn't find it on the map) or just the name of the farm itself.

Buses were waiting outside the station in Stoke-on-Trent. I inquired about Hope Farm, but no one seemed to know where it was. But, when I mentioned the Brindley family, I received more information than I had hoped for. James Brindley had made the name Brindley famous in the area. In 1752 he had designed and built a water-powered corn mill in Leek, a nearby town. My great-great-grandfather, John Brindley, had a brother named James. I wasn't sure if James, the famous engineer was one of my ancestors, but I was assured that if my roots were in this area it was likely, as all of the Brindleys who had lived in Staffordshire were related in some way.

I took a bus to the town of Hanley, then a double-decker to the town of Leek. I asked the woman sitting next to me if she would tell me when we came to Leek. She asked if I were visiting relatives in the town. When I told her of my quest, she became very excited and announced my presence and my intentions to the other passengers. The bus driver drew me a map showing where I could see a bridge and a canal that James Brindley had designed. He suggested I buy a "fareday" ticket; it would save me money, and I could ride the buses in the area all day. The woman was on her way to her doctor's office in another town, but she insisted on going with me to Leek, and introducing me to the staff at the tourist office. When we alighted from the bus, she phoned her doctor to change her appointment. In all of my travels I have never encountered such friendly, helpful people. I felt proud to have my roots in such a place.

Leek is a lovely little market town on the Churnet River. The staff at the tourist office gave me plenty of information, including the news that the Bible and the wooden chest (handmade by my great-great-grandfather) that had been donated to the museum by my ancestors were sold in the 1950s (along with other artifacts) to private collectors. I could have learned so much from the entries in that Bible.

The mill and museum wouldn't open until Easter; I was a little early. One of the staff members telephoned Mr. Peter Copson, a member of the Brindley Mill Preservation Trust. He came to the tourist office and drove me to the mill and museum, opened it just for me, showed me around, and even let me run the mill. I was delighted to hear of the Brindley International Historical Foundation, based in Brentwood, Tennessee.

Mr. Copson invited me to stay and see more of the area, but I needed to get back to my train travels. It was a great day for me, and I'm indebted to those who made it so easy for me to discover a part of my heritage.

As I walked through the square on my way to the bus stop, I saw a monument set in the center of the street. It was a war memorial with the names of those who gave their lives in battle. There were several Brindleys listed.

I spent the next two days traveling over new routes in England and Scotland, making miles by changing trains often. I ended up in Edinburgh again, and connected with the same overnight train I had taken previously from Edinburgh to London. There aren't many overnighters in Britain.

I had planned to detrain at Crewe and take a new route back to London, but the lights had been off all night in the second-class carriages; I couldn't see in the pitch-blackness enough to gather my things and find the door. None of the crew came in. There was nothing to do but try to sleep, which wasn't easy without heat. It was freezing.

At 5:00 a.m. it was light enough to find my way into the special all-night snack carriage, the "First Class Sleeper Lounge." A conductor was sitting at a table. He was surprised when I told him the second-class carriages had been without heat or lights all night. I said we were unable to warm ourselves with a cup of tea, as we were not welcome in the sleeper lounge, adding that some of the small children in the unheated carriages were crying because they were cold. I asked if we "non-sleepers" could at least buy a cup of tea or coffee. The conductor was very sympathetic; he announced that all the passengers in second class could have complimentary hot drinks (not in the lounge, we brought them to our seats). I felt much better after the hot coffee. However, in the darkness I had missed my stop; the train would go all the way to London before stopping.

From London I took a few short routes. In the early evening I stopped for the night in Bath, the beautiful spa town.

I woke early; I wanted to see more of the town. The Roman Baths and the Pump Room were built in the first century, but not discovered in modern times until 1878, when workmen were repairing a leak in the King's bathroom. Buried under silt, the baths and the Pump Room were preserved by the flooding of the Avon River long ago. I spent some time walking over the beautiful old bridges.

By noon I was on a train to Newport, and then, to wherever I could make new mileage. After a rough day of traveling on seven different trains, I caught up with the overnight train to Edinburgh again. Another hotel bill saved, but I wonder if the crew is getting tired of me. On one of the trains I rode today, the sliding door of the WC closed on my hand as I tried to exit during a particularly rough curve. At the next stop the conductor escorted me into the stationmaster's office to have my hand bandaged. My sore hand added discomfort to my fatigue. On the bright side, the train didn't lose power, the carriage was warm, and the lights worked.

Arrival in Edinburgh was in the early a.m. I went on to Glasgow to catch the West Highland Line to Fort William, an extremely scenic route. A remnant of Emperor Hadrian's Wall (also called the Roman Wall) appeared outside my window. It stretches for seventy-three miles, from Newcastle upon Tyne to Bowness. It was built to protect the English lands of the Roman Empire from the wild Scottish Highlanders, at the cost of the lives of 10,000 slaves. It is over one thousand years older than the Great Wall of China.

The train passed the bonny banks of Loch Lomond. When we came to Rannoch Moor, we crossed a portion of its peat bogs, passing boulders and streams. The train bounces over the bogs, because the track was laid over tree roots, brushwood, earth and ash; the railway workers found no solid foundation on which to lay the tracks.

Keppoch House, the ancient abode of one of the Clan MacDonald's Chiefs is on the left side. Ben Nevis, Britain's highest mountain (4,406 feet) is seen from the right.

Shortly we came to Fort William, and I detrained. Many passengers go on to Mallaig for the ferry to the Isle of Skye. Flora MacDonald is buried there, and there is a Clan Donald Centre with information on the MacDonald Clan. At Trumpan, on Skye, one can see the remains of a church that a raiding party of MacDonalds set afire in 1597. Members of the MacLeod Clan were at worship in the church at the time. Before I read these facts in a brochure that I was given on the train, I had only known of the Campbell's massacre of the MacDonalds. Now, I find we have a dark past also.

In Glasgow I boarded the *Strathclyde Transport Train* for a new route to Carlisle. Arrival in Carlisle was late in the evening; I checked into the beautiful Cumbrian Hotel on Court Square. The hotel is joined with several other buildings. They have all been painted white, and roofed in blue tile. Together, they look like a huge castle.

From Carlisle to Newcastle upon Tyne the train runs very near the Roman Wall. Newcastle received its name when William the Conqueror built his "New Castle" there. The "upon Tyne" was added because it is on the Tyne River. Today wasn't all accredited mileage, but I traveled mostly new routes from Newcastle to London, over Sunderland, Middleborough and Leeds. When the snack trolley (mini-cart) came through on one of my trains I asked for a cheese sandwich, and mentioned that I was a vegetarian.

" We don't have cheese sandwiches; would you like a salad sandwich?"

"You mean you'll put a salad on bread?"

"No," she said, "We have salad sandwiches made up, fresh-cut." She showed me a salad sandwich; it was what we call a lettuce and tomato sandwich. If I had asked for a vegetarian sandwich on all the other trains instead of a cheese sandwich, perhaps I could have eaten. I asked for a cup of tea.

"We are out of tea. Would you like coffee?"

"Isn't that tea in the thermos?"

"Yes, but we are out of milk."

"But, I don't take milk in my tea."

"We don't do black tea, Madam."

"Please let me have a cup of *plain* tea, then." Reluctantly, she poured me a cup of tea. How British do they get?

I was in London by 10:30 p.m. As I walked out of the station to find a hotel, I paused, looking for a wastebasket. A man asked if he could help me find my way. I explained that I was looking for a place to put my trash. He spoke with a heavy Cockney accent.

"They removed all them dustbins on account of so many bums."

"Bums have to check the dustbins in order to find food sometimes," I said indignantly.

"Not bums. Bummms... Boom!" He meant bombs! The IRA had been suspected of placing bombs in trashcans and wastebaskets (dustbins, as the English call them). I couldn't resist acknowledging with a quote from Peter Sellers in a Pink Panther movie; I said, "The exploding kind!"

"Yes. Booom!" He then asked if he could help me find a hotel. I declined, but he insisted, and walked along beside me; he was concerned for my safety. It was rather late, but I assured him I was not afraid and he finally let me continue alone.

There weren't many hotels open in the vicinity of the station. I rang the bell of a small hotel on a side street. They had just closed and the family was having a late dinner. The owner told me she had a vacancy on the third floor. When I asked to see the room first, she became very rude, and said that I had my nerve wanting to look at the room first when she had quoted me such a low price, and I had interrupted her meal. She had a thick Eastern European accent. I was glad she was not British. So far, no one in Great Britain had been even slightly rude to me. After I remarked that I wouldn't stay in her hotel at any price, she slammed the door, and then opened it again, and called after me, "I hope you have to sleep in the street tonight, Yank!" In Britain, perhaps I should call myself the Ugly Yank, instead of the Ugly American.

Walking deeper into the residential area, I found a three-story brick building with a vacancy sign. After I rang the bell several times, a man and a large German shepherd answered the door. The man said he was renovating the hotel, but still renting rooms. A sign on the door listed several credit cards that were honored, including the American Express Card. I asked, to make sure, and he confirmed it. When I asked to see the room first, he wasn't too happy about it, but told me to leave my gear in the hallway and follow him. I said, "I must take my backpack with me. I'm carrying important documents." There were ladders, planks of wood and cans of paint along the way to my floor. When we reached the room (the dog came up too), I looked out the window and explained that I was checking for an escape route (travel books recommend the procedure, particularly in older hotels such as this one, in case of fire). His reaction surprised me; he seemed furious. The dog sensed a problem. His stance and stare frightened me. The man spoke to me in a gruff voice. He looked absolutely apoplectic. "I will not rent to you. I don't take American Express. You'll have to leave!" I reminded him that the sign says he takes the card, but he replied, "I don't want you in my hotel. Leave now!" With the dog standing by, I had no choice; I left, but I couldn't imagine anyone becoming so angry over what had happened. He was the only British person to be rude to me. After walking a few more blocks I checked into the County Hotel. Thinking further about the confrontation with the owner of the last hotel, I wondered if he had thought I was some kind of fugitive or spy because I was looking for an escape route, and I had said I was carrying important documents. I hadn't mentioned they were my mileage documents, and the escape route was in case of fire.

Chapter 11
Over the Irish Sea

I had miles to go before crossing the Irish Sea to begin my Irish Rover Ticket.

All four of my trains to Holyhead, Wales were InterCity trains. I had plush, first-class seats and complimentary coffee all the way. Crossing the causeway from Anglesey Island (also spelled Anglesea) to Holyhead, on Holy Island was at night; I didn't see much. I was thrilled to learn that Anglesey Island's ancient Welsh name was Mona (Roman, and Old English spelling). It was also one of the ancient names of the Isle of Man, in the Irish Sea, between England and Northern Ireland. I planned to thank my mother for giving me the name. The name I had complained about to her in my childhood because it was unusual. All my friends had ordinary names. However, there is another side to my name. In several languages it means "the moon." The dictionary says the moon is "the heavenly body that revolves around the earth once about every twenty-eight days." It is taking this "heavenly body" a lot longer.

Just after 1:00 a.m. I boarded the ferry in Holyhead to Dun Laoghaire (pronounced Dunleary), Ireland.

Arrival in Dun Laoghaire was at 5:30 a.m. I made my way to the station to catch a Dart (Dublin Area Regional Transit) Train to Dublin. The station was closed; I couldn't change money or get my rail pass validated. I was feeling the effects of my travels. My ankles were swollen and I ached all over.

When the train came, the station was still not open. I seemed to be the only passenger without a pre-arranged ticket. The conductor couldn't validate my rail pass, but he let me board anyway.

I detrained at Dublin's Connolly Station. The North Star Hotel is directly across the street. I checked in and was given a double room for the price of a single. In a few minutes the room began to shake. I had been in several earthquakes in California, and I was sure we were having one. Then I heard the sound of a train, like the sound the wind makes just before a tornado strikes (I've been in my share of tornadoes too). I was wondering if we were having an earthquake or a tornado. Could we have both at once? When the shaking stopped, I looked out. A train bridge was just outside my window. I couldn't get away from trains when I was away from trains.

As the trains passed by my window I could see their shadows on my ceiling. In the hall outside my room I discovered just how close my room was to the railroad bridge. There was a window

92

with frosted glass across from my room. If the window hadn't been barred with iron, I could have reached out and touched the trains as they went by. Anytime I am in Dublin this will be my first choice in hotels. I'll be sure to ask for a room on the station side.

By noon I felt rested and went out to see the city, first the old buildings around the bridges over the Liffey River. Connolly Bridge is wider than it is long. The Ha' Penny Bridge was named for the price the townspeople were charged to cross it in olden times. I didn't recognize Dublin Castle at first; it looks more like a large courthouse than a castle. It has been rebuilt many times since its beginning in the early 1200s. Anticipating lots of rain in Ireland, I bought another umbrella.

Intending to begin my train travels right away, I woke early, but when I started up the stairs to my room after breakfast I experienced a weakness that unnerved me. I felt as though I would collapse. Even though I had been climbing the stairs at a normal pace, I had to sit down on the landing of the second floor. I took it as a warning and reserved my room for another night.

Feeling much better after a few hours of rest, I went out in search of lunch. It was market day in a nearby pedestrian area; women were pushing baby buggies laden with bananas or household items. Singsong cries of, "Nannies, six for a Pound!" and "Nannos, eight for a Pound!" filled the air. Vendors were using several different pronunciations for banana. The Irish write the Pound (their currency) as "Punt." Some of the market people were saying Pound, but pronouncing it "Pay-ound." The prices of bananas ranged from six for a Pound to twelve for a Pound. Tobacco vendors carried their wares in jacket pockets, calling out, "Bacco! Bacco!" Adding to the excitement, a live band was playing and singing Irish songs on a bandstand in the square.

Buyers were tempted with row after row of sweets and bread. Clothing, household items, and antiques were available. I walked down to the far end to the vegetables, fruit and flowers. But then, I saw the meat and fish tables, so I decided to cross the street to the shopping center. As I hurried to get away from the meats, one of the fishmongers thought I was heading for her stall. She held up a silvery monster toward my face, and said, "Fish today, Madam?" Stifling a gag, I ran into the shopping center. The modern stores inside were quite a contrast to the outdoor market.

I had a plate of vegetables, a fairy cake and a cup of tea in the cafeteria of one of the department stores for less than three Pounds. But then, I could have bought anywhere from eighteen to thirty-six "nannos" in the market for three Pounds.

I didn't do any sightseeing; I thought I should rest a little more. Back in my room, I was literally rocked to sleep by the freight trains that sped by my window. For me, a perfect lullaby.

Waking from a long nap, it took a few seconds for me to remember where I was. It was late evening. I could have visited a pub for dinner; I felt fine, but as a precautionary measure, I decided to turn in early. I called room service. It was enough to enjoy my private, specially prepared meal at the small dining table in my room, listening to the news in Irish Gaelic, while the room shook intermittently from fast freight trains.

I slept well and woke early. In the breakfast room I was chatting with the man at the table across from me, a Scotsman who was combining a holiday with a business trip. He was wearing a dress shirt and a necktie. When he stood up to leave, I was surprised to see that he was wearing a kilt, complete with a sporran (a purse worn around the waist, which dangles in front, just below the waist). No, I did not ask him what he was wearing beneath the kilt. Neither did I drop my napkin and peek up from under the table.

After checking out of the hotel I walked across to the station and had my rail pass validated, leaving most of my luggage at the station. The North Star was booked up for the night.

There are no overnight trains within Ireland; I would have to take day trips, returning to Dublin to sleep after the shorter routes, sleeping wherever I ended up on the longer ones. An InterCity to Sligo was ready to board. I carried only my documents; I would return to Dublin tonight. When I asked the conductor the number of the train, he said it had no number. "It's just called the 8:40 to Sligo."

Sligo (Sligeach) on Donegal Bay, in the Atlantic Ocean was only three hours away. When we were ready to detrain the conductor announced, "Please move forward, toward the front of the train in order to reach the platform." The platform is too short to accommodate the longer trains. I walked around Sligo for a couple of hours. As I stood admiring an old church, the bells struck twelve just above my head. The peals were deafening, but I recorded them to enjoy again in the future. I find it interesting that the bells of each church or cathedral sound so different. A brown, fuzzy dog followed me for several blocks. His friendliness toward me was a welcome change over the 'bad attitude' dogs of my experiences in Continental Europe. Before I returned to the train station I walked back to the house where the dog had first attached himself to me. He seemed to sense it was time to say farewell; he went back into his garden without so much as a wag of his tail.

I returned to Dublin on another InterCity and checked into the Bronton Hotel. When I went back out to have dinner I was nearly hit by a car. I have trained myself well, looking both ways several times before crossing a wide street, especially in Britain, where vehicles drive on the left. But I didn't see the curved street that sneaked into the one I was crossing. Running for my life, I barely

halls, chasing each other in and out of a couple of the rooms across from mine, but noise doesn't bother me, and I like to see young people have a good time.

In the night I smelled smoke. Fearing the building was on fire, I grabbed my documents and my flashlight and ran into the hall. There was no fire. Guests were smoking in the room across from mine. I knocked on the door. A man about twenty years old opened it.

"What do you want?"

"Excuse me, this is a no-smoking floor, and the smoke from your room is bothering me. Is it possible for you to go downstairs to smoke?"

"I'm not smoking."

"Someone in the room is." He closed the door all except a tiny crack.

"Hey, is anyone in here smoking?" Several people yelled, "No! We aren't smoking!" Then there was laughter and the man who had answered the door said I must have been mistaken, and if I didn't like smoke I should move to another floor. OK, no more Mrs. Nice Guy! This warranted my alter ego, the Ugly Yank. "Listen Jerko! If anyone changes rooms, it's going to be you. This is not the smoking floor! Furthermore, if you don't stop smoking, I'm going to start farting." Hurrying back to my room, I had to laugh. I don't know what came over me; I don't often talk that way.

When I entered the hall in the morning I was overwhelmed by an acrid odor. The hall was full of feathers; my rude neighbors had had a pillow fight last night. Feathers were stuck to the walls and the floor. I figured they had poured water on them. As I entered the elevator, I knew it wasn't water. The odor was overwhelming. They had urinated on the feathers in the hall and in the elevator. I told one of the staff about it and was informed that several rooms were rented to a rock group (and their groupies, judging from what I had seen), and they had been warned about their behavior, and threatened with eviction. They would be barred from the hotel in the future. I thought they should be barred from society.

Breakfast in the Bronton Hotel is something to look forward to, although the smell in the elevator had almost caused me to lose my appetite. Almost, I said. I still ate enough to hold me until dinnertime.

My rail pass is running out, but I need to fly back to the States anyway, to ride Amtrak while the unlimited-stopover special is on. My return flight is for a London departure. Before beginning my train day I booked a flight from Dublin to London for tomorrow's flight.

My mileage to Cork (Corcaigh) today will be the last in Ireland. Leaving Ireland won't be easy for me. Even if you aren't of Irish descent, the Irish make you feel as though you have "come home." Except for the rock group last night, I was never treated badly by anyone in Ireland (perhaps the group wasn't Irish). The Irish Railroad personnel went out of their way to answer my questions, giving me more information than I had asked for. Not one Irish conductor refused to sign my documents. " *When Irish eyes are smiling, sure they steal your heart away*!"

I caught the train to Cork, which would take the route over Limerick (Luimneach). On arrival back in Dublin I went straight to the North Star Hotel, and was taken aback when the receptionist said there were no vacancies; I hadn't expected difficulty on a Sunday night, in off-peak season. The Bronton was fully booked too. I wandered around for a long time, finding nothing available. It was raining, but I couldn't use my umbrella; I didn't have a free hand, because I had my luggage with me, as I wasn't sure where I would be tonight. I couldn't find a room in Dublin anywhere, and there were no more trains out. It was getting late. I was tired, and there weren't many people on the street, so I went into the only hotel I hadn't checked (because it looked so expensive). The receptionist gave me some hope. She said she was expecting a cancellation or two, and I could wait if I wanted to. Soon, a cancellation was called in, but there was a man ahead of me on the waiting list. The receptionist said, " I am sorry, but after all, he was here first." I assured her that I wouldn't dream of infringing anyway. He should get the room. In fact, I would have insisted he take the room even if I had been first on the list. The young man was obviously ill. He could hardly stand up. I had noticed him when I came in; he was leaning his head on the reception counter.

Soon it was midnight, but the lobby was still filled with revelers. Some of the people who came in after I did were actually asking guests if they would let them share their room. I was just about to try it too, when the receptionist called me over. She had found a private room for me near St. Stephens Green. Earlier, I had checked for hotels in that neighborhood, but I didn't know about the private room for rent. I was tired; I took a taxi and checked in. It was a very nice house and my room was spotless. I hadn't taken time for dinner, but I still had a couple of packets of coffee and a packet of instant oatmeal. I couldn't believe my bad luck; this was the one and only place I had stayed in Great Britain or Ireland that didn't have a "Teasmaid," an electric pot for boiling water. When I went down to ask the landlady for some hot water, the lights were out and all was quiet. My luck didn't get better. It got worse. When I sat down on the toilet seat, it broke with a loud snapping sound. It pinched my behind badly; it was caught in the crack (no pun intended). After wresting my bottom out of the cracked seat, I washed the wound with antiseptic and went to bed. So much for my last night in Ireland! There aren't many parts on my body that I haven't injured on my journeys. But, I have a long way to go, there's still time.

It was quite a distance to Heuston Station, but I decided to walk, luggage and all. I followed the River Liffey most of the way, seeing all the beautiful bridges once more. As I passed the Guinness Brewery at St. James Gate, I thought about going in, introducing myself, and bragging about my upcoming record. But, it looked closed, and I was a little concerned about missing my flight to London. As I passed a Turkish fast-food restaurant, I was amused by the name, "McDoner" (*doner* is a Turkish pita bread sandwich). When I arrived at the airport in London, I was told I would be on standby. One of the agents came to each of us standbys, asking why we needed to travel on short notice. The passengers with the most urgent causes would have priority. I was surprised when they called out my name. My next train would be on American track.

Culzean Castle, Near Ayr, Scotland

Chapter 12
Out of Little Rock

Who said Americans don't ride trains? Someone must be riding them; it was a month before Amtrak could get me even half the reservations I needed to complete my trek across, up, down and around the United States by rail. In that month I spoke with many information agents, upsetting some of them with my complicated requests. I began calling as early as 4:00 a.m., beginning again after midnight, taking advantage of Amtrak's round-the-clock information and booking system. The unlimited stopover special had appealed to many travelers. Ordinarily, with an "All Aboard America" fare, one could make up to three stopovers per ticket. With the unlimited special, rail buffs and vacationers could embark on a dream journey.

Each time I called Amtrak I was disappointed. I was unable to get seats on more than six different routes at a time; it seemed that everyone was going everywhere. Most of the many agents I spoke with were extremely patient with me, considering my complicated requests for routing and reservations. Only a few of them were rude to me, probably because it became too difficult to figure out the next step. When I gave an agent several different routings to check, and if one segment was unavailable, we had to start over again with plan-B. I finally accepted plan-Q, although I would have to break the journey, stay in hotels, and buy three All Aboard America tickets.

If it had been possible to get all the reservations I had requested, a single ticket, valid for forty-five days would suffice, but I bought two separate thirty-day tickets (one to be used after my Canadian journey). My third All Aboard America ticket would be purchased, and seats reserved later.

My husband drove me to Little Rock to board train # 22, the *Texas Eagle* to Chicago. My 631-mile journey began just before midnight. Seats on the two-story Superliner are comfortable and recline further than the European ones. I slept most of the night with more comfort than I had expected.

Breakfast was served in three shifts. The friendly crew was busy making sure everyone had heard the announcement. An attendant walked down each aisle, asking if anyone needed a reservation for breakfast, repeating the complete menu if asked.

I was having coffee in the café downstairs when we stopped in St. Louis, but I took it with me and detrained; we had a thirty-minute stop. It was good to walk for a few minutes in the morning air. As we pulled away, I could see the 630-foot "Gateway Arch," the tallest monument in America. Soon we passed under the Eads Bridge, the oldest in St. Louis (1874). Then we crossed the Mississippi River on the Merchants Railroad Bridge, leaving Missouri for Illinois.

I checked my easy-to-read Amtrak brochure for information. At Granite City we had switched from the tracks of the Terminal Railroad Association of St. Louis, formed (according to my brochure) by several railroads to escape the high tolls levied by Jay Gould, the "robber baron" who owned the Eads Bridge in the later years of the last century. At that time the bridge was the only way to cross the river. The Association solved the problem by buying the bridge. We were now on Southern Pacific's tracks.

From the domed Lounge Car (also called the Sightseer Lounge) I could see from either side of the train. We crossed Lake Springfield and then the Sangamon River before arriving at Springfield, Illinois, our next stop.

At Lincoln, I caught only a fleeting glimpse of the "Watermelon Statue" commemorating Abraham Lincoln's christening of the town with watermelon juice (the melon was from a cart standing nearby). If I sought out every view and monument fully described in Amtrak's informative brochure I would be cross-eyed and have whiplash.

After our stop at Bloomington-Normal I was wondering if there was also a Bloomington-Abnormal, but according to my brochure we would soon pass "Normal," a town named for a teacher's college (Illinois Normal School), which became Illinois State University. Bloomington-Normal is a combination of the towns of Bloomington and Normal.

I chose to ignore the next sight listed in the brochure, a nuclear power plant, opting instead for a slice of pizza and another cup of coffee in the café. We switched tracks again, this time to those of the Illinois Central and Southern Pacific Lines. At Lockport we traveled parallel to the old Illinois and Michigan Canal's tow-lined paths. Two more stops and we would be in Chicago. I went upstairs to gather my things.

I had five hours in Chicago before # 30, the *Capitol Limited* was ready to board; I put everything in a locker and went out to see a few sights and pick up some food supplies. The Sears Tower, the tallest office building in the world, is only a couple of blocks from the station. I stood staring at its amazing height. The 110 stories reach an imposing 1,454 feet; its TV towers stretch it to 1,559 feet. It only took me a few seconds to become dizzy, just looking up at it. I decided not to ride up on the elevator (one of the fastest in the world) to look down from the sky deck (103rd floor). I was dizzy enough from riding trains.

Just after 6:30 p.m. I was settled into the *Capitol Limited,* and was on my way to Harpers Ferry, West Virginia, an overnight trip. Among the buildings in the city skyline, I saw the Sears Tower once again as we eased out of the station. Comiskey Park, home of the Chicago White Sox came into view before we crossed the Chicago River, known as the "backwards river," since the early 1900s when engineers reversed its flow to prevent pollution of Lake Michigan. Not long after we crossed the Calumet River, darkness fell.

In the early morning we stopped in Pittsburgh, but for only fifteen minutes. I stayed on the train, waiting for the café to open; I needed a cup of coffee.

I didn't sleep much last night; a second cup of coffee couldn't keep me awake. I felt drained, even though traveling on Amtrak is so easy. I couldn't concentrate on my bookwork, or the passing scenery. I don't know how long I slept, but when I woke we were in a tunnel. We had entered the mile-long Sand Patch Tunnel. On emerging, we were on one of the longest, steepest (2%) grades in the Alleghenies. Several horseshoe curves followed. Within an hour we were traveling through the Cumberland Gap, and then stopping at the city of Cumberland, Maryland, places I had visited in my youth when I lived in Washington, D.C.

Another bridge, another river crossing, and then we entered the Graham Tunnel. We were in West Virginia at the entrance and exit of the tunnel, but at one point in the tunnel we were in Maryland. Twenty minutes later we passed Hancock, a small town on the Potomac River that lies in three states, West Virginia, Maryland and Pennsylvania. Exciting, but when we stopped at Martinsburg, West Virginia I saw something even more noteworthy. The station is the oldest working station in the United States. Built in 1847, it has been in service constantly except when it was under siege during the Civil War. The only building in Martinsburg to survive the war, it is a National Historic Landmark.

Somewhere between Martinsburg and Harpers Ferry, General Stonewall Jackson engineered a plot to steal the railroad. His troops, under the command of Colonel Thomas R. Sharp, captured fourteen engines and many cars on this line that were loaded with supplies and new track. Impressed with Sharp's daring, the officials of the Baltimore and Ohio Railroad employed him as Transportation Master after the war. Amtrak's brochures were providing me with a much-needed history lesson.

The train was an hour late arriving in Harpers Ferry. My sister Joan and her husband Jim were waiting for me. I would spend several days with them in Maryland. They brought the sad news that Amtrak's *Silver Star,* on the way to Florida from New York, had struck a tractor-trailer that was stuck on the track near

Sycamore, South Carolina. Fifty-five people out of the 265 on board were taken to hospitals. None were seriously injured. Two engines and fourteen cars were derailed. I remembered how hard I had tried to have the *Silver Star* added to my itinerary, settling for the *Silver Meteor* instead when Amtrak agents were unable to get me a seat at the All Aboard America fare. I would have had to switch to the *Silver Meteor* anyway.

Feeling rested after a good night's sleep, I took the Metro to downtown Washington to the Russian Embassy. I wanted to discuss my record-breaking journey, hoping to get permission to travel on the "BAM," the *Baikal-Amur* main railway line along the northern side of Lake Baikal, and also to apply for a visa. The receptionist asked me to wait a few minutes. In less than five minutes she called me back to her desk, and said no one could speak with me, they were too busy. I pointed out that I was the only visitor. She said they were busy answering the phones. I reminded her that the phones hadn't rung, getting a typical red tape answer. "But the phones will start ringing soon." She went back to her paperwork. I no longer existed. When I called the Russian Consulate in New York I was told I could ride the BAM Railway, but I would have to get the ticket on my own. I called "Intourist" in New York; they couldn't sell me the ticket on the BAM railway, and I couldn't buy it in Russia because all of my trains and hotels would have to be reserved in advance. I settled for all the routes Intourist agreed to. Arranging travel through Intourist was still much easier than I had been led to believe. I went back to the Russian Embassy. This time the staff was fairly congenial. Nothing I could say would convince the visa officer that my route from Kazakhstan to Russia would not cross a portion of Kyrgyzstan (Kirghizstan). She showed me a map, and it did look as though it would. I was so grateful for the multiple-visa, unattainable (for me) in the embassy in Germany that I paid the extra thirty dollars to cross Kyrgyzstan, although I didn't think I would actually cross the border. The train travels just beside it at one point, according to the schedule. I hope it does cross over; I can add another country to my travel total.

Chapter 13
Tracking Memories

The next step was a twenty-six-hour ride from Baltimore to New Orleans on # 19, the *Crescent*, with 1,195 added miles. The train was called the *Crescent* because the Mississippi River cuts through the city of New Orleans in a crescent shape. So far, making miles on Amtrak has been a lot easier than most of the European routes, because of the longer runs. But, having to reserve every train is a big problem for me, considering the scope of my journeys. Also, Amtrak runs only one long distance train in each direction per day, per route. On several western routes trains run only three times per week, which will cause some layovers for me.

Shortly after I settled in my seat in the single-level train, we stopped in Washington, D.C. Somehow I missed spotting the Capitol and the other national monuments after we exited a long tunnel, catching only a glimpse of the Washington Monument. But I was raised in Washington, and I have them all etched in the childhood corner of my memory.

The dogwood trees surrounding the beautiful colonial homes are in full bloom. Most of the blossoms are creamy white, but a few of the trees are glorious in pink. White dogwood grows wild along the banks of the small creeks. The train had become noisier and shakier; it was like being on an older train.

Knowing that darkness would obscure most of the Blue Ridge Mountains and all the other beautiful scenes, I went to sleep.

I had slept through most of the Carolinas; I woke as we were going into Georgia. Soon the train rumbled over Well's Viaduct, high above the trees.

Just before noon we arrived in Birmingham, Alabama. Smoking is not permitted on board between Birmingham and New Orleans; I hurried to the Lounge Car to secure a smoke-free seat. I envied the couple sitting with me; they had secured reservations around the perimeter of the United States. In the beginning I had planned to travel that way, closing up the circle by doing all the shorter routes. It would have been much easier, and cheaper for me.

We had gone through Alabama and Mississippi (crossing only a small portion of each), and were traveling along the bayous of Louisiana by early evening. The ghostly-gray Spanish moss hanging from the trees brought back memories of my life in Florida. Once, in fright, my daughter (at about age five) had said, "Daddy, please don't park here! The trees are haunted!"

There were houses built on pilings out in the lakes, with bridges leading to them. Each bridge had a small wooden gate. Most of the houses had screened-in porches, and one had a gazebo built onto its bridge. Crossing the Lake Pontchartrain Bridge was scary. The bridge is so narrow I couldn't see it once we were underway, and if there were railings on the bridge, they were very short. I didn't see them at all. It was as if we were slowly moving over the water like a boat. Now I understand why a two-story Superliner isn't used on this route.

Only the familiar train noises confirmed the fact that we were on a railroad track. It took about fifteen minutes to make the six-mile crossing. The huge lake (644 sq. miles) is beautiful. Looking to the right it seemed more like the ocean; I could see the horizon.

Near the end of the bridge there is a sign, warning that a drawbridge is 1000 feet ahead. I was hoping it was down. It was a long 1000 feet for me, but the drawbridge *was* down. Once, my sister Joan and I were standing on a bridge in Oostende, Belgium watching the boats on a sunny afternoon. Joan remarked that the Belgians seemed very friendly; everyone on shore was waving at us. We waved back, calling out a cheerful, "Ahoy!" A man ran to the edge of the bridge (we were in the middle), and told us the bridge was about to open. We barely made it safely to shore before it opened. In the middle! We hadn't realized it was a drawbridge. Thereafter, I have been apprehensive when crossing one.

Soon after we were safely across the Lake Pontchartrain Bridge, I could see the front of the train as it rounded a long curve. The engineer sounded the whistle as we went curving through a flashing railroad crossing, the engine and several cars still visible from my window.

As we approached New Orleans I was suddenly faced with the Rosedale Cemetery, the largest I have ever seen. Mausoleums and gravestones seemed to stretch for miles, at times on both sides of the freeway we were paralleling. The graves are above ground because of the high water table. Minutes before the train stopped in New Orleans, a young girl asked me to sign her ticket stub. My first autograph request. Now I *must* beat the record! The *Crescent* had afforded me a memorable rail journey, from beginning to end.

In New Orleans I caught up with train # 2, the *Sunset Limited,* on its way to Florida, from Los Angeles. The *Sunset Limited* is aptly dubbed "Amtrak's Southern Transcontinental." Boarding at New Orleans, I would travel 1,033 of the 3,066 miles across the Continent. The other 2,033 will be done after my Canadian journey.

Usually on Amtrak trains, coach passengers choose a seat when they board. Tonight the attendant on the platform told me to sit in seat # 38. As soon as I sat down, a young woman with long brown hair walked up to me. She frowned, and said, "You can't sit here, both of these seats are mine. I have an injured leg and Amtrak said I could have two seats."

I got up and went to the only empty one. It was the first aisle seat on the front of the car, next to a little boy. When the attendant came to check tickets, she said, "I told you to sit in # 38!" My explanation of the seating problem prompted her to berate the young woman, who reacted by trying to crowd me off the seat when I sat next to her again. I went back to the front seat, brought my gear back to # 38, and proceeded to stow it overhead.

"You can't put anything up there. I boarded this train in California, and I have an antique picture frame up there. It takes up the whole section."

"Well, I have to have a little space, unless you want to hold my gear." I was getting a little tired of being hassled.

Her answer to the problem was to step (with her injured leg) onto the seat across from us (a little girl was sleeping across both seats), and rearrange some of her bags above to accommodate mine. Fine, I didn't care anymore; I just wanted to rest. Five minutes later, a traveling companion (with short blonde hair) of the young woman came to me. "I am going to let you sit in the two seats up front. I'm going to my sleeper anyway." Let me? Who was she, an assistant attendant? She transferred the child from the front seat to the seat behind it. She and her two kids were taking up six seats, and her friend and her child were using another four. Surely the attendant was unaware of that. I moved again, but used only one seat; I didn't want to hear the attendant complain. But, I did hear her. The next time she came through the coach, she spotted me, out of my cage. You guessed it; she made me go back to # 38. I did, but I decided it would be my last move for the night. It was way after midnight. Lucky for me, my seatmate decided to join her friend in the sleeper.

I vaguely remembered stopping in Mobile, Alabama in the middle of the night, but that's all I remembered until morning.

Tired of sweets, I ate a cheese pizza for breakfast. So far, I've had great coffee on Amtrak's trains. I had a clear view of the small town of Chipley, Florida from the window in the café as I lingered over my second cup of coffee. According to my brochure it is an old railroad town. In 1883 a line linking Tallahassee and Pensacola was completed, providing transport for Chipley's cotton industry.

The two young California women seemed to have disappeared; they didn't come back from the sleeper to supervise their children. One of the older girls (about thirteen years old) went down to the café and brought back breakfast for them. A boy about seventeen years old came and sat with the kids too, helping to care for them.

Before noon we had stopped. A freight train was stuck on the track next to us. I sat in the Sightseer Lounge for a long time before the freight train was hauled away by several engines. It was the longest freight train I have ever seen. The Sightseer Lounge was full; everyone wanted to see what was happening.

On one of my trips downstairs to the restroom I was surprised and shocked to spot the thirteen-year-old daughter of the blonde being kissed and fondled by the teen-age friend. Who was watching the little ones? I wondered.

The latest word was that we would arrive in Miami about three hours late. I would hardly have any time to sleep in my pre-paid hotel room. The train picked up speed, but we would still be very late. Someone announced over the PA system that passengers connecting at Jacksonville would be met, and shown to their train. At Sebring, Florida I could see the famous International Grand Prix Racetrack.

Arrival in Miami really *was* three hours late. I called a taxi, but when it hadn't shown up in thirty minutes, I called back and was told there was no train station in Miami. Where was I then, in the Twilight Zone? Before I could call another company, one of the baggage clerks came over and asked me to remove my bag from the cart; he wanted to close the station. By that time there was only one other passenger left in the station, a young man from New Zealand. The clerk rushed us out and locked the door. It was close to three o'clock in the morning.

The New Zealander wasn't having any luck with the cab companies either. Having read that Miami has a high crime rate, I decided that a taxi was our only recourse; we would keep trying. At least there was a phone outside. My luck was running out, and so was my change. After putting the last of my coins in the phone slot, I begged the dispatcher to send someone who knew the area to rescue us. I insisted we were in the Miami station, but the dispatcher said the train station was really in Hialeah. When I lived in Miami there was a station on Flagler Street, right downtown. He informed me that the Flagler street station was now a Metro station. So that's why the first taxi never showed up.

When our taxi finally came, the driver wouldn't take both of us; the New Zealander was going in the opposite direction. I refused to leave the young man alone outside the station. The driver called another taxi and waited with us until it arrived.

The receptionist charged only day rate because I had arrived late, and would check out early. I had less than two hours to sleep, but I was so hungry I took time to mix a packet of instant oatmeal with tap water for a snack. Then I had even less time to sleep. As soon as my head hit the pillow the phone rang. My husband was worried; he had called several times before I arrived, only to be told I had not checked in. I explained all the problems to him, and went to sleep.

When my travel alarm went off I thought it was my wake up call; I picked up the phone and said, "Thank you, I'm awake." I repeated the procedure twice before I realized it was my alarm still ringing. I was still tired, but I repeated my slogan, "Today is the First Day of the Rest of My Guinness Journey," and plodded on.

Another taxi ride and I was back at the "Miami/Hialeah" Station. The *Silver Meteor* travels along a portion of the Atlantic coast; I would see the ocean in daytime. From Miami to Jacksonville would be a repeat route for me, but from Jacksonville on, it was new, so I could claim 753 miles on arrival in Washington, D.C. I had no problem getting the conductor to sign my document, but then, on Amtrak I had never been refused. The problem was waking up all through the night to catch each conductor before a crew change. Distances are long; there are several changes on each route.

We were an hour late arriving in Washington, but I would still have a seven-hour wait for train # 51, the *Cardinal* to Chicago. My sister Joan and a friend met me for lunch. The multiple-restaurant complex downstairs in the station is a vegetarian's paradise, and I proceeded to make up for all the meals I had missed.

Walking around Washington's Union Station brought back childhood memories for us. It has been restored to its former glory, and beyond. The big difference between now, and then, is the presence of all the shops and boutiques. Joan bought me a T-shirt imprinted with a picture of the *Empire Builder*, a train I plan to take after my Canadian routes. I couldn't resist having my picture taken with the life-size cardboard images of President and Mrs. Clinton. Playfully, I stood behind the President, pretending to choke him.

I bade farewell to Joan and our friend and went to the platform. More memories emerged from the childhood corner of my mind. When I was twelve years old, I came to Union Station to say good-bye to friends. As the train pulled away, blasting its whistle, I experienced a deep feeling of sadness that bordered on loneliness, not because my friends were leaving, but because the train was leaving and I wasn't on it. Then I understood why authors of books and songs used the words "lonesome whistle." The whistle *does* give one a feeling of loneliness, but my interpretation is different from that of the writers. Now, after so many trains, I have finally sorted out the "lonesome whistle" emotions. If I am not on the train when it leaves, or I hear the whistle from afar, I feel lonely because I'm not riding the train. When I hear the whistle as a passenger, I may feel lonely because I *am* lonely, because I'm away from loved ones.

This time I was watching for some of Washington's memorials, although we were heading in a different direction. The Tidal Basin and the Jefferson Memorial passed by my window, framing my memories. I had played beside them both in early childhood. My first train ride, at age four, was on this route. It was during the depression, and my father had gone to work for the government in Washington, D.C. My mother, brothers, sister, and I traveled by train from Indiana to join him.

I was tired, and kept drifting in and out of a light sleep. In the early evening we were pushing through the Blue Ridge Mountains, a different section from the one I had missed on the *Crescent* because of darkness. The views were of trees, waterfalls and creeks. After finishing up my extra lunch I had brought from Union Station (as dinner), I went down to the café for coffee. I sat with two women from my coach. Andrea is a wife and mother who works in a real estate office in Chicago. She was on her way home from a visit with her mother in Virginia. Jenny was going home to Indianapolis after getting her engineering degree from a college in Maryland. We celebrated her triumph with coffee and wine.

Overnight on the *Cardinal* was a disaster (in our coach). One of the attendants kept poking anyone who slumped over, or otherwise used an empty seat next to them, claiming that the seat would be needed at the next stop. Once or twice that was true, but mostly it was just a show of power. There was an empty seat next to me, but after some of the sleeping problems I had encountered on European trains, I didn't need two seats. One of Amtrak's seats is as comfortable as two seats on European overnight coaches. Jenny and a young man were the prime targets of the nasty attendant. Every time one of them would spill over onto an adjoining seat, she would wake the culprit, repeating her contrived threat. Later, I overheard a man talking to the attendant. He asked her where all the passengers were who were supposed to board and take the empty seats. "Oh, I just tell them that sometimes to keep them from sleeping too soundly." What she really meant was that they should be kept from sleeping too soundly because they didn't pay for a sleeper. If everyone traveled in a sleeper, she wouldn't have a job. I wondered how anyone could sleep at all with her constant whining. She acted as though she was paying for the passengers out of her own pocket. The nasty attendant got her comeuppance from Jenny. After she tired of the scolding and the poking, Jenny refused to move from the empty seat unless a passenger actually needed the seat. I silently cheered Jenny. No one needed the seat; Jenny sat alone the rest of the trip, stretching out over both seats whenever she felt like it. In Chicago I had an eight-hour wait for the *Lake Shore Limited*. I was so tired I could easily have slept on a bench in the waiting area, but I felt the need for a little exercise. A brisk walk for about six blocks tired me even more; my eating habits and sleeping patterns are taking their toll.

Chapter 14
North to Canada

It seemed like days instead of hours before I boarded my overnight train. The *Lake Shore Limited* would take me to Albany, New York to connect with train # 69, the *Adirondack* to Montreal.

In the morning, I looked out the window. We were just out of Buffalo, New York. I hadn't expected to see Niagara Falls from the train window. I can only imagine how spectacular they must be up close; I saw only a portion of them from a distance. After sitting for so long, on so many trains, I am beginning to feel like a "couch potato," viewing one travel video after another, with the window of the train as my television set.

I detrained in Albany-Rensselaer to catch the *Adirondack*. It was good to be traveling in daylight. We traveled through the Adirondack Mountains, and along the shores of Lake Champlain. Burlington, Vermont is just across the lake, but the train stays on the New York side.

In Montreal, it was easy to find my hotel, Le Reine Elizabeth; it's in the train station.

My alarm went off at 5:30 a.m., and I hurried downstairs to find a cup of coffee. It was somewhat difficult to convince the man at the ticket counter that I was to pick up my prepaid CANRAILPASS. When I asked him to hurry because my train was leaving soon, he said I had about twelve hours before it would leave. I had mistakenly thought Canada used the twenty-four-hour clock as the Europeans do, and assumed that 6:50 was in the a.m. The desk clerk let me back into my room, but the two cups of coffee I had gulped down kept me awake.

The shops beckoned; I spent a couple of hours shopping and eating. I didn't buy anything except food. It would be inconvenient to carry gifts with me.

I couldn't resist having a caricature of myself drawn by a street artist. At my suggestion he drew a train passing through my head. Adding his own ideas, he showed me reading a Guinness Book. He drew a suitcase at my feet, adorned with stickers of Rome, Paris and Montreal.

My overnighter, train # V014 to Truro, Nova Scotia has wide, comfortable seats. The conductor was too busy to sign my document, but he promised to come back later. He didn't; he detrained in Levis (the town, not the trousers). The beautiful skyline of Quebec City is just across the Saint Lawrence River from Levis. Passengers going to Quebec take a ferry across. The buildings on the shoreline remind me of Europe. The "Chateau

Frontenac" poses pompously, as if on a pedestal, above the city.

The Dome Car (also called the Observation Car) differs from those on Amtrak trains; the seats face the front of the tracks. It's almost like being in the cab of the engine. There is a window in front and all along both sides.

The next day we arrived in Truro, a long way from the Truro on the southern coast of England I had traveled through.

I changed to train # 15. A group of teen-agers was on board with their chaperone. They almost filled the Dome Car, not just with themselves, but with noise. Some of them were so rowdy that the conductor threatened several times to run them out of the Dome Car. When one of the girls said a vulgar word over and over again, I went back downstairs, but not before I told her why I was leaving, and asked her if her mother would approve if she heard her speak that way. The girl apologized, and things quieted down.

The two nights on trains passed quickly, and I had slept comfortably. Not long after arrival in Montreal, I changed to train # 33 to Ottawa. The schedule listed another way back to Toronto. I secured seats on both trains, giving me extra mileage. The total was only 633 kilometers, and took a total of nine hours, but I had spent more time, for less mileage sometimes in Europe. I will begin converting kilometers to miles again. Of all the countries I'll be traveling in, only Great Britain, Ireland, and the United States measure in miles.

I was back in Toronto, and in my hotel room by 8:30 p.m. I find it hard to believe that the thriving metropolis of Toronto was once called "Hogtown."

I went out to look for a restaurant. A road crew was blocking one side of the street with their vehicles. They were tearing up the street, leaving a trench that stretched for more than a block. Carefully, I picked my way through the debris to the other side. It was difficult; the asphalt street was as black as the night, but I was determined to have a hot meal. I found an Indian restaurant a few blocks away. The waiter asked if I wanted onions on my takeout dinner. I replied that I liked them, but didn't want them tonight. When he brought the food, he gave me *two* forks and a handful of mints. "Have a special evening," he said; winking and smiling in a way that suggested I didn't want onions because I had a companion waiting in the hotel room.

The *Canadian* is a beautiful train, called Le *Canadien* in French. It is Canada's transcontinental train. The conductor and his assistant signed for me. At dinner, I was served a platter of fresh vegetables. The coffee rivaled Amtrak's.

Before I began my journeys on Amtrak and VIA I had asked the public relations departments about taking showers in the sleeping cars, even though I would be traveling coach class. I was told it would be up to the sleeping car attendants, and so far I have not been refused.

We stopped at Hornepayne for thirty minutes; I walked around the platform for exercise. It was after three o'clock in the morning and I was hungry again, but it was a long time until breakfast. I was surprised when a member of the crew brought me a cup of coffee. So, it pays to brag about making a Guinness Record. Actually, on the Canadian Railroad, I was recognized as soon as I showed my CANRAILPASS, or asked for a signature. In the main computer (along with my name and the dates and train numbers) they had entered "Passenger is accumulating rail miles for the *Guinness Book of World Records*." It was also on the computer printout of my itinerary. What an ego builder!

At Edmonton I went into the station to have my document stamped. Most of the stops on Amtrak and VIA weren't long enough to walk to the station, stand in line and get a stamp. I usually only try if we have at least ten minutes before departure. The signatures and stamps of the conductors will be proof enough of my travels.

Once when we had a long break for a crew change and the adding of a couple of coaches, I came back to my place to find it completely empty, with no sign of my luggage or my mileage notebook. In Europe I had always kept my notebook and documents with me, even when going to the WC. Before I began my North American trek I changed to a see-through plastic backpack, the documents and journal visible as the only contents. Would anyone want to steal someone's journal? I found a conductor and had him follow me to my coach. A woman overheard me complain that my things were missing. "She was not sitting there. I have never seen her before." The conductor told me I was mistaken about the coach number. I said, "I know I was in coach number four, and I left important papers on this very seat. If my Guinness Book is missing, I don't know what I will do! " Finally, another conductor admitted (quietly) that number four was now number five, because the last crew had made a mistake in the numbering, and the new crew had corrected it. So, I wasn't crazy, or dreaming after all. We went to the next coach, and there I found my things exactly as I had left them. The conductor said, "Now, please sit down." I sat down, clutching my documents, and vowed never again to let them out of my sight.

I went up to the Dome Car in the evening. A man introduced himself as Stan Leslie and asked if I would answer a question. I said I would. He hesitated a moment, and then he said,

"Some of us heard you talking about losing your Guinness Book. We were wondering why you became so upset over a book that could be replaced at the end of your trip."

I laughed, and explained, "My book could never be replaced. It isn't a book from a bookstore; it is a record of my hard-won mileage. I hope to be listed in the *Guinness Book of World Records*. I am trying to break the world record of "Most Unduplicated Train Miles Traveled." He agreed that it would be difficult to redo those miles. I asked him to explain it to the other passengers in his coach; perhaps I hadn't imagined that some of them had given me odd looks.

Jasper, in Alberta Province, is the gateway to the Jasper National Park. We had a thirty-minute wait, so I went to the Whistlers Inn across from the train station where they exchange currency, and have personal check, and travelers' check-cashing service. I needed more Canadian dollars. After securing a station stamp I still had time to have my picture taken on the old black locomotive # 6015, that is on display. The locomotive was in service from 1923 to 1958 between the East Coast and the Rocky Mountains, carrying passengers and freight.

Standing on the platform waiting to board, I could see snowcapped mountains. Fruit trees were in bloom in the valley beneath. We would be traveling along the Rocky Mountains all the way to Vancouver; I anticipated some of the most beautiful scenery possible from the window of a train. I was not disappointed.

In Vancouver my hotel was quite a distance from the station; I rode the "Sky Train" (the monorail). There was no conductor or driver on board; it was all remote control. Just as I have done many times on subways and streetcars all over Europe, I caught a train going in the wrong direction. When I realized it, I jumped off and caught the next one going back. It was great to ride above the city for a change. I felt like I was riding a roller coaster without the speed and the fear.

I retired early; it had been a long, four-day ride.

It was warm enough to swim, and it was the first day of the pool season. I would be the first in the freshly filled pool. But first, I had a cup of coffee, just relaxing, looking out my third-floor window at the tables with umbrellas, and the pool. As soon as I changed into my bathing suit and went down to the pool, carrying a plastic cup of ice water, hundreds of white, fuzzy flakes floated into the pool from the trees. The fresh water in the pool was now full of the white fuzz, and so was my cup of ice water.

Tomorrow I'll leave Vancouver at 4:00 a.m. on an Amtrak connecting bus. In a few days the *Mount Baker International* train will begin running between Vancouver and Seattle, the first rail service on the route in fourteen years.

My 2:00 a.m. wake-up call startled me out of a deep sleep. I went out to a pay phone to call a taxi, but I had problems getting through. As I stood out on the edge of the street looking for a taxi, one of the hotel guests arrived in a limousine. He was from India. I had seen him earlier in the evening, talking to the receptionist. He was dressed for his nightclub act, wearing a black tuxedo, a ruffled shirt, and a black bow tie. The white turban around his head was a striking contrast to his black beard. I declined his offer to ride to the Sandman Hotel in his limousine. He managed to get the phone to work, and soon a taxi was at my disposal.

Train # 11, the *Coast Starlight*, left Seattle at 8:00 a.m. I sat on the window side of a double seat. When we stopped in Tacoma, Washington I was in the dining car. I returned to my coach to find a young woman sleeping in my seat, so I sat on the aisle seat. Amtrak's way of keeping track of passengers is to place a "hatcheck" above the seats with the destination, and whether one or both passengers are going to the same destination. I had no idea where the woman in my seat was going; the attendant who collected her ticket evidently thought another attendant had placed the hatcheck with "Oxnard" (my destination), and the number "one" for one passenger (me) on it. She assumed it was placed there for the newly arrived passenger, because I was out of my seat. Later, when an attendant saw that I was sitting there, she told me that wasn't my place, and said I should go back to my original place.

"Excuse me, but this is my seat. I boarded in Seattle. That hatcheck is for me." The new passenger woke up and put her two cents worth in, "I was here first. I boarded in Tacoma, and it comes before Seattle." Since when? I thought. And if so, why did it take an hour to get to Tacoma from Seattle? Next, the attendant had her say, "I'll go and get someone to settle this right now." She came back with a conductor. "Who moved?" He said. I couldn't believe he said that. Who moved? What kind of a question was that to ask a passenger? "If you call going to the dining car moving, then I moved. But I boarded in Seattle where the train begins, and I sat here. My things are on the rack over the seat." "Well, show me your ticket, and we'll see where you boarded." I showed him my ticket. He wrote out a hatcheck for the new passenger, placed it above the seats and walked away.

Before I started down to the café for breakfast, they announced that we would be arriving momentarily at Jack London Square in Oakland, California. I decided to get coffee in the station, and I was glad I did. A welcoming committee awaited us. It was a celebration of the first time an Amtrak train stopped at the new station. We were served pastries and coffee. I was taking seconds back to the train when a newspaper reporter caught up with me. The man who served me coffee had told her I was working on a

Guinness Record. She was looking for a story, and I could have been it. But the train was about to leave by the time we got together; she barely had time to get my name and a few facts before the train pulled away. When I detrained in Oxnard, California, it was like coming home. It's only a few miles from my former home in Thousand Oaks. My daughter, Loretta met me at the station; I will spend one night with her and my son-in-law, Randy before my next train.

Chapter 15
Cowboys and Indians

A line of passengers snaked along two corridors in the Los Angeles Union Station. I joined the line; it was for the *Sunset Limited*. Passengers who were part of a group were passing out balloons to the children. Being fond of balloons myself, I asked for one, and was given a blue one. A little black boy about eight years old was holding a red one. When it slipped away, floating to the high ceiling, he began screaming like a banshee. His mother tried to shut him up, but he just kept screaming. I gave him my blue balloon, but instead of thanking me, he whined. He said he wanted another red one. Just as the line started moving toward the boarding gate, the man who had given me the blue balloon handed me a red one. I didn't trade it to the whiny little rascal; I tied it to my satchel, leaving it there as a souvenir, even after all the air leaked out (many trains later).

I was taking the *Sunset Limited* as far as New Orleans (2,033 miles). I had taken it from New Orleans to Miami (1,033 miles) before I began my Canadian journey. This would complete the 3,066-mile transcontinental route for me, with new credit from Los Angeles to New Orleans. There would be several crew changes on the two-night, three-day run; I would have to stay alert to catch the conductors. Sometimes the attendants collect tickets, and I have to look for the conductors. Although, time permitting, some conductors actually come through the coaches and greet each passenger personally. An Amtrak exclusive, I think. After the first conductor signed my document, I ate a candy bar and went to sleep.

By the time we reached Phoenix I was ready for breakfast. I brought my coffee up to the Sightseer Lounge, seeking a seat before the crowd from the first sitting in the dining car stormed in. The Amtrak Route Guide informed me that Phoenix was built on ruins left by the Hohokam Indians, who lived in the area from the time before Christ to the fifteenth century.

Out of Tempe, Arizona in the Superstition mountains, lies the "Lost Dutchman Mine." The Lost Dutchman was actually a German, Jacob Waltz, who had struck a rich silver vein before disappearing. The mine *and* the miner were lost.

When we crossed the Gila River at Coolidge (still in Arizona), we came to the Gila Indian Reservation. The remains of a 600-year-old communal dwelling left by the Hohokam Indians can be seen from the train. Soon after we crossed into New Mexico, the "Face of Cochise," the mountaintop that resembles a giant face (looking upward) came into view. It is the highest peak of the Chiricahua Mountains.

Between Lordsburg and Deming we crossed the Continental Divide. I will cross the Continental Divide several times during my journeys.

There is a point near the El Paso train station where the Mexican border is a mere thirty feet from the tracks. The Mexican city of Ciudad Juarez can be seen across the Rio Grande. The fence along the border seems inadequate; I can see how easy it would be to sneak across in darkness. We had a twenty-minute stop in El Paso; time enough for a quick jog. The station (built in 1904) is listed in the National Registry of Historic Places. Suddenly, bells pealed from the belfry on top of the station. I switched on my recorder. It was the first time I had ever heard church bells ringing from a train station.

Just out of Marfa, Texas, unexplained sightings of lights in the sky, known as the "Marfa Ghost Lights," have been seen over the town constantly since 1938. Although I looked from both sides of the train, I didn't see them.

I slept through Langtry, headquarters of Judge Roy Bean, who changed the name of the town from Vinegarone to Langtry because he was in love with Lily Langtry, the actress.

We had a long break in San Antonio to shuffle cars. Heading east the *Sunset Limited* and the *Texas Eagle* separate in San Antonio, with the *Texas Eagle* going to Chicago via Little Rock, and the *Sunset Limited* continuing on to New Orleans, ending in Florida. From east to west, the two trains combine, the *Texas Eagle* going on to Los Angeles with the *Sunset Limited*.

In the afternoon we crossed the Sabine River into Louisiana, passing through cypress swamps. When we crossed Bayou Blue I wondered if it was the bayou in the song "Blue Bayou." We passed another bayou, the "Bayou Des Allemandes" (Bayou of the Germans).

Crossing the Huey P. Long Bridge is one of the highlights of the journey. It stretches for four miles, high above the Mississippi River.

I had secured a dozen signatures from conductors and assistant conductors between Los Angeles and New Orleans. I had a bonus signature from the bartender.

I reserved a room in New Orleans; my next train would leave the following afternoon. As soon as I stepped outside the station, a man whose head was swathed in gauze walked up to me. He said he was on vacation and had been robbed and beaten, and now needed five dollars to buy a train ticket home. It was probably a con, but it could be true. I gave him the money.

After a quick phone call to my family in Arkansas, I went out for dinner. The streets of New Orleans were full of party people, having a great time, but I thought I needed my rest, and I knew I needed my beauty sleep. I can almost feel myself aging.

The *City of New Orleans*, train # 58, was leaving at 2:45 p.m. Outside the station, I spotted the now un-swathed head of the man I had given the five dollars to last night. He was getting into a taxi (probably paying with my five dollars). He was a con after all.

Shortly after leaving New Orleans we traveled through the Louisiana Bayou area, home of Cajuns and Creoles. In less than an hour after departure we crossed the Louisiana/Mississippi State Line. At McComb, Mississippi I saw old railroad cars parked by the station. According to Amtrak's brochure they were historic cars of the Illinois Central & Gulf Railroad. The last steam engine is there too, but I didn't spot it.

At Jackson, Mississippi the golden dome of the Capitol building (patterned after the one in Washington, D.C.), topped with a flying eagle, is visible from the train window. According to my Amtrak Route Guide, the city of Jackson began along the banks of the Pearl River as a trading settlement called LeFleur's Bluff. After being burned to the ground by the troops of General Sherman in the Civil War, Jackson was nicknamed "Chimneyville."

By the time we stopped in Memphis it was 10:30 p.m. The thirty-two stories of the "Great American Pyramid" rise up against a myriad of lights. Memphis was named after the ancient capital of Egypt.

I was fast asleep before we passed Fulton, Kentucky, the Twin City of Fulton, Tennessee. A street runs through the towns, separating them. I wanted to see the Fulton on the Kentucky side, not because it is known as the "Banana Crossroads of the United States," but because it holds the Guinness Record (unofficial) for the largest banana pudding in the world. Two tons!

In Chicago the next morning, I took the subway to a hotel near the airport. My cousin Bonnie will fly in from Los Angeles in a couple of days. Amtrak couldn't get me out of Chicago on the *Southwest Chief* for four days. I will have a welcome three-night stay.

About two o'clock in the morning I was startled out of a deep sleep by a loud pounding on my door. A man's voice was demanding, "Open the door! Now!"

"What do you want?"

"The manager sent me, open up!"

"I'll call the front desk and see if he sent you." He didn't; the man had mistaken my door for the one next to mine. The manager apologized; he had sent the man to warn my neighbors to quiet down.

The next day I went to the airport to meet my cousin. Bonnie and I had never met before, but somehow we recognized each other. We spent the evening getting to know one another. Bonnie has been researching the family tree; I have learned so much from her. It's too bad I hadn't known some of the facts before traveling in Canada; I had been in some of the areas where the families had lived when they arrived from Great Britain.

Bonnie flew to London today to meet my sister Joan for more research on the Brindley side. I boarded the *Southwest Chief,* train # *3* to Los Angeles. After three hours of traveling in Illinois we crossed into a corner of Iowa before going into Missouri.

We were in Dodge City, Kansas before I stirred. My first view of the morning was of Boot Hill and the Hangman's Tree. The aroma of freshly brewed coffee drew me down to the café. In less than an hour we had crossed out of Kansas and into Colorado. An old Atchison, Topeka and Santa Fe engine, # 1819 is parked in the yard at the station in Lamar. Trinidad is another old Wild West town. Bat Masterson was once the town sheriff.

When we arrived in Los Angeles at 8:15 the next morning I had a quick change to the *San Diegan.* I had thirteen signatures from conductors and assistant conductors and 2,259 miles added to my total. My daughter met me in Simi Valley. I had a couple of days between trains.

The *Desert Wind...* what a great name for a train. I was on my way to Chicago again, but over a different route, gaining new mileage.

Passengers were warned via the PA system before we stopped in Las Vegas, "The train will be leaving in fifteen minutes, with or without you. You don't have time to try your luck, so don't press your luck!" Of course, we all ran into the casino just to look. I wanted to play roulette, but I didn't want to miss the train; I stayed by the doorway, with one eye on the train. The Plaza Hotel and Casino doubles as an Amtrak station. As far as I know, no one missed the train.

We were supposed to stop in Salt Lake City at 3:30 a.m., with almost a two-hour wait. We were behind schedule; we stopped for only about thirty minutes.

There was a five-minute break at Helper, Utah. I barely had time to walk the length of the platform before it was time to board. The small station is surrounded by rock formations that resemble castles. Huge helper engines were needed to power the train up the steep grade, so the town was given the name of "Helper."

An announcement was made, inviting passengers to watch for a geyser that erupts every seventy minutes. With luck, we'll pass at the seventieth minute. We did, and the geyser obliged; it slowly eased up, and then spouted for us.

Near Rifle, Colorado we sat on a single track in a narrow, boxed-in canyon for a long time. I was hoping the other train (coming from Chicago) wouldn't run into us. The conductor announced that we were waiting for a rockslide to be cleared away. A perfect time to take my shower, I thought. But then, if more rocks came tumbling down, I wouldn't want to be rescued in the nude. I stayed in the Sightseer Lounge, gawking out the window like everybody else. A crew was on the way to clear the tracks. We were already running late. Lunch was late, and dinner would be late. The staff had run out of coffee and cups.

The road crew arrived with heavy equipment vehicles, and began clearing the tracks. Just as the train pulled away, we heard this request, "Will those of you with the window open downstairs, with your heads sticking out, please get your heads back in and close the window! This is very dangerous. Do not do this! Please close the window for your own safety!" The train picked up speed and we were on our way.

We didn't make up enough time, although we traveled fast when possible. An announcement was made, "Those passengers connecting to the *City of New Orleans* train in Chicago will detrain in Galesburg, Illinois. You will be bused to Champaign-Urbana where you will meet your train. Baggage checks will now be collected. Your bags will be put on the bus for you at Galesburg." That included me. Since I had been unable to secure reservations on more new routes, I was heading home to begin a new All Aboard America ticket. I wasn't able to travel home on the direct route; all coach seats were booked for the next five days on the train to Little Rock. Rather than be stuck in Chicago for so long, I planned to take the reverse route (no accredited mileage) of the *City of New Orleans,* detraining in Memphis, and travel home to Arkansas by auto.

What a jolly crowd we were on the bus out of Galesburg. Now that we would make our train after all, it was easy enough to joke and laugh about the delay. The station in Champaign-Urbana was confusing. We finally figured out we needed to go up an outside ramp to reach the platform. Honky-tonk music from a little bar (across the tracks and down a steep hill) enticed a couple of the waiting passengers, but they came back to the platform after one beer, fearful of missing the train. Several patrons of the bar came out the back door and invited all of us for a drink. About three passengers scooted down the hill to accept, but I heard the train approaching, and warned them. They barely made it up the hill before it pulled alongside the platform.

Chapter 16
Under the Big Skies

I purchased my third All Aboard America ticket, with reservations for the remaining western routes, although it meant repeating many miles, without credit toward the record. It was necessary to connect with new routes. The *Texas Eagle* would take me to Chicago over a repeat route. With an 11:40 p.m. departure, there wasn't much to do on the train, except sleep.

The connection to train # 27, the *Empire Builder* was within two hours of my arrival in Chicago the next day. In the café downstairs, I sat with two young women. Pearl is Japanese and Erika is Swiss. They had first met in New York, on a train. Although their limited English was their only means of communication, they decided to travel together. Erika suggested we jog when we stopped in St. Paul-Minneapolis. We had almost forty minutes, but my jogging lasted only about five minutes. Actually, we were running. I really thought I could keep up with the young women. Catching up with them once more, I had to admit I couldn't keep up the running. I could hardly breathe. They were tired too, and were glad to be given a reason to stop. Extensive travel steals some of the sparkle out of you, no matter how young or how old you are.

It was midnight when the train pulled away; I went to my seat. So far, I had a double seat to myself. If I had wanted to, I could have used both of the seats; the attendants on this train wouldn't complain.

In the night we had slipped into North Dakota. I was in the café early in the morning when Pearl and Erika came down. In a few minutes the scenery had become so wildly beautiful that we took our coffee up to the Sightseer Lounge. The train was beginning the part of the route that closely parallels the Canadian border. We traveled through wide, grassy prairies, and followed the Red River and then the Missouri River to the Rocky Mountains. I hadn't realized that the Missouri flowed so far north. An Arapaho Indian joined us; he makes and sells jewelry in Arizona. He invited each of us to choose an item from his handmade collection; it was a difficult choice. I settled on a necklace made of braided rope, intertwined with stones striped in rainbow hues on a background of sapphire blue, with a yellow stone in the center.

Back in the café I ate a pastry and stared out the window again. I decided I wouldn't eat another pastry for dinner. One at breakfast and one at lunch should be enough. Amtrak should serve cheese or lettuce and tomato sandwiches for vegetarians. On every train so far, the sandwiches were made with meat.

My supply of snacks had run out. I went to the dining car and asked about the dinner menu, and I was told they would fix me a vegetable plate. My reservation was for the last sitting. The young woman who had spoken to me earlier brought me a large plate of salad. I reminded her that I had asked for a vegetable plate. "But those *are* vegetables," she said. "Never mind, it's OK," I said. I ate the salad. As I was finishing my second cup of coffee, one of the cooks sat down at the table across from me. He was eating mashed potatoes and some kind of greens. Why couldn't I have some? I called the waitress over and asked if I could have a small plate of the hot vegetables. The cook said, "I think they have been thrown away already."

"What! You threw away hot vegetables when you have a vegetarian on board who is practically starving?" I was only halfway joking.

"Well, I'll go check," the waitress said. "What kind of vegetables do you want?"

"Just a little of the mashed potatoes and a blob of greens."

"What are blobba greens, Ma'am?"

"I don't know what kind of greens you have, but I'll take any kind. I meant a blob, a pile, or a dipperful."

She came back up the stairs with a plate of potatoes and "blobba greens." They were delicious. When I finished eating and paid my bill, a waiter came up from the kitchen with a Styrofoam container of potatoes and blobba greens. They were the remaining vegetables from the pot, and after what I had said about a vegetarian starving, they didn't want to throw them away. I was really full, but I thanked him and walked back to my coach. Not wanting to waste the food, I ate every bite of it, including the juice from the blobba greens. Then I pushed the recliner lever and leaned back in my seat. The blobba greens were gurgling in my stomach. I was content.

We traveled the Glacier Park area in the night; I missed some spectacular scenery. But, I will be traveling the same section in daylight on my way home. I have three more new routes out west, and then I have to repeat the miles back; I will have done every route to and from the West Coast, some more than once, receiving no credit for repeat miles.

In the early hours of the morning we had crossed into Oregon. Arrival in Portland was at 10:30 a.m. Some crewmembers were going to the Park Lane Inn; I rode with them in the shuttle. Amtrak passengers receive a discount on room rates.

We were driven back to the station on the shuttle. A sign on the clock tower of the old, brick station says, "GO BY TRAIN." Is there any other way?

I had a few hours before departure. Not wanting to stray too far,

I walked about a mile, then looked for a place for lunch. There wasn't much in the area, just a health-food restaurant, which looked unhealthy, and a fast-food snack bar. From where I sat inside the snack bar, I could see two men and a woman standing by an outdoor table. One of the men and the woman sat down and began kissing. The other man was dressed in black leather; he was trying to look like a real punk, with a dog chain around his neck. He swung the chain back and forth, hoping to impress (or frighten) the other diners. He came inside to order. I was sitting alone at a table for four. There were plenty of others vacant, but he wanted mine.

"Get up. We want to sit here."

"I am not finished with my food. You can sit somewhere else."

" I want this table!"

"You can have it when I am through with it." I spoke without looking at him. It was easy to be brave with other people around. I wish I had been brave enough to say, "I didn't pull your chain!" He went back outside with the food. If he only knew that compared to dog-chain punks in Europe, he looked like a little boy in a Halloween costume. He wasn't even wearing a dog collar to fasten his chain to. He didn't even have a dog.

By the time I got back to the station the train was ready to leave. I was on # 26, the *Pioneer* to Denver, with all new mileage.

We crossed the Willamette River on the Steel Bridge. Traveling along the Columbia River Gorge (dividing Oregon and Washington) in daylight was great. I saw waterfalls, huge dams and many bridges. Rooster Rock is a shaft of black volcanic rock, visible from the train windows.

In the café I purchased a thermal coffee mug with the *Pioneer* logo printed in gold. On all my future Amtrak trains I will have complimentary coffee. I wish I had known about the mugs many trains ago. I would have saved a bundle.

As we went through the Lewis and Clark State Park, I saw several waterfalls cascading down a mountain. Then, almost immediately the Multnomah Falls appeared outside my window, exploding over a wall of greenery. According to my Amtrak brochure they drop 620 feet. Watching for the next splendor, I dashed to the wrong side of the train, then, just in time going back to the other side to see the narrow canyon that is never touched by sunlight. The next spectacular view passed quickly on the left side, the Beacon Rock; a sheer wall of rock, reputed to be the largest of its kind in the United States.

By looking out one side of the train and then the other, I managed to see the Bonneville Dam, the Cascade Locks, and the silver "Bridge of the Gods," built on the site of a natural formation used as a bridge by the Indians, before volcanoes destroyed it.

Daylight was fading fast.

Darkness notwithstanding, I saw the entire length of the train as we rounded a horseshoe bend. We were climbing the Encina Pass, near Durkee, Oregon. We Crossed the Snake River several times, switching from Oregon to Idaho, and back to Oregon.

When we crossed into Wyoming, I was drawn back to the Sightseer Lounge by the magnificent scenery. We stopped in Rawlins where local mines produced a special red pigment (Rawlins Red) that was used to paint the Brooklyn Bridge in 1878. Rawlins is also famous as the town that scared off twenty-four outlaws. Vigilantes had lynched a train robber, and sent warning notes to twenty-four known outlaws. Each of the outlaws bought a one-way ticket out of town at the station the next day. At Rawlins we had crossed the Continental Divide. Later we crossed it again; I was losing count of the times I had crossed it by train.

We stopped in the famous cowboy town of Laramie. In 1877, Jesse James, suspected of a stagecoach robbery, was jailed in Laramie.

I went back to the Sightseer Lounge again, just in time to join the bingo and trivia games. I lost at Bingo, but I tied with another passenger for first prize in the trivia contest. My prize was an Amtrak blanket. When the Chief of On-board Services heard (from me) about my attempt to break the record on train travel, he gave me a set of wineglasses etched with *"Pioneer."*

In Denver I checked into a downtown hotel, and went in search of dinner. It was close to midnight when I left the restaurant, and raining lightly. A man on the other side of the street was walking along with a parrot on his shoulder. The man looked at me, crossed to my side of the street, and walked beside me. He didn't say anything, but the parrot shrieked all the way to my hotel. I thought it a little strange, but I wasn't afraid, there were other people on the streets. When I went into the hotel lobby, the man and his bird kept going.

In the morning I boarded the *California Zephyr*, train # 5. From Denver to Salt Lake City was repeat mileage for me; it's the same as the *Desert Wind's* route. Between Denver and Salt Lake City the train passes mountains and cliffs that were carved by the wind into statues of people, animals and a likeness of the Sphinx. Nature has carved cliffs into castles, amphitheaters, Inca Temples, and a giant, smiling cat. The show goes on for miles and miles. The scenery is spectacular all the way. *America, the beautiful.* When we stopped at Sparks, Dorrie Crooks, a narrator for Amtrak boarded the train. She is a representative of the California State Railroad Museum in Sacramento. In the Sightseer Lounge we were treated to some of the history and legends of the route, including the true story of the ill-fated Donner Party that set out by wagon train in 1848 from Springfield, Illinois to the Pacific Coast. Miscalculating the time it would take to reach the coast, and encountering unforeseen problems, they were stranded in an extremely cold and snowy winter near Truckee, California. About half of the party died during the winter. Those who survived were reduced to cannibalism to keep from starving to death. I gained about 1,400 miles on the stretch between Salt Lake City and Martinez, California, where I connected to train # 718, the *San Joaquin* to Bakersfield. The route gave me an extra 283 miles, but it meant staying over in a hotel. I'm going home now, leaving from Bakersfield. No matter which route I travel, I can't claim mileage; I've done them all. Nonetheless, I have chosen the long way home, traveling again on one of my favorite trains, the *Empire Builder*. But first, I have to get to Portland via the *San Joaquin* and the *Coast Starlight*, to connect with the *Empire Builder*. After it takes me to Chicago, one last train, the *Texas Eagle* will take me home to Little Rock. Once you have seen America from the window of a train, you have seen America.

Chapter 17
Arctic Circle: Summer

It was late evening when I arrived at my base in Bad Kreuznach after my flight from Baltimore to Luxembourg. I had left enough clothes in my closet at Rosi's apartment to last until I broke the record. The suitcases I brought with me were filled with clothing for the homeless, donated by a church near my home.

One night of rest was enough. I headed for Finland, traveling over a new route through Amersfoort and Hengelo, Holland. My third train of the day was an overnighter that crosses the German border at Bad Bentheim. It was a rough night; I was in a second-class compartment with seven other passengers. The young man across from me had very long legs, so I kept my feet under my seat all night, causing my ankles to swell.

The train pulled into Berlin at 7:30 a.m. Two hours later I was on a train to Copenhagen over a new route, via Warnemunde, in the former East Germany. From Warnemunde, several carriages go inside the ferry for the crossing to Gedser, Denmark. From there, I would go to Stockholm.

All my trains were late; I would have missed the night ferry from Stockholm to Finland, so I decided to stay overnight in Copenhagen and go on to Stockholm tomorrow. By the time I got to the Mission Hotel Hebron the extreme swelling had caused my ankles to bump together as I walked, bruising my ankles. My room was tiny, but clean. The bed was the size of a youth bed; the springs creaked under my weight.

I walked the few blocks to the famous Tivoli Gardens, a gigantic amusement park, built in 1843 on the site of the old city walls. All the castle-like buildings, the Chinese Pagoda, and the trees are strung with twinkling lights. A casino, carnival rides, restaurants, snack bars and gift shops are just a few of the things that await the visitor. My ankles were really hurting; I thought it better just to sit on a bench and listen to a concert until I was ready for dinner.

On the train to Stockholm I deciphered a newspaper article in Dutch about the bomb that exploded in Paris yesterday, in the Saint Michel Metro station. Several people were killed, and eighty-six were wounded. (Three weeks later a bomb went off near the Arc de Triomphe, in Paris, wounding seventeen people.)

On arrival in Stockholm I took the underground to the docks to board the Silja Line's *Scandinavia*. The Eurail Brochure says a $16.00 fee entitles EurailPass holders to a cabin. All the cabins were taken, but the "airplane chairs" are free.

I went to the pool area to shower. It costs thirty Finn Markka to use the pool, shower, sauna and Jacuzzi. There were no doors on the shower stalls; I went to the receptionist and asked where the showers with doors were. "There are none. We don't do that." She shook her head in disbelief, as if she couldn't imagine why anyone would want to shower in private. Also, a door leading to the pool was open, so I showered with my bathing suit on. The Jacuzzi was filled with tiny little kids (mostly unsupervised), so I tried the pool. Rowdy teen-agers kicked and splashed me every time I tried to swim. I gave up, and took another shower with my bathing suit on. I put my wet towel and suit in my satchel, not caring if they mildewed or not.

The airplane chairs were wide and comfortable, but most of the younger Eurailers and backpackers slept in their sleeping bags on the floor. I had to step over a few to get to the WC.

I slept well enough; I didn't wake until 6:00 a.m. The ship goes on to Helsinki, but I got off in Turku. A train to Tampere was waiting at the harbor; I just made it before it pulled away. I was in a first-class compartment. The seats were upholstered in orange velour. There was an orange carpet in the compartment and in the corridor. The foldaway tables were Day-Glo orange. Everything was so bright, that I could have used a pair of sunglasses to counteract the glare.

From Tampere I could take a direct route to Kemi Jarvi, at the end of the last stretch of passenger train track in Finland, but I discovered I could take a couple of detours and get in some extra mileage, without waiting for the direct train. I detrained in Pieksamaki, and caught a train to Riihimaki, changing to a night train to Kemi Jarvi.

The train to Kemi Jarvi has an all-night café called the "*Railerei*," with cherry-red tables, and folding chairs with black seats. When I went into the *Railerei* it was crowded with passengers in a party mood. Most of them were just drinking beer and talking. I think I was the only one eating. The cook fixed me a concoction (she called it macaroni) of shredded potatoes, turnips, pimentos, peas and carrots in a cream sauce. It would have been good if she hadn't added some green beans that were still frozen. I washed them down with hot coffee, and enjoyed the meal.

Taxis were waiting outside the station in Kemi Jarvi to take passengers into town. I went into the station to have my document stamped, and when I came out all the taxis were gone. The information agent gave me a map, with directions into town. My ankles were still slightly swollen, but I didn't mind walking. The sun was beating down on my head. I hadn't expected such hot weather above the Arctic Circle so late in the season.

It was about three miles to the bus station in town. I was the only one waiting for the bus to Rovaniemi. The famous Santa Claus Village is only ten kilometers from Rovaniemi, and right on the Arctic Circle, but my train leaves within fifteen minutes of my arrival in Rovaniemi, so I must save it for another time. How often I have said that. From Rovaniemi I took a different way back to Turku, over Kontimaki and Kouvola on an overnighter.

On arrival in Kouvola at 5:15 a.m., I took a train to Joensu. Then, just one eight-hour train ride would get me to Turku to catch another overnight ship, the Silja Line's *Europa*.

When the ship docked in Stockholm I rode the underground to the train station for the trip back to base, which would take all day and one more night of travel. The total time for the trip to Finland and back will be seven nights, eight days. To claim the 4,764 kilometers, I will have taken twenty trains; two underground trains, one bus, four ferries and two cruise ships.

Back at base, I slept most of the day. Waking in the early evening, I felt rested enough to spend a couple of hours at the *Liedertafel*. I sat with several friends. Just before midnight, a sandy-haired German man sat down at our table, and introduced himself as Dieter, a tour bus driver from Koblenz. Speaking German, he said, "I don't like to drive Americans on my bus. They always complain because the bus is not air-conditioned." A few minutes later, he repeated the same words, adding, "Complain, complain. Americans always complain." Then, he leaned toward me (I was across from him) and said, "It is late. I am sleepy. Will you come and spend the night with me on my bus?"

"No! Your bus is not air-conditioned." The bus driver was the only one who didn't laugh.

With Sankt Nikolaus in Bad Kreuznach, 1953

Chapter 18
Easy Railing

On Saturday I took a day off to be a typical tourist. Bad Munstereifel is a spa town, west of the Rhine, in the Eifel Mountains, not to be confused with Bad Munster Am Stein, the spa town a few kilometers from Bad Kreuznach. Bad Munstereifel is off-the-beaten-path for Americans; visitors to the town are mostly German tourists. To reach it, one can take a train or a Rhine ship to Bonn, a train to Euskirchen, then a train or a bus to Bad Munstereifel; the end of a secondary rail line. My day called for a short cruise along the Rhine before catching a train at Bonn.

The travel brochures were right. Bad Munstereifel is a beautiful town. To enter the town from the station, I walked through one of the old city gates. Sidewalk cafés were lined up along the narrow river. It seemed that every little café was done in a different color scheme. Not even in Paris have I seen such an array of colors. I chose a café, not for its menu, but because the umbrellas were purple, trimmed with white fringe. I heard only German and Dutch spoken.

Every few feet a stone bridge arched across the river. Ducks were nesting at the foot of the steep banks, stirring only to honk and fight over the bread and nuts thrown to them by the children. Planters held geraniums of pink, red and white. Lavender and white petunias were everywhere. Rectangular planters were hanging on the fence rails like window boxes along the river. Huge round pots of flowers were hanging from the eaves of most of the shops.

The *Kurhaus* sits atop a hill in a wooded park. I was tempted to spend the night in a hotel, but I needed to go back to base to get my gear ready for my next trip. When I first arrived in Bad Munstereifel I had checked the schedule, somehow misreading it. It was Saturday; the last train leaves an hour earlier, and I missed it. I took a bus to Euskirchen and a train to Bonn. Transferring to another train to Bingen, I would have barely enough time to connect with the last train to BK. On Saturdays, the trains to BK don't run as late as they do on weekdays and Sundays. My train was only four minutes late arriving in Bingen, but the last train to BK was gone. I should have stayed in Bad Munstereifel. This wasn't the first time I had been stuck in Bingen on a Saturday night. I took a taxi to BK. It was almost midnight when I arrived at the apartment. Although I had only planned to play tourist today, I did have forty-eight kilometers (from Euskirchen to Bad Munstereifel) to my credit. Ships, buses and taxis don't count.

Hoping to cover the rest of the long routes, and some of the shorter ones between my base and Berlin, I started out early. I was in Lichtenfels before 10:30 a.m. "The Largest Gift Basket in the World" sits in front of the City Hall, filled with pink and red flowers. Lichtenfels is famous for its basket weavers. One can watch the weavers at work in the basket market, and visit the Basket Museum nearby. There is even a school where one can learn the skills of basket weaving.

My next two trains took me over Jena, Gosschwitz and Gera. A few more local trains and an InterRegio and I was as far north as I could go in Germany on the route. I didn't go to Berlin after all. A night train back to Frankfurt was already boarding; I had a train to sleep on, and in the morning I could start again. It had taken eight trains from Frankfurt to get me this far today, but just one overnighter took me back.

When I arrived in Frankfurt after a restless night on the train, I decided to go on to base to shower and repack before traveling on. A couple of hours later I headed northeast to Warburg. Then, on a third train, I was cutting across on a secondary line to Hagen. I was alone in a first-class compartment, trying not to fall asleep in my comfortable seat. The route was new to me; I didn't want to miss anything. At Marsberg I saw old churches and a castle with towers on a hillside. Several little bridges cross a narrow waterway near the cream-colored train station.

The train station at Brilon Wald is extraordinary. Two huge three-story buildings make up the base. A "bridge house" unites the two buildings, and white towers flank the station on both sides.

On my InterCity from Hagen to Mainz the conductors were busy serving coffee and sandwiches to commuters at their seats. When one of the conductors signed my document, I said, "Nobody has time this evening." He laughed. "I am not nobody. Nobody means *Nieman*. I am somebody, and I give you my signature." From Mainz I took a local train back to BK, and called it a day.

Today I stayed in BK. I went to the "Fisherstecherfest," a festival that includes a contest between teams of men representing different countries. Each team consists of two men to row the boat and a main player who stands on the bow of the boat. He uses a long pole to knock the man on the opposing team off his boat, into the river. The winner of each bout goes against the next team, and so on, until one team has beaten all the others.

The men in the boats dress in costumes of the country they are representing, but the man on the bow wears bathing trunks. Today the countries represented were Portugal, Greece, Scotland, Yugoslavia, Germany and the United States. The German team won for the third consecutive year.

The music was wonderful. There were Scottish pipers, a United States Army band, a German brass band, and a German choral group. The Scottish pipers were actually Germans wearing kilts and tasseled knee socks. A few were wearing Glengarry hats with ribbons hanging from the back. Some of the Germans were wearing white running shoes, and white T-shirts (printed with their names), and kilts. The German names had been Anglicized, complete with a Scottish "Mac." Fuchs was now Mac Fox, Klein was Mac Little and Zimmerman was billed as Mac Carpenter. Those are the only ones that stick in my mind.

A mobile crane was set up for bungee jumping. I have thought about trying it, but have never had the nerve. Today I was feeling brave, but when I found that the price was 100 Marks, I opted to go up in the basket of the crane instead, for only ten Marks. Three people can ride up with the jumper. The jumper rides on the outside edge of the basket, and after the jump, he or she is rescued from a dangling position over the river. I took a picture from the top; it was scary up there. If I had tried to jump I probably would have balked at the last minute, making a fool of myself, and wasting a lot of money. It would have taken hours just to check out the souvenir stands, food stalls and tents. At one of the tents they were serving wine in a large pumpkin shell. Knowing that most Germans dislike the taste of pumpkin, I asked the young man selling the wine if it was pumpkin-flavored. He gave me a sample; it was delicious. It was made with white wine, pumpkin juice and diced pumpkin. After two more glasses of it I realized I hadn't eaten all day; the wine was getting to me. I bought a funnel cake and a cup of coffee to counteract the effects of it. A Turkish man was handing out Muslim literature, but only to women. The brochures were printed in German. I took one and was shocked to read the excuse they gave for having four wives. "Because of the many men who died in World War II, there are not enough to go around for all the women who need a husband and a family." Do they think the non-Muslim world is stupid? If the men who died in the war were still alive, they wouldn't be young enough to start a family for all those "poor women" who need a man. What a crock! We all know why they want more than one wife. It went on to say that women would be much better off if they covered their heads and bodies. "Men will look you in the eye, instead of the leg." Most of us "wanton Western women" wear blue jeans; how are they going to look us in the leg?

When I got back to the apartment in the evening our friend Erich was there. When I told him I almost bungee jumped, Erich said, "You are crazy. You are too old! Old people can have a heart attack doing that." He was right. It was a crazy idea; I was glad I hadn't done it. Erich and Rosi thought just riding up in the crane basket was crazy, but Dirk thought it was "cool." The German kids use the expression too. He had wanted to ride up in the basket, but Rosi forbade him. To assuage his disappointment, I took Dirk to the *Liedertafel*. Children are allowed (up until 10:00 p.m.) if accompanied by an adult. A couple of people at our table spoke English. We were joking about Germans having difficulty pronouncing "th" correctly, and I gave my idea for solving the problem. "I can teach you to pronounce "th" in five seconds. Just pretend you have a lisp."

Chapter 19
Return to Poland

Laden with two suitcases (World Traveler and a slightly smaller one), I boarded a train in Frankfurt on my way back to Wroclaw. Both suitcases were filled with giveaway clothing. I decided to name the other suitcase. It is now called "Tagalong." I was traveling a repeat route as far as Erfurt and then a new route to Wroclaw; I had several new routes to do in Poland. It was difficult to change trains so often with the extra luggage. I also had my backpack, a lunch kit and a small satchel with me.

By the time I arrived in Cottbus, near one of Germany's borders with Poland, it was almost nine o'clock in the evening. I sat on a wooden bench waiting for my next train; I was the only person on the platform. I put my satchel and lunch kit down on the bench, and walked over to check the train schedule. A large sea gull perched up in the rafters above the bench. He let fly a barrage of nasty droppings on my satchel and lunch kit. For once, my timing was perfect; I was sitting in that spot not two minutes before. Never mind the train schedule; the droppings had permeated my lunch kit and the umbrella that was strapped to my satchel. I decided to check into a hotel. The lunch kit was ruined; I threw it away, along with the umbrella. To be on the safe side, at the hotel I threw away the satchel and the top layer of clothing. My room was clean, and the bed was comfortable. I have never seen such a mix of colors and styles in a hotel room before, but somehow they blended. A black-and-white chair sat by the window. The drapes and the valance were violet silk. My bed was covered with a yellow-plaid spread. There was a Bonsai evergreen tree in a white oriental planter, sitting on an oak end table. A red ornamental bird perched on top of the tiny tree. I didn't need to be reminded of birds.

I wanted to enter Poland at the German town of Forst, a border I hadn't crossed before. The information agent in the station said I could take a train up to the border, and either walk or take a bus into Poland. When we stopped at the border, I got off the train with my luggage. A woman in a blue uniform called out to me in German, "Are you going farther into Poland?"

"Yes, where is the bus?"

"The train is going. Get back on. It will leave you!"

"But I need my PolRail pass validated."

"The conductor will do it. Get on the train."

The conductor couldn't validate the pass. He told me to get off in Zagan (Sagan) and have it validated in the station. A freight train passed, blowing its whistle long and loud. Purple heather was growing everywhere. From Zagan I would take three more trains to Wroclaw. I should have brought the extra suitcases of clothing another time, on a more direct route.

We stopped in Zary (Sorau) for a few minutes. There were two train stations in Zary. One was an old brick building, covered with vines. The windows were boarded up. Old wooden train carriages were sitting on a siding. On the other side of the tracks I could see an old house with a green façade, trimmed in yellow. I would call the style "Victorian Gingerbread." Nearby was an old, brick church with a green steeple. In the midst of all the antiquity stood a several-storied modern apartment building. Each apartment had a bright-orange balcony. I discovered I could transfer to another train at Zary, and take a more direct route to Wroclaw, saving several hours and riding one less train. But the conductor had signed for me as far as Zagan. I'd have to go on.

Soon after we pulled out of Zary the track turned curvy. The whistle sounded often. It sounded more like a ship's whistle than a train's.

After I had my pass validated in Zagan, I set out to buy something for lunch. Everyone I passed stared at me. Zagan is not a tourist town; the people seemed to know I was not only a stranger, but also a foreigner.

When I passed the fire station the gardener walked over to me, and pointed down a side street. He must have assumed I was looking for a store; I found one in the direction he had pointed. The sign on the door said "*Pickarnia*." I knew that meant bakery. One of the women in the store spoke a little German, but I surprised her by ordering bread, cheese and milk in Polish. She came out from behind the counter, shook my hand, and refused my money. I put the money on the counter, said good-bye in English, and thank you in Polish. As I stepped out the door and headed back down the street, she came running after me. She handed me a piece of cake, wrapped in a paper towel. I went to the station and caught a train.

The constant jockeying of luggage up and down the steep steps of all those trains was exhausting; I was glad when I boarded my last train to Wroclaw. Three of my trains were slow locals.

In Wroclaw I stored the two suitcases in the station and checked into my old standby, the Grand Hotel. The same owners have four other hotels, practically next door to each other. I had planned to try a different one this time, but I couldn't resist the Grand. Despite the spooky feeling it gives me, I love being there. It doesn't give me the feeling of stepping into a fairy tale, as many hotels in Europe do. Rather, it gives me the feeling of stepping into a Gothic novel.

I went back to the station and retrieved my World Traveler suitcase; there were lots of homeless people on the benches in the waiting area. Two women and three men were sitting together; I took out the clothes I thought they could use. I laid the clothes on the bench, nodded, and walked outside to give toys to the Gypsy children. A group of Gypsies came down the stairway behind me; one of the women was carrying a blond-haired, blue-eyed boy about two years old. I wondered if the Gypsies had kidnapped him. He grinned as I handed him a little stuffed bear. I took out the rest of the clothing and toys for them; I had another suitcase of things for tomorrow.

Back in the station, I sat on a bench for a moment. Two of the homeless people I had given the clothes to came toward me. The woman was wearing the coat I had left on their bench; the man was carrying the brown sweater. When he saw me, he put on the hooded scarf (meant for a woman), turned from side to side like a model, and laughed.

Suddenly, all the homeless people, including the winos, went out one of the side doors of the station. It was as if some kind of signal had sounded. Had one of them spotted the railway police, and given a secret warning? I followed, wondering about the sudden exit. They went over to the park across from the station and sat down, some on benches, and some on the grass. Loaves of bread, scraps of bread, bits of chicken and a half-eaten pizza were laid out on newspapers. It was time for dinner, and the day's pickings were shared. I was touched; I wanted to cry, but then, I realized the significance of what I had witnessed, and smiled instead. Most homeless people, particularly winos, spend their days and nights completely alone. No one loves them. But this group was sharing more than a picnic in the park. I learned a new meaning for "brotherly love."

I rose early; I needed time to give away the other suitcase of clothing. It was easy, and fast. Gypsies claimed most of the things. I saw a young Polish woman pushing two tiny boys in a stroller. She didn't look poor, but sometimes it's nice just to have something from another country, especially from America. I offered two little sweat suits, imprinted with the logos of football teams to the young woman, and she accepted them gratefully. She read the logos and said, "America?" I nodded, and walked away. Now, I had two empty suitcases; travel would be easy. Very easy, the empty Tagalong fits inside the empty World Traveler.

One train would take me all the way to Elk, Poland, near the Lithuanian and Belarus borders. The first conductor wouldn't sign my document because there were no other signatures on it. I showed him yesterday's document with other signatures, and he signed (also on yesterday's document).

In Elk (Lyck), I had five hours to wait for my next train. I left my suitcases (one inside the other) on a bench in the waiting room, and went out to find something to eat. I went into the Bar Olenka, a tiny little café just to the left of the station. Three young women came out of the kitchen to greet me. I tried my funny Polish. Milk (mlecko) got the biggest laugh. I ended up with a salad and a cup of coffee. *Kava* is easy to remember, and a salad is what you always get, anywhere, if you say you don't eat meat. The café was reminiscent of those in America in the 1950s. The tables and chairs were wooden with a coating of red lacquer, and the red tablecloths were made of oilcloth. Each table was set with a vase of paper roses and a blue candle dish. Having nowhere else to go, I stayed awhile. From time to time one or two customers would come in, and order something to go. When I went back out into the square later, all three of the workers watched me from the window. They weren't the only ones staring at me; I was beginning to think I was the only American who ever stopped in the town.

I boarded the last train to Warsaw (a local) at midnight. It would take me over a different route, via Bialystok. I was alone in the compartment. In the dim lights of the stations, I could barely read the names of the towns. We stopped in Grajewo, Ruda, and Osowiec, all within the first two hours. At Osowiec, the conductor led an old man into the compartment. He stood his cane in the corner, and sat by the door.

At the next stop several winos got on the train to check for drinks. I stepped out onto the platform to check for vendors. There were none. Back in the compartment, I discovered that my two-liter bottle of orange soda was missing. The wino that took it probably thought a passenger had detrained, and left it. He certainly needed it more than I did, but I wondered why my seatmate, the old man, hadn't told him it was mine. Later, when the old man got off the train, the conductor led him out of the compartment. It was then that I noticed his cane had a white tip. He was blind; he didn't know the wino was taking my drink.

Awake before dawn, I watched the black night fade slowly into the gray of a rainy morning. My compartment was cold, and my bones were aching from the dampness. Munching the last of a package of chocolate wafers, I checked my timetable for trains from Warsaw to Berlin. If this train made it to Warsaw on time, I could catch the EuroCity to Berlin.

As I stepped off the train in Warsaw (we were on time), I almost fainted. Something is wrong with me. I'm not sure if the flu is catching up with me, or if I just have a chronic case of rail lag.

I felt a little better after having a roll and a cup of coffee on the EuroCity. A couple of hours later the conductor told me to change to another carriage; mine wasn't going all the way to Berlin; it would be uncoupled at Poznan.

In Berlin, I saw an InterCity Express pull in. It was going to Frankfurt; I couldn't resist, and I boarded. I had taken the route and the ICE before, but I needed the rest more than the miles. I never thought I'd say that. My base was still a long way off, and I was past tired.

In spite of my condition, I enjoyed the ride. We had outrun the rain; the sky was blue, with a few gray clouds scattered here and there. I was able to catch up on my bookwork; converting the kilometers into miles, and double-checking the routes for repeat mileage. From Frankfurt, one train took me back to base.

I slept late. Rosi brought me some liquid cold medicine. She was surprised that I agreed to take it. I usually refuse any over-the-counter medication other than cough syrup or aspirin. Whatever it was, it works. Within two hours I felt better, but I still couldn't shake my weakness, so I stayed another night.

My plan to rise and shine was ditched. I slept in again. Feeling fine by noon, I took off with only my lightweight backpack and a small satchel. After taking a local from base to Frankfurt (Main), I took one EuroCity, an InterRegio, and a Regional train, reaching Frankfurt (Oder) at 11:00 p.m. I wanted to go into Poland on a slightly different route, but there were no trains going my way at that late hour. There was a night train to Warsaw; I could get off somewhere across the border and change trains. Three young men were standing in front of the steps to the carriage I was going to board. I stood behind them, waiting. One of them pointed to his unfinished cigarette; they weren't ready to board. The steps were high, and I stumbled as I tried to step up onto the first one. The man with the cigarette gave me a boost. The ashes from his cigarette burned my wrist. As I turned to say something to him, he laughed, and grabbed my travel purse, but It was strapped across my shoulder. I don't think he was trying to rob me, or he would have tried again, or cut the strap. He was probably just showing off. I called him a jerk and a *Zlodziej* (thief, in Polish, although he may be German), and went to an empty compartment. After they boarded, I got back off the train; I didn't want a problem in the night.

Checking the schedule in the station, I saw that the *Saint Petersburg Express* was leaving soon. It was going to Russia, crossing the border into Poland after only a thirty-minute ride. If I took that train, I could get from the Polish border to the Baltic with another train or two. The information agent said I could take the train without a reservation. I hurried back up the stairs to the platform; the *Saint Petersburg Express* was still there. It was an old train, but a special one. I had always wanted to ride it.

A Russian conductor spotted me, and asked for my "Bed Card." I said I didn't have one; I only wanted to cross the border, and would stand in the corridor for the short ride. He said he was sorry, but I couldn't board without a Bed Card, because the train had only sleeping carriages. A German Railway policeman was on the platform; he asked me if I spoke German. He wanted to know what the problem was. I explained, in German, that if I didn't get on that train, I would be stuck. Then, I said the magic word, "Guinness." I told him I needed the mileage to beat the world record. He spoke to the Russian conductor, and all was well. The conductor told me I could go, but only as far as the Polish border.

A Russian man about fifty years old came out of the first sleeping compartment while I was standing in the corridor. He pointed to the empty bunk next to his, and then pointed at me. It was easy to understand; he was inviting me to share his room. He was just being polite. On Russian trains, the sleepers, like the European couchettes, aren't allotted according to gender. Before I could explain that I was only going a short distance, the conductor brought me a small chair, and placed it in the vestibule. It was the kind we call a boudoir chair, and upholstered in gold brocade. For thirty memorable minutes I sat on a brocade boudoir chair in the vestibule of the *Saint Petersburg Express*, riding into Poland.

It was difficult to explain to the Polish border guards why I got off the Russian train in Poland at one o'clock in the morning. Why would I board a sleepers-only train for a thirty-minute ride? One of the guards said something about my passport having so many border stamps in it. Again, the magic word, "Guinness," and an explanation of my attempt at a rail record did the trick. I waited two hours in the station for my train. The route didn't give me time to sleep. By the time I boarded the night train to the Baltic, I had only two hours before changing trains to Kolobrzeg, Poland.

Kolobrzeg (Kolberg) is a beautiful health resort on the Baltic Sea, in the province of Pomerania (Pommern). Pomerania was divided between Germany and Poland in 1945. I was glad to have four hours to explore Kolobrzeg before my next train.

I walked through a park and down a broad avenue, hoping I was walking toward the sea. To be on the safe side, I began asking directions, first in English, then in German. Getting nowhere with either language, I tried my Polish. Three middle-aged men walked toward me. I said, *"Gdzie jest woda? "* Trying to remember the phonetics from my phrase book, I pronounced it *Gdshe yest vah-ta*. Later, checking my phrase book, I realized I should have pronounced it *vo-tah*. Instead of, "Where is the water?" I had said, "Where is the cotton?" That made their day; they had a good laugh. Finally, after getting the same response from a young couple, I just kept walking until I found the sea. Why hadn't I just asked where the Baltic was? *"Gdzie jest Baltyku?"*

The sea was dark blue, and as smooth as velvet. Boats were barely moving in their moorings. A small sightseeing ship built in the Viking style, with a red-and-white sail came into view. People were lining up for tickets. Families were picnicking along the shore. Summer was over, but Kolobrzeg was still warm. I went into a couple of snack bars, but didn't find anything I could eat. I sat for a few minutes at an outdoor table, sipping a Pepsi.

Only a few people stared at me. I'm sure American tourists come to Kolobrzeg, since it is a health resort. Sweden is just a day's sail across the Baltic, and so is Denmark. I had heard Swedish being spoken by a tour group in the train station.

As I headed back toward the station, a red train came down the middle of the street. It was full of tourists, going to the sea. When I got back to the main part of town, I heard church bells. I couldn't see the church, but I followed the sound, recording the bells as I walked. I still had two hours before my train; I went into the Hotel New Skanpol, a modern, multi-storied building with 164 rooms, and a sauna, solarium, beauty parlor and fitness center. The receptionist speaks English. I asked her to write a veggie note for me; my own version wasn't perfect. She wrote the note, and told me that the waiters in the hotel's restaurant also speak English. The cook came out of the kitchen to help me order. As soon as I finished my meal I went to the station to board a train. I had decided to go to Zakopane, the famous Polish ski village in the Tatra Mountains.

It was 5:45 a.m. when the train pulled into Zakopane. I wasn't planning to stay; I was just passing through. Everyone else seemed to be staying. A line was forming outside the tiny tourist office, although it wasn't yet open. I caught the next train out; it was going to Czestochowa and then to Warsaw. The conductor refused to sign or stamp my document. He wrote on the front of my PolRail Pass too. The back of the pass was already full. Conductors had written times, dates, train numbers and towns where I had boarded. Most of them added their signatures or employee numbers; my pass was almost illegible. I could probably prove my mileage from the back of the pass. Some of the conductors try to keep the pass, as if it is only a one-ride ticket.

I got off the train in Czestochowa to take a couple of short routes, but the schedule on the platform didn't show any routes that were new to me. The same train was still sitting on the platform. I got back on before it pulled away. There was a crew change at Czestochowa, and the new conductor saw me board. When I asked him to sign, he was furious; he didn't know I had already made the miles. He thought I was cheating. The conductor didn't speak English or German, so I tried to explain in Polish, and handed him a pen. He yelled at me, and threw the pen back toward my notebook. I felt bad. I didn't want anyone to think I would cheat for even one mile of the way. I was earning every mile.

By changing trains off and on all day, I managed to travel some short routes in Poland. I ended up in Terespol, on the Belarus border. Signs were printed in Polish and Russian. There was a customs office in the station. I asked if I could get a visa to cross the border, returning on the next train, but I was told I would have to get the visa in Warsaw. Everyone in the waiting room stared at me.

I found a couple of ways to do short routes that weren't on the Polish map in my timetable. First, I took a local train to Lukow. I watched the soft rain falling on green meadows where bright-orange deer were grazing. In one small village there was a large puddle of water by the train station. Oblivious to the train, and the people outside the station, four yellow ducklings were following the mother duck around in the puddle.

From Deblin I doubled back to Lukow on another local, by a different route. I went into the station café and showed my new veggie note to the young woman behind the counter. She said, *"Ogorek, grzyby, cebula."* I understood; she was naming all the vegetables she had (cucumbers, mushrooms, and onions). I said, *"Tak, chleb."* I was saying yes, to the vegetables, but I wanted them on bread, like a sandwich. She showed me a big bowl of dough, and said something like *Knedliky*, the Czech word for dumpling. I figured it must mean dumpling in Polish too. I said *"Tak!"* She rolled the dough, made a huge football of it, and then dug a deep hole in it, showing me that she was going to stuff it. *"Kaczka,"* she said. Oh, No! She was going to stuff a duck into that gaping hole. *"Nie, nie,"* I said. *"Nie kaczka!"* My new "real Polish" veggie note wasn't working out too well either. I sat down to eat my cucumber, mushroom and onion sandwich; I didn't dare try the Polish word *(musztarda)* for mustard. There was a bottle of catsup on the table, so I gave my sandwich a squirt. Ordering a drink to go was easy. I just said, "Pepsi *do pociag* " (Pepsi to train).

As I was walking out to the platform to board the train to Warsaw, a man about seventy-five years old caught up with me. He asked if I would have dinner with him in Warsaw. We spoke in German. I told him I would be leaving Warsaw on a night train, so it would be impossible. I thanked him for the invitation. Then he hugged me. He said, "No, I thank you. I thank America for what it did in the war."

It was the first time a Polish veteran had hugged me because of our role in the war, but several times German veterans had hugged me for the same reason. And each time, I cried because our former enemy understood that we were in the right. I was never more proud to be an American.

As soon as the train pulled into Warsaw, I caught a night express to Berlin, over a slightly different route. I looked into the first compartment in the corridor, and saw only a briefcase on the overhead storage rack. That was encouraging. I figured the owner of the briefcase was a commuter who would soon detrain, leaving me a private place to sleep. I put my backpack on the rack, and stepped quickly into the corridor to look out the open window. From the corner of my eye, I saw only the dark suit of the man who grabbed my head from behind. He forced me around toward the compartment door, and slammed the right side of my face into the doorjamb. I saw stars! He pushed past me, grabbed his briefcase, and disappeared down the corridor. When the stars stopped blinking, I tried to find the conductor, but the door leading to the sleeping carriages was locked; I couldn't go through to check the rest of the train. I hadn't seen the man's face; I couldn't identify him, anyway. He must have thought I was going to steal his briefcase. My face was bleeding, and my eye was swelling. How could he have done that to me? I was afraid to go to sleep. In the washroom I discovered the source of the blood, a deep gash on the side of my face, just under my eye. Afraid of infection from the non-potable water from the tap, I wiped my face and eye with an alcohol pad. Ouch!

In the morning, I boarded InterCity # 501, the *Schauinsland*, to Frankfurt; I still had a day's journey ahead. I didn't go to the restaurant car (my face looked pretty bad). I bought a sandwich and coffee from the mini-cart. From Frankfurt I caught the last train to BK. I didn't travel for a week; I was ashamed to go out, because I had another black eye. It looked worse than the one I had been given on the street in Berlin.

Chapter 20
The Balkans

With only a faint rainbow around my eye, the last reminder of a black eye, I set out for the Balkans via Budapest. I felt a keen sense of excitement; I had never been to Bulgaria or Romania. But first, I wanted to spend a day in Budapest. No other city compliments the Danube River so well, not even Vienna. In Mainz, I boarded EuroCity # 25, the *Franz Liszt*; I had taken it before, so there would be no credit for mileage, but I had exhausted almost all of the routes from Mainz to Budapest, anyway. The ten hours of travel would be easy; I had been sequestered for a week. Today I felt like a real tourist. I was on a fancy train, with nothing to do but lean back and watch the passing panorama.

In the restaurant car I was seated with a Viennese. I don't use the proper, German name of a person from Vienna because to our ears it sounds comical. Since Vienna is really Wien, a person from Wien is called a Wiener. I was impressed when the Viennese said he is a music critic. He travels around, attending concerts and recitals of classical music. When I told him about my journeys *he* was impressed with *me*.

"Madam, when I ride this train for eight hours, I am exhausted. You are amazing."

"Oh, many tourists travel this way." But, I was tempted to agree with him.

I arrived in Budapest about 9:30 p.m. As I stepped out of the station, a young man sidled up to me and offered me a packet of white powder. I made a sound that can only be described as the sound of an exclamation point, unaccompanied by a word. Then I said, "I am a vegetarian! I care about my health." He spoke in English. "I have something for vegetarians. Here, buy this health pill. It will make you feel good." I turned and ran. I went directly to an apartment building I had heard about. Some of the tenants rent out rooms. I saw a vacancy sign on the third floor balcony. A middle-aged woman answered my knock; a large yellow dog accompanied her. She led me to a room that appeared to be her living room. Family pictures adorned the walls and the shelves. An antique, mahogany china cabinet displayed beautiful old dishes and crystal glassware. My door wouldn't close tight; the dog kept pushing it open. He sat on the floor at the foot of my bed and watched me unpack. I was glad he accepted me. Most of the dogs I had encountered in Europe had growled at me, chased me or tried to bite me. Or all of the above.

My landlady brought me a cup of tea and explained the bathing procedure to me. I must light the gas burner on the water heater, which is fastened to the pipe above the tub. The procedure has to be repeated every couple of minutes; the hot water container is about the size of an eight-cup coffeepot. It was getting late, but I decided to brave the bath; I wanted to start my day of sightseeing early the next morning. The bathroom door wouldn't shut tight either; the dog came in, leaving the door wide open. I got out of the tub, and tried to shoo him out, so I could push the door to. He wouldn't budge. As if the open door wasn't enough of a problem, I singed my eyelashes when I tried to light the burner. But I slept well, and so did the dog (beside my bed).

Breakfast was a cup of coffee and a box of cookies, served in my room. Not certain if the whole box was for me, or if I should take only a few, I ate three of them.

First on my agenda was the Gothic Parliament Building. It sprawls like a giant fairy-tale castle on the Danube. The Danube was green today. I wonder if Johann Strauss just thought "The Beautiful Blue Danube" sounded more romantic, or if the river really was blue before our modern-day pollution of it. I walked along the river until I reached the Chain Bridge. Seven bridges connect the Buda and the Pest sides of the Danube. I crossed over to the Buda side of the river to Castle Hill. The thirteenth-century Matthias Church (reconstructed in the nineteenth century) is officially called the Church of Our Lady. It once served as a mosque for the invading Turks. Budapest has the largest source (from one city) of curative mineral waters in the world; I couldn't resist taking a peek at the most famous spa hotel in Budapest, the Gellert.

My wandering brought me back to Keleti Pu (East Station) in time for the *Balkan Express*. It would take me to Sofia, Bulgaria via Belgrade, Serbia (Yugoslavia). All of my seatmates were Serbian. Magda, a young blonde, and her twelve-year-old daughter, Irina, were traveling to Belgrade (they live in Germany) to visit relatives. Others in the compartment questioned me about American policies concerning the Serbs and Bosnia-Herzegovina. Magda interpreted for us.

In three hours we were in Kelebia, on the Hungarian side of the border. Customs officials checked passports on the train. A Yugoslavian crew replaced the Hungarians.

The Serbian conductor refused to sign my document. Magda acted as a go-between, relaying the questions and answers that flew back and forth.

"Why should I sign anything for you while your country bombs mine?"

"I cannot control my government. I am an ordinary citizen like you."

"You are thinking of train rides while my countrymen are dying! I do not care if you win the record or not!"

He turned and walked out of the compartment. I wasn't angry with him; I understood his point of view. Another conductor came in, but before he could sign my document, the other one came back and signed it, said something to Magda, and left again. She said the conductor was sorry; he knew it wasn't my fault, as it wasn't his fault that his country was fighting a civil war. I hadn't been watching the news lately, and I didn't know that NATO had been bombing Bosnia off and on for the last few weeks, and were still bombing. No wonder the Serbian conductor was mad. Bosnia borders Serbia, and it is the Serbs we are bombing in Bosnia. I had thought he was talking about previous bombings.

I was concerned about crossing into Serbia; I didn't have a visa, but I had heard from other tourists that it was possible to get a transit visa at the border for twenty dollars. About two months before I began my train journeys I had a nightmare so real that I woke in a cold sweat. In the dream I was in a stone customs building with one barred oblong window. Two soldiers in olive-green uniforms with red epaulettes were interrogating me. Not satisfied with my vague answers, they were going to kill me. I can't forget the dream. Tonight I was remembering it vividly.

We stopped for the border check at Subotica, Serbia. A soldier came into the compartment, took my passport and motioned for me to follow him. I thought he was taking me to another compartment for questioning, but he stepped off the train, waiting for me to follow him. I asked him to wait; I hurried back to the compartment, and told Magda they were taking me off the train. I said, "My name is Mona Tippins. If the train leaves without me, call an American Embassy." Magda jumped up, told me to stay in the hall, and went to the doorway of the train. When she came back, she said, "Go with him. He is going to get you a visa. It is all OK."

I followed the soldier into a small building. It was just off the platform, and not made of stone, as in my nightmare. I sat on a wooden bench while an officer checked my passport. In a minute or so, he handed it back to me. I said, "I need a visa." He smiled, and said, "You have a visa. I gave you one." I was relieved. When I tried to pay for the visa, he said, "No. Go to your train." The train was pulling away without me; I dragged myself up through the door, just as it closed. Magda gave me her address in Germany, and her brother's address in Belgrade (Beograd). She asked me to get off the train in Belgrade, and stay with her in her brother's house. I was tempted; it would be an interesting experience, but I needed mileage. Also, I wasn't sure if the rest of the Serbs in Belgrade would be as receptive to me as Magda, my other seatmates, and the customs officials. Anyway, I had only a transit visa for Serbia. I was lucky the soldiers didn't take me hostage, considering the circumstances.

When we arrived in Belgrade, Magda, her daughter, and the other Serbs in my compartment detrained. The train sat in the station for over an hour, but I didn't see anyone board the train. Some of the carriages were uncoupled. I moved to a through carriage going to Sofia, Bulgaria. It was 11:00 p.m. when the train pulled out of Belgrade. For me, it had already been a long night, and I still had miles to go in Serbia.

I was awake by 5:00 a.m., and wondering if I would have trouble getting into Bulgaria. An hour later the train stopped in Kalotina, just across the Bulgarian border. Customs were handled on board; this wasn't the border of my dream either. I didn't need a visa, but I was asked to fill out a statistics card. The authorities needed to know where I was coming from, and where I was going. It was the conductors I had a problem with. Evidently they had never encountered a Bulgarian Rail Pass before. I showed them the instructions in Bulgarian on the second page of my pass, and my note requesting a signature for the mileage. They signed my document and stamped my rail pass.

In one hour we were in Sofia. I had my Bulgarian Rail Pass validated, and checked the schedule. A train to Varna (a port on the Black Sea) was leaving in a few hours. I would wait.

A ditch surrounds the remains of a large decorative fountain in the courtyard outside the lower level of the station. Two little boys were sleeping in the ditch, under an army blanket. A pile of wood served as a makeshift stove. The blazing fire reached to the top of the pot. A wiry young man, presumably their father, poured some of the hot water into a basin, and mixed it with cold water. He woke the boys; they took off their shirts and began to wash themselves. The man took a chunk of meat from a brown paper bag, and put it on the fire in a large skillet. There were kiosks and vendor's booths all around the courtyard. I bought a cup of coffee and a pastry for myself, and a loaf of bread and some milk for the man and his boys.

I caught a streetcar outside the station, and rode around the city. Vegetable and fruit markets were everywhere; I bought three bananas and a loaf of bread. I was cutting it close; it was almost time for my train, and there wasn't a streetcar in sight. I hailed a taxi, and hoped for the best.

The driver looked like a pudgy version of Rambo. He had long, dark hair, and wore a red bandana tied around his forehead. His abdomen protruded over the waistband of his khaki pants, which he had slit up the sides. When he smiled I noticed the wide gap between his two front teeth. He was eating a banana, and there were two lying on the dash. As soon as we pulled away, he picked up one of my bananas and exchanged it for one of his overripe ones. I gave him an odd look, and he switched them back.

He wouldn't start the meter; he wanted to make up his own price at the end of the ride. I finally persuaded him to start the meter just before we got to the station. It ran up to 1500 Leva (about $18) in thirty seconds. I got out, shook my finger at Rambo, and gave him a five-dollar bill. He squished banana through the gap in his teeth, and laughed. The train to Varna was waiting on the platform. I could relax; it was an eight-hour ride.

In Varna I walked a long way, looking for a hotel. It was difficult to figure out the signs in the Cyrillic alphabet. I looked in the window of a building and saw a row of washing machines. I had my satchel with me; I figured it was a good time to get my laundry done. A woman was standing by the first machine. I went to the last machine in the row and opened my satchel, then turned to ask the woman if she spoke English; I needed change. She spoke German to me, "What are you doing?"

"I want to wash my clothes." I think her laughter could be heard out on the street.

"This is a shop! We sell washing machines. We do not do your laundry." I laughed almost as loudly as she did.

When I saw a tour bus parked outside a several-storied building, I knew I had found a hotel. It looked expensive from the outside, but I was there, so I went in. The receptionist speaks English and German. The price was much less than I had expected. I set my gear down in my room, and went out to have dinner. There was a restaurant in the hotel, but I had seen lots of sidewalk cafés on my way to the hotel, and I wanted to sit in the fresh night air; it was almost warm in Varna. With help from my veggie note, I was served at a sidewalk café around the corner from the hotel. Children chased one another, bumping the chairs as they darted between the tables. It wasn't the restful, people-watching evening I had hoped for.

Back at the hotel, I stopped in the restaurant for coffee and dessert. Four young women sat at a table across from me. They were all extremely beautiful, and all appeared to be under twenty-five years old. Each one was dressed in a different style. One woman, with long blonde hair, was wearing a dress like Alice wore in Wonderland. She actually had a white pinafore over her dress. The other blonde was wearing a long, sheer gown. One of the brunettes was dressed in a red evening gown; the other was wearing white shorts (very short), khaki blouse, and thigh-high black boots. I was sure they had appeared in a modeling show, or a play. They weren't eating or drinking, just smoking. I never assume that women are prostitutes, no matter how they are dressed. I first suspected they were 'Ladies of the Evening' when a man walked over to the table and chose the 'Lady in Red.' They walked arm in arm, out of the restaurant, and up the stairs. Any doubts I harbored about their characters were dismissed, after the woman wearing the shorts made vulgar motions to a man who had just entered the room.

I went to the bar upstairs to buy a bottle of mineral water. There were three more 'Ladies in Red' standing by the bar. One was wearing a long evening gown with sequins, and the other two were wearing short cocktail dresses. All were wearing red.

I attempted to walk up the thirteen flights of stairs to my room, but on the fifth floor, I took the elevator. I've had a cold hanging on for a couple of weeks, and I tire easily.

My room is furnished with a peach silk-covered sofa and a full-sized bed, covered with beige silk. French doors open onto my brick balcony; I could see the shoreline, a brightly-lit bridge and the sea. Varna reminds me of Paris, with its sidewalk cafés and bright lights above the boulevards. And, as in Paris, people were milling about, even though it was very late. It was as though they didn't want to go to bed, lest they miss something. I didn't want to go back inside, because the view was so beautiful, but the air was getting colder. When I tried to record something, I discovered I had lost my voice. It was time to escape the night air.

There was a train leaving at 3:20 p.m. for Plovdiv via Karnobat. I could change to an overnighter to Sofia, over a new route, and head for Turkey or Greece, or both. A day in Varna sounded fine to me. Varna is believed to be the oldest inhabited area in the Balkans; Thracian tribes settled it twelve centuries before Christ. Gold artifacts from 3600 BC have been uncovered nearby.

I set out to see a little of the city. I still felt ill, but my voice was back. After riding a bus for twenty minutes I saw the sea, so I jumped off the bus at the next stop. The streets looked familiar; I was back at my hotel.

I walked down to a park by the sea. Several women were sitting on folding chairs, and some were sitting on the grass, crocheting tablecloths and scarves for sale. Clotheslines were strung between two trees to display their work. The sea was calm; wavelets were barely bumping the shore. A few clouds dappled the sky.

I sat at a sidewalk café, drinking cola. Food was served, but nothing for me except sweets. I went into a restaurant in a mall-like building. Lunch was over; there were no other customers. The piano player was leaving, but when I walked in, he sat back down, and played just for me.

I headed for Istanbul by way of Plovdiv, Bulgaria.

We arrived in Plovdiv in the late evening. In the station, I sat on a bench near the door. A man, obviously inebriated, sat down by me. He kept touching my shoulder, so I went outside to the kiosk for a cup of coffee. The man behind me in line said, "*Guten Abend*" (good evening). He thought I was German. I asked if he spoke English, and he said he did. His name is Josep; he works in Plovdiv, and was waiting for a local train to his home. He said he usually drives, but his son had taken the car to a university in Sofia. Josep interpreted for me, but there was nothing I could eat except potato chips.

The train to Istanbul was canceled; the next one would leave at 8:30 in the morning. I could go back to Karnobat on a local at 1:00 a.m. or to Sofia on the 3:00 a.m. train. That was it; no more trains would leave Plovdiv (except locals) until 6:00 a.m. I opted for Karnobat.

After Josep's train left, I sat next to a young woman who speaks English. She was waiting for a local train. The cleaning ladies ran everyone out so they could mop the floors. The young woman and I sat on a park bench across from the station. While we were talking, two cars pulled up and parked a few feet from us. Several Gypsy men jumped out of the cars. They started fighting, with fists and clubs. Two of them pulled knives from their pockets, and slashed at each other. We just sat there talking, as if nothing was happening. I must have been tired; I felt as though it was a dream. When two police cars drove up, we went back in the station. The floors were dry.

After the woman left, the drunk came back in and started bothering me; I walked out to the platform, pretending to catch a train. I didn't go back into the waiting room; I went into an anteroom, and lay facedown on a large table that was slanted like a drafting table. Exhausted, I fell into a deep sleep, still wearing my backpack.

Feeling a nudge against my shoulder, I looked up, expecting to see the drunk. Two policemen were standing by me. One of them spoke to me in Bulgarian. I knew he wanted to check my ID. Both of them seemed surprised when I showed an American passport, and a rail pass. They probably had thought I was a homeless person or a wino, the way I was sleeping so soundly, leaning forward across the table, and using my satchel as a pillow. My hair was a mess, from sleeping facedown. The drool on my chin didn't enhance my appearance, either.

They had wakened me just in time for my train. I walked out to the platform, and was ready to board, when Josep found me. His son had returned home from Sofia with the car, so Josep drove back to Plovdiv to rescue me. He knew I didn't want to take the train back to Karnobat, repeating miles, and he was concerned for my safety in the station. He said his wife would be home from her night job by the time we arrived at his apartment, and I could rest until time to take a train to Sofia. It would save me some time, so I accepted. I had heard about the rough roads in parts of Bulgaria, but I wasn't prepared for that ride. Josep drove over potholes and shoulders at the same speed as he did on the asphalt. When a bus needed to pass, Josep drove us into the ditch, slowing only slightly for the maneuver.

The apartment was on the second floor, in a small town near Pazardzhik. There was a black wreath with a picture of a smiling, white-haired woman on the door. Josep said his mother had died recently; the wreath was for her. He kissed her picture before he opened the door. His wife was not home yet, but he woke his son up to meet me. I went to the bathroom, but didn't see a sink. I asked Josep where I could wash my hands. He twisted the shower around, and pulled it over to where a sink should be. Voila! It was a foldaway sink. I have seen many different contraptions in European bathrooms, but not one like that.

Josep fixed me some toast and tea. He showed me a cot in the kitchen. Flat dishes lined with burning candles lay in the center of the cot. A Bible and a few sprigs of fresh flowers lay on the pillow. Josep said, "That was my mother's bed. She died there." I didn't say so, but I didn't want to sleep there. He must have sensed it; he said I could sleep on the couch in the living room.

I only slept for three hours; it was time for us to drive to Pazardzhik, to catch up with the train to Sofia. Josep's wife had arrived while I was sleeping; she rode with us to the train station. They insisted on paying for breakfast in the station restaurant. Josep wrote down their address, and asked me to write to them.

In Sofia I talked to an information agent, and she said it would be better for me to go to Istanbul from Greece. She suggested I spend the night in Sandanski, Bulgaria before going to Greece, because there might be some delays on the through trains to Turkey.

The next day I boarded a train to Thessalonika, Greece, arriving at 3:20 p.m. Five minutes later I was on a night train to Istanbul. There were rumors that the Turkish Railway workers would go on strike, but the train pulled away on time. It was an older train. The WC was dirty, and there were no paper towels, toilet tissue or soap, but it was nothing new; most of the trains I've been on lately were without those items. I was alone in a compartment; I made myself a place to sleep. Around 11:00 p.m. we stopped at Alexandropolis Port, on the Aegean Sea. It looked as though all the passengers were detraining except me. One of the conductors saw that I was still on the train. "You didn't get off the train!"

"I am going to Istanbul."

"Do you have a ticket for Istanbul? The Turks are going on strike." I told him I didn't.

"Then get off the train!" He grabbed my satchel. I put on my backpack and ran with him to the door.

"But the train is moving!" I said.

"Get off the train!" He set my satchel down, and tried to help me step off the train. I turned around and tried to step off backward. The conductor held my arm. I held the metal handgrips with both hands; one leg was dangling toward the ground. We were no longer in the station; if I jumped I would fall in a ditch. I saw that I couldn't make it, even though the train was barely moving. He realized it too; he helped me climb back in. Then he spoke to someone on the radio, and the train backed up into the station. I figured out what had happened when I saw the rest of the carriages sitting at the station. They had been uncoupled from the engine and left there, but the engine and my carriage were going on to Istanbul.

I saw other passengers on the carriages of the waiting train, so I started to board the nearest one. The same conductor was on the platform, and he said I couldn't get on the train.

"Where is the train going?"

"Back to Thessalonika, but you can't go."

"Where can I go then?"

"You can go to a hotel!"

"Well, I'm sorry, but if the other people are going, I'm going too." I started up the steps again.

"They have tickets. You don't have a ticket. You can't go!" Passengers were leaning out of the train windows, looking and listening.

"I don't have a ticket for Istanbul. I have a EurailPass. I can go anywhere in Greece I want to."

"Get on the train."

I was exhausted. Thinking again about the "*Throw Momma from the Train*" incident, I couldn't imagine why I attempted such a thing. I should have screamed and held on to the inside rail, refusing to get off a moving train, no matter how slow it was going. It was different when I jumped off the moving train in Poland. I jumped to help someone.

It would be several hours before we arrived in Thessalonika; I stretched out across three seats.

When I woke, the other passengers had detrained; I was alone on the train in Thessalonika's station. I had just missed a train to Athens, and the others were either locals or were traveling routes I had already done. I had heard that Americans no longer need a visa for Romania, but the information agents in Thessalonika weren't sure. To get to Romania, I needed to go back to Sofia. I had more than six hours to wait for the next train.

I stored my gear in a locker, and went out to the sidewalk café in front of the station for coffee. Pale peach-colored umbrellas and awnings shaded the tables and chairs. The air was already warm, although it was not yet 8:00 a.m. Buses run between the station and the rest of the city, but I knew I would fall asleep from the motion. Instead, I took a long walk.

I went back to the station for lunch. In the cafeteria I had a bowl of spinach cooked with olive oil, the only hot food I could get. I took my coffee out to the sidewalk café.

A blond-haired man in his early forties was sitting at a table next to mine. He smiled at me, and I smiled back. He came over and showed me a roll of lottery tickets; he was one of many vendors who sell them in the stations, and on the street. I saw lots of people buying them, usually in strips of ten or more. He said, "English?" I nodded. He didn't say anything else; that seemed to be the only word in English he knew. He sat down beside me. When I finished my coffee, I said good-bye and went for another walk.

When I came back to the station, he was gone. A few minutes later, there he was again. He followed me everywhere. We didn't speak. Greek is a language that really is "all Greek to me."

He followed me down to the lockers when I was ready to board my train. I finally realized he was retarded. Without a word, he took the satchel from me and walked beside me. We went upstairs to the platform. He took the lottery tickets from his fanny pack and handed it to me. I shook my head, but he insisted, so I accepted it, and gave him a purple baseball cap.

When the train pulled in, I shook hands with him, and boarded. He motioned for me to open my window, and held up a pen and a notepad; he wanted my address. I shook my head, pointed to myself, and said, "Mama. Grandmama." Then he spoke English, "You no Mama. You no Grandmama. You my heart."

He wanted to exchange watches. I hesitated, for I was wearing a beautiful designer watch my sister had given me as a bon voyage gift. He started to cry. It was just a watch, after all; I exchanged with him. I closed the window as the train pulled away.

The customs officials collected passports when the train stopped in Strimon, and returned them in Promachon, still on the Greek side of the border. The Bulgarians checked at Kulata, and I was issued another statistics card.

A second-class ticket from the Bulgarian border to Sofia cost me 164 Lev (about two dollars). The same conductor that signed for me a couple of days ago was on duty. I handed him the money for the ticket. He remembered me. "No, You have a Bulgarian Rail Pass. You don't pay." I showed him my pass that had expired. He understood after I pointed to yesterday's date. Later, I bought a croissant and a cup of tea for 164 Lev from the mini-cart. I thought it odd that I could ride a train for 200 kilometers for the same price.

In Sofia I bought a ticket to Bucharest, Romania. There was only one first-class carriage on the train, and I was the only passenger in it.

In the night I went to the WC. I locked the door behind me before I realized I had forgotten my flashlight. The room was dark, except for a tiny glimmer of light coming through the frosted window. The floor was flooded with water and urine. There was no paper or soap. The toilet seat was missing, and so was the light bulb. I wasn't about to use the toilet under those conditions, but I couldn't get the door unlocked. It was made of thick metal. I hit it and kicked it, but it didn't budge. I called out, but there was no one to hear me. About ten minutes later we stopped in a station. The platform light helped a little. The window was hinged, and could only be opened a few inches at the top. I called out the window, but no one answered. If the opening had been large enough, I would have climbed out the window. As a last resort, I prayed. On my next try, the door opened. I should have tried prayer first.

We stopped at the Bulgarian checkpoint at Ruse (Rousse). Thirty minutes later we crossed over the Danube River on the Friendship Bridge into Romania, and the checkpoint at Giurgiu. I didn't need a visa, only a statistics card. The train sat in the station for forty minutes. There was a beautiful bright-blue, self-propelled train parked on the opposite platform. Soldiers were guarding it as officers in blue uniforms were boarding. Books and papers were lying on a long table inside; it must have been a conference or a treaty signing. A soldier was standing outside the door to my carriage. I asked him if I could take a picture of the blue train. He shook his head, and crossed his rifle in front of him. I took that as a "no."

Two young men approached me as I walked into the station in Bucharest. One of them asked, in English, if I wanted to change money. I said no, and walked on. They followed me to the door, so I stopped, and put my back to the wall, just in case. They went outside, so I relaxed, and went to look for an exchange bureau. The men came up to me again. I had just taken a one-hundred-Mark bill out of my purse. One of the men asked me again to change money. When I said no, the other man stepped behind me, grabbed my wrist and twisted it to my back. He said, "Be still!" I felt something against my back; I didn't know if I was being robbed at gunpoint or finger point, but I took no chances; I didn't move until after he wrenched the money from my hand, and they both had walked away. There were no railway police in sight.

The *Dacia Express* goes all the way to Vienna in eighteen hours. I was in a second-class compartment with two Romanian women. One is a College Professor, and the other is an Engineer. With only three of us in the compartment we had space to stretch out.

I knew I could make the EC # 26, the *Joseph Haydn* from Vienna to Mainz. I had taken it before; there would be no new mileage. If I made it to Mainz on time, I could be in BK tonight. That was a pleasant thought.

On the *Joseph Haydn* I sat in a first-class parlor carriage, in a plush lavender seat. From a selection of side orders, the waiter in the restaurant car fixed me a vegetable plate. I felt better, and more rested than I had in days.

In Mainz I had six minutes to go down the stairs, through a tunnel, and back up a flight of stairs to another platform to board the Regional Express to BK. I would make it "home" tonight.

I still have a few days travel time on my Romanian pass; I packed World Traveler and a shopping bag on wheels with toys and clothing, and headed for Romania by way of Austria. In Frankfurt I boarded the *Donau Kourier*, # 223. I rode it earlier in my journeys, when it carried sleepers and seating carriages. It has been changed to a EuroNight (EN), an overnighter carrying only sleepers and one carriage with wide chairs called *Liegesessel*. I paid for one of the wide chairs, and slept until I detrained in Linz, Austria.

In Linz, I took a train to Summerau, and waited for a train across the Czech border. The ground was covered with snow. As soon as I stepped into the station to get warm, the little red-and-yellow, self-propelled train pulled in. I tried to board on the wrong side, which brought smiles to the faces of the six Czech women, already on board. They had been shopping in Austria. The little train swayed back and forth all the way to Horni Dvoriste, in the Czech Republic. It was one of my most memorable rides.

I traveled for three days and nights through the Czech Republic, Slovakia and Hungary, adding many miles to my total, but without pausing until I arrived in Romania. My cold is still hanging on. I feel a little better, but I'm terribly congested, and my neck is stiff from sleeping in a sitting position, and wearing my backpack makes it worse. A couple of aspirins didn't help much.

It was late at night when the train crossed the Hungarian/Romanian border. I sat up to prepare for customs check. I wadded my Mylar blanket into a big, wrinkled blob. The Romanian customs officer punched it with his fist, and said, "What is it? What is it?" When I said it was a blanket, he said, "I don't know blanket. What is blanket?" I smoothed the Mylar blanket out, laid down across the seats, covered with the blanket, and pretended to snore. He laughed then, but he still asked me to open both pieces of luggage. I thought he would ask me about the toys and the extra shoes, but he didn't. Then, he asked me why I wanted to come to his country. Suppressing the urge to say, "Because it is there," I showed him my note in Romanian about breaking a record.

In the morning five ragged little boys came into my compartment and asked for candy. I didn't have any candy; if I had, I would have already eaten it for breakfast, there was no restaurant car. But, I did have a pair of shoes for each of them. Then I brought out shirts and pants. They started undressing immediately to change to the new clothes. At that precise moment, two conductors came in to check tickets. I had been mistaken for everything else; hopefully the conductors wouldn't think I was a child molester. Evidently they were used to the little beggars riding the trains for a short distance to see what they could bum from the passengers; they ran them out and asked if I wanted my door locked. I declined. In their haste to run from the conductors, the boys left my compartment in disarray. Dirty, ragged clothing and shoes surrounded me. When the boys passed by again, I asked them to take their things away. They threw them away. Later a little Gypsy boy came into the compartment, and sat across from me. He didn't ask for anything, but I assumed he had seen the clothing I had given the other boys. I gave him a pair of hiking boots, a pair of socks, and a warm jacket. He pointed to his dirty, blue-plaid pants. I had given all the pants away, but he was happy when I gave him a baseball cap imprinted with an American logo. He told me his name was Florian.

I detrained in Brasov, in the Transylvanian area of Romania. A taxi driver asked if I wanted to see the thirteenth-century Bran Castle. I said I did, but I was taking a bus. He offered to take me for ten dollars. That was a bargain (the castle is 28 km from Brasov). He put my luggage in the trunk, and we took off for Dracula's former haunt. I have heard stories from tourists who experienced weird feelings when they entered the castle. When we passed a field close to the castle, I felt worse than weird. I had chills. My goose bumps got goose bumps. Later I read that Vlad (Dracula) had murdered many soldiers and townspeople in a field near the castle, impaling them on stakes, row by row.

Bran castle rises like a huge specter, on a hill above a cobbled square. The steep walkway to the castle was covered in ice. The interior of the castle seemed musty, but I didn't experience any weird feelings, but then, much of the castle was closed for repairs. I saw only the "homey" rooms. Who knows what lurks in the nether rooms? The square below the castle was filled with kiosks and vendor's tables. The driver took me to see the Gothic "Black Church," so called because it was blackened by the fire set by the Austrians in 1689.

When we got back to the station it started to snow. The driver asked for another ten dollars; he said the price he had quoted was for one way. He then offered to spend the day with me. For an additional twenty dollars he would show me all the sights, and find me a place to stay for the night. I declined; I wanted to be in Bucharest before nightfall. In the station I walked up the stairs to the waiting area. I had a special doll with me. She was a golden-haired German doll, with tiny, white teeth. A Gypsy girl about ten years old smiled shyly at me. I gave her the doll. She hugged the doll, and hugged me. Then, at least a dozen Gypsies swarmed around me, chattering away. One old lady tried to open my suitcase. I took some of the clothes from my shopping bag on wheels, and passed them around. The old lady grabbed the bag, held it over her head, and reached in and pulled all of the clothes out of it. Some of the other women started fighting her for the clothes. I was still in the middle of the group; I was hit on the head and on the arm (accidentally, I'm sure). In the fracas, one of the wheels on the bag was bent (probably on my head). I gave the bag to the old lady. Some of the passengers on the lower floor seemed amused by the scene. We were at the top of the stairs leading to the mezzanine. Later, when I was waiting on the platform for a train to Bucharest, I saw two Gypsy boys trying to pull the bag along, despite the damaged wheel.

At first I was alone in a first-class compartment on the train to Bucharest, then a young Romanian businessman joined me. He wanted to know what I thought of his country. I told him I thought it was beautiful, and I liked the Romanian people very much. He tried to convince me that Dracula was really a good guy, and had done a lot for his people. I knew that the story of Dracula is a sore spot with Romanians, but I couldn't resist asking why, if he was such a good guy, was he called "Vlad, the Impaler?" He had no answer to that. The two conductors signed my document, but argued with me over the validity of my Romanian Rail Pass. After reading the instructions in Romanian, they accepted it, but insisted I pay for a seat reservation, even though reservations weren't required.

In Predeal, about 25 kilometers from Brasov, the snow was coming down fast and thick. As soon as a crew swept the snow from the tracks, they were covered again. We waited about thirty minutes before we could travel again. As we moved a little faster, the train was blowing snow from the tracks all over the evergreen trees along the banks.

The resort town of Sinaia looks like a Swiss resort town. Most of the buildings near the station are chalets. Icicles were hanging from a concrete bridge that was broken in half. An old green freight train was sitting in the station. The flatbeds had about four feet of snow in them. A little farther on I saw a man walking through the woods; the snow came almost up to his waist.

In Bucharest the snow had turned to rain, making it easier for me to give away the clothing; the homeless had moved from the park to the station, to escape the rain. It didn't take long to empty my suitcase, but I had several hours to wait for a train back to Budapest, because I wanted to take a different route to gain mileage credit. I walked around inside the station for awhile, eating a pizza. A young woman dressed in a blue sweat suit sat begging in a corner of the station. Her dark hair was cut in a short, pixie style. When I approached her she screamed and kicked as though she were crazy. I hurried away. Later, when I stepped out of the waiting room, I saw her again. She had changed to a stylish outfit of tan pants and white ruffled blouse. Her hair was neatly combed. Suddenly she started heckling an elderly couple. When they moved away, she followed them. She spit on the old man, and laughed about it. Only when she hit the man did anyone intervene. I had walked away, but she saw me. She came running toward me, spitting as she ran. I ran, pulling World Traveler behind me. It kept tipping over. Once she almost spit on it. That really made me mad. I stopped, and shook my fist at her. She kicked World Traveler before I could stop her. I hurried to the platform with her after me. Some of the waiting passengers were amused by the scene, but I didn't find it funny. She caught up with me, and hit me on the back of the neck. I felt a sudden rush of adrenaline; I knew I could kick her butt, but since she was obviously crazy or on drugs, should I? I didn't have to decide, the train pulled in and I jumped on the first carriage. The only others on my carriage were several young people, two compartments down, who spent most of the night chasing each other up and down the corridor.

Just out of Bucharest it began to snow again. I was in a compartment alone, but I didn't want to sleep; I wanted to watch the snow. When the snow became deeper, the train slowed. I could see the engine and the forward bright-blue carriages as the train curved around the track. I have seen many places covered with snow, but none looked as beautiful as the Romanian snowscape I was seeing tonight.

From Budapest, I took a few short routes between Hungary and Austria, catching up with the *Orient Express* in the late evening two days later. It's not the luxurious *Orient Express*, but it travels the same route and still carries the name. And sometimes just the name of a train is enough to make you want to ride it.

I detrained in Karlsruhe, Germany at 4:00 a.m. While waiting for my next train, I thought back about some of the sadness I had seen in and around the stations. And the last few days have been Hell. I have seen so much sorrow. Sorrow that reaches beyond winos, beggars and the homeless. There have been many times on my journeys when I have been heartbroken. I have decided not to burden my readers with the details. They will remain in my personal journal, and my memory.

Mentally and physically exhausted, I climbed the stairs to the apartment, and actually fell into the hall, as I tried to go through the door. Rosi heard the noise, and came out of the bedroom. She asked about my trip. I said, "I will tell you a little about it, but some things will go to the grave with me."

Central Station in Varna, Bulgaria

Chapter 21
To Russia with Love

On a postcard to my husband, I wrote, "Having a great time between catastrophes!"

I took a few days off to prepare for the long journey from Germany to Russia and beyond. I shopped for food and bottled water; I have heard about the shortages in Russia. Erich bought me several packages of a special cracker that is loaded with vitamins and minerals. I will survive.

It was 11:00 p.m. In Frankfurt's main station, the train to Moscow backed up alongside the platform. I felt a great sense of excitement and expectation. It was my first trip to Russia, and my first night in a sleeper. All the railways in the countries of the former Soviet Union require passengers to have sleeping accommodations on overnight trains; there are no seats. My trains and sleepers were reserved in advance. I'm traveling hard class, which is comparable to second class in Western Europe. Soft class is comparable to first class. I was wearing a special jacket my daughter-in-law, Crissy had made me. A colorful train snakes across the back of the jacket, with the words "To Russia With Love" written under it.

Two conductors were on the platform to assist in boarding. One of them spoke to me in German, and showed me to my sleeping compartment. There were three bunks, all on one side of the compartment. The middle one folds down from the wall. I had the bottom bunk, a young Russian woman the top. An elderly Russian woman came into the compartment and tried to move my things from my bunk to the hall. When I questioned her (in German) she became very angry, and went into the hall to call a conductor. I had no idea what she was upset about until the conductor came in and said the woman wanted my bunk, instead of the middle one. Since she was older, I agreed. She was still rude to me, and she complained to the conductor again. He took my things and led me to a first-class sleeping compartment. He said the woman didn't want to be in the same sleeper with me, but he didn't say why.

Later I was standing in the corridor, and she spoke German to me. "I can speak German. I have been visiting my son in Germany, but I do not like Germans. I will not speak to you." Who was she speaking to then? So, that was the problem; she thought I was German. I answered in German; "I am an American. I speak German because I am in Germany, and I speak to everyone." Then she changed her attitude toward me. She even ordered me a cup of tea. Actually, it was a glass of tea. In early nineteenth-century Russia, women drank their tea from a cup, while men drank from a glass, set in an elaborately carved holder. Now, everyone is served in such a glass.

There were only two bunks in my sleeper. The bottom bunk was also a seat, with a thin pad as a mattress. My table was shaped like a toilet, but when I opened the lid, I discovered a sink.

As we pulled out of Fulda it began to snow, but soon it turned to rain.

There was no restaurant car on the train; the conductors were cooking steak and onions in their compartment. They invited me to join them, but I told them I was a vegetarian. In a few minutes a conductor brought me a plate of hot vegetables.

At 7:45 the next morning we came to the German/Polish border. Papers and passports were checked on the train.

Throughout the two-night journey to Moscow, the conductors brought me tea or coffee whenever I asked. I fixed oatmeal and instant potatoes with some of the hot water.

We crossed into Brest, Belarus on the second night. The border check was on board the train. I am proud of the Belarus stamp on my passport. In fact, I couldn't suppress a squeal of excitement when the border official stamped it. He was taken aback, but I could tell he appreciated my enthusiasm.

In the early afternoon the next day we crossed into Russia. The conductor gave me a customs declaration form to fill out. He was surprised when he saw my American passport; he said he thought I was German. The border check was at Smolensk. Two control officers checked my passport and visa. We spoke a mixture of Russian, German and English (at least I did) to establish my reason for traveling to Russia.

The older Russian woman came to my compartment and said, "The taxi drivers will try to cheat you because you are a foreigner. They will ask for fifty Marks or fifty dollars. Do not pay more than twenty dollars."

Arrival in Moscow was at the Smolenskaya Vokzal (Smolensk Station). Russian stations are called Vokzal because in the 1830s the Czar saw his first train at London's Vauxhall Gardens. When the Russian Railway was built, the Czar used the word "Vokzal" for station. The taxi drivers outside the station were charging outrageous prices; some asked for eighty dollars. I had been warned, so I bargained. One man in an unmarked car agreed to take me for ten dollars. He couldn't find the Hotel Bellegarde, so he stopped to ask directions. Then he backed up for five blocks down a busy street, and we were in front of the hotel. Security guards checked ID inside the lobby.

My bed was very narrow, and so was the room. But, for one

person, it was adequate. The carpet was beige with dark brown flowers, and ferns outlined in black. A small table, a white lamp and a brown swivel chair filled the rest of the room. I stood looking out the window, overwhelmed by the wonder of being in Moscow.

Chapter 22
The Trans-Siberian Railway: Moscow to Vladivostok

The taxi to Yaroslavskiy Vokzal (Yaroslavl Station) cost me twenty dollars. I had one large suitcase (Tagalong), a satchel, my backpack and a large food bag, so I stood inside near the exit to the outdoor platforms. Most of the world refers to the train that crosses Siberia as the *Trans-Siberian*. The Russian name of it is the *Rossia* (also *Rossiya*, or *Rossija*), the *Russia*. The railway is called the Great Siberian Railway, or the Trans-Siberian Railway.

The sign above the entrance listed the *Rossia,* my *"Trans-Siberian,"* as leaving at 2:15 p.m. As soon as I snapped a picture of the sign, two older women wearing official railway armbands scolded me. I pointed to the sign, put up one finger and said, "A'deen!" I was trying to show that I had only taken one picture, and it was of the sign. I know the Russians are still touchy about tourists photographing trains and train stations, but why couldn't I take a picture of the sign? One of the women said, "Tree! You tree!" She held up three fingers, accusing me of taking three pictures. The other woman pointed to the waiting room sign and squatted, to show me I should go and sit down. I pointed to my luggage and shook my head; I wasn't about to drag it with me to the waiting room and back. I brought a large suitcase because I will be on the train for eight days, and need more clothing than usual. There will be no washing of clothes on the train.

The train pulled in a few minutes before departure time. I struggled out to the platform with my luggage. The *Trans-Siberian Express!* There it sat, in all its glory. And I had a ticket to ride. For eight days! Standing on the platform so long admiring the *Rossia,* I almost missed it. Russian carriages are larger than European ones, due to the wider gauge of the tracks; it was difficult to hoist my luggage onto the train. The conductor helped me on, in the nick of time.

Still in a daze, I found my carriage and my sleeper. Luckily, I had been assigned a bottom bunk. A Russian man had the top bunk across from me. When the conductor came in, she said, "We have a problem here." She asked the man to move to the next compartment. Although the sleepers are not allotted according to gender, the Russian Railways try to place foreign tourists in a room with others of the same sex or with a family.

The bunks were upholstered in red vinyl. A blanket, thin pad and a pillow, all rolled together were on each bunk. In addition, I was given a sheet and a towel. The small table by the window was set with a tea service. There were tea bags and sugar packets on a small tin tray, and a box of cookies wrapped in gift paper imprinted with flowers and fairy-tale characters.

I had a note written in Russian, requesting a signature, and I had no problem getting my document signed.

We crossed the Volga River at Yaroslavl. I was standing in the corridor with several passengers. They laughed when I said "*Matryoshka Volga*" (Little Mother Volga). It is the name the Russians fondly call the Volga. The Volga flows for 2,300 miles before it empties into the Caspian Sea.

In the night another man came in and took the bunk opposite mine. He kept the light on so he could read his paperback book. About three o'clock in the morning two young men took the two top bunks. The only word I had spoken to them was "Hello," but as usual, I was mistaken for a German, and treated rudely. The man assigned to the bunk above me stepped on my shin as he climbed up. He was portly, and I couldn't help but yell, "Ow!" He actually smirked at me (the light was still on). I was tired of being punished for what the Germans did in the war. It was time to declare my nationality. I stood up, and exclaimed, " I am an American!" Then I said it in German. *"Ich bin Amerikanerin!"* For good measure, I threw my Russian at them. *"Ya Amerikanski!"* Not one of them acknowledged my outburst, but I read their expressions. They were surprised. Thereafter when the man climbed up to his bunk, he stepped only on the foot of my bed, and he stepped carefully. Nonetheless, I was glad when they detrained.

I went to the samovar down the hall for hot water. I still had a couple of packets of oatmeal. Some of the passengers tried to converse with me, but none spoke English or German. Most of the Russian I had learned escapes me, now that I need it. After speaking so many different languages in my travels they have all mixed together in my mind. Sometimes I feel as though I'm standing beneath the Tower of Babel, and all the languages have been confounded. All of mine, anyway. The high-pitched Asian music coming from speakers in every compartment didn't help either.

Before noon a family of four moved in. The two little girls shared an upper bunk. The family spoke only Russian. In addition to my limited Russian, we used gestures, and expressions to communicate. If a word or phrase is spoken often enough, in a particular tone, one suddenly becomes aware of its meaning.

The father set a large container of food on the bottom bunk opposite me, and placed several bags on the table. He offered me a fried chicken leg. One of the few phrases I didn't forget in

Russian is, "I am a vegetarian." He laughed. Then he said something like "margarina," and I thought he was offering me butter or margarine. I said, *"Ya nyet khlep"* (I have no bread). He pulled out a Styrofoam container of instant noodles, and repeated "margarina." He had meant macaroni. The ingredients were listed in English (the noodles were produced in China). I had been craving pasta; I hurried to the samovar for hot water to "cook" the noodles.

At Perm we crossed the Volga again, and somewhere between Perm and Yekaterinburg we had crossed into Asia. The Ural Mountains (Ural'skiye Gory) form the border. There is an obelisk near the tracks that marks the boundary between Europe and Asia, but it is written in Cyrillic. The marker is at mile 1,110 (1,777 km) from Moscow. Although I stood looking out the window, straining my eyes, I missed it.

We had a half-hour break at Yekaterinburg, on the eastern slope of the Urals. I couldn't help thinking about the assassinations of Czar Nicholas (Romanov) II and his family. It was here that the murders occurred in 1917. Ironically, the Russian Railway was started in 1891, during the reign of Czar Nicholas. The last track was laid in 1916, completing a stretch from the Pacific to Europe. The name of Yekaterinburg was changed to Sverdlovsk in 1924, and changed back to Yekaterinburg in 1991.

The Romanovs were in my thoughts so much that I dreamed about the murders last night, seeing them as vividly as if I had witnessed them.

We were now in Siberia. I stepped off the train at the first stop of the day. The man from my compartment motioned for me to follow him to a kiosk. He showed me the instant noodles, and checked the price for me. I bought the only two packs available. I ate one for lunch and the other for dinner. That was the only time I found pasta of any kind for sale.

By the next day I had eaten all the food I had brought with me except some bread and the special crackers Erich had bought me in BK, so I made tomato soup with my last plastic packets of catsup. Here's the recipe. Add hot water, and stir.

There was a dining car on board. Plates of raw grated beets or shredded cabbage with vinegar were my vegetarian choices because the hot vegetables were cooked with meat. I wanted to try the Russian borscht, but it too was made with meat. Why do Europeans talk about the Russian meat shortage? From what I have seen, the Russians eat as much meat as anyone else. In fact, I haven't seen food shortages of any kind, except for vegetarian dishes. And that is only because the Russians have so much meat that they put it in most of their cooked vegetables.

With hot water from the samovar I had all the coffee and tea I wanted. I really didn't enjoy the coffee so much. Russians drink their coffee black, so there was no cream or milk. But everyone brought along a jar of sugar or sugar cubes for their coffee.

At each stop I saw at least one vendor selling ice cream. It needs no refrigeration in the below zero weather, and it doesn't melt before you can consume it. Some of the platform vendors had pots of boiled potatoes, and dumplings stuffed with potatoes. The Russian passengers had bowls to take away the hot food, but I hadn't been that smart. Instead, I had the vendors put my potatoes or dumplings in a plastic bag. My hot food was always cold by the time I got back on the train. I learned to begin eating the piping hot potatoes immediately, as I walked back to the train.

It had taken me a few days to realize it was the many time zones that caused me to knock on the door of the dining car, only to be told it was the middle of the night, although it was still light out. I had forgotten that all the Russian trains run on Moscow time. The *Trans-Siberian* crosses seven time zones. I will never keep up. Later it didn't matter what time it was; I didn't know what day it was either. I am on the other side of the International Dateline, which further confuses me. Thinking about my family, I figured I was in their tomorrow, while they were still in my yesterday. Yet, we are all in our own today.

The name Siberia (*Sibirsk*) comes from the Tatar word, *Sibir* (the sleeping land). The vastness of Siberia can only be imagined until one travels across it. It is not a small world, after all.

Suddenly I realized that while the train was moving over the Earth, the Earth was moving under the train. Having nothing better to do, I took out my pocket almanac and my pocket calculator, and figured. The *Rossia* was traveling 70 miles per hour. The Earth rotates on its axis at 1,050 miles per hour, and the Earth revolves around the Sun at 66,600 miles per hour. But then, our solar system circles within our galaxy at 648,000 miles per hour, and our galaxy is moving through space at 612,000 miles per hour. That means I'm traveling at 1,327,720 miles per hour! Wow! How many G's am I pulling?

After the stop in Irkutsk we veered south to Kultuk, near the Mongolian border. From there we skirted Lake Baikal (*Ozero Baykal*); the world's oldest lake. It is also the world's deepest lake. At the bottom of the lake lies the world's deepest land depression. The lake is 375 miles long, and its width varies from eighteen to more than fifty miles. There are over 2000 species of fish and mammals within the lake, including sea cows, and the freshwater seal called *nerpa*, found only in Lake Baikal. The twenty-seven islands in the lake provide a place for the seals to rest from their swimming and fishing.

More than 300 rivers flow into Baikal, but it flows into just one, the Angara. There is a five-mile-deep rift in the lake, causing earthquakes several times a day, usually too mild to be felt.

I took a picture of the frozen lake through my ice-framed window. In the dead of winter the ice may be over thirty feet thick. Trucks use it as a road.

We followed the lake for a long time, then about 100 kilometers past the town of Babushkin, we curved away from the lake toward Ulan Ude, the capital of Buryatia.

I think it was day five (or six?) when two men from the *National Geographic* heard me saying, "Skolka?" I was asking a vendor on the platform how much the potatoes were.

"What are you doing here?" One of the men asked.

"Actually I'm winding up a Guinness World Record on train travel."

They wanted to interview me and photograph me, but I was afraid the train would leave without me. Almost every time I thought we would stay in a station for twenty minutes, the train left in five. Also, I had hurried off the train without putting on my coat or hat, or boots. I was wearing running shoes and a quilted plaid shirt, and I was freezing. They filmed me asking for the potatoes, but it was so quick, I don't think they will use the footage.

In the dining car I was seated for my daily raw cabbage. The bench doubles as a storage compartment. I misunderstood when the waiter wanted me to get up; I thought he was tired of grating cabbage and beets, and was asking me to leave. But he wanted me to move so he could put supplies under the seat. A boy about fourteen years old sat at my table. "I speak English. Tell me about America." We talked awhile, mostly about sports and schools. Then the waiter ran him out. The boy was waiting for me outside the dining car. "Please, come to our compartment. Others want to meet you." I followed him down the corridor. Three young girls and another boy, all about fourteen or fifteen years old, were waiting to greet me. They all spoke English. I took a couple of pictures of them, and we exchanged gifts. I gave them white soaps in the shape of angels, perfume samples, and shampoo. They gave me pens and pencils. Later when one of the book vendors came through the train the kids bought me a Russian detective magazine, and a hardcover romance novel. All five of them signed the novel, the Russian version of *"Broken Vows"* by Shirl Henke. If I can find the book in English when I return, I'll read it.

Sometime after dark we stopped long enough for me to take a picture, but as soon as I pointed my camera towards the station the attendant said, *"Nyet!"* I pointed to the train. She said, *"Nyet!"* I can ride this train for eight days, but I can't take one picture of it? The Russians have a lot to learn before they can entice masses of tourists to their land. My camera was cocked and ready to shoot. I pointed it upward to the star-studded sky, clicked it twice, and said (in English); "The sky belongs to everyone. I can take a picture of it."

A chill woke me; there was little or no heat. Curly patterns of ice framed the edges of the windows (from the inside). I hurried to the samovar for hot water; a cup of tea would warm me. The samovar was ice-cold.

Every time I try to walk through to the third-class carriages the attendant stops me and sends me back. It's not easy getting that far, because the door handles and the floors between carriages are coated with ice. The floors are slippery, and the icy wind whips through the spaces where the carriages are coupled. Today I got through several third-class carriages before the attendant caught me. She told me to go back. I said, "I want to have tea here."

"You have tea in your own wagon." I didn't tell her my samovar was cold.

There are no compartments in third class, just vinyl bunks, stacked one above the other. Passengers bring their own blankets or sleep with their coats on. Some sleep with fur hats, and gloves on. The carriages are not heated. Sometimes I wear my coat and gloves to bed, although most of the time my carriage is heated. I can only imagine how cold it must be in third class. Intourist had refused to let me ride third class. Intourist doesn't even mention it, and the railways call it "Lying Class," and *Platskartny*.

Gypsies and other vendors ride in third class for short distances, selling their wares to other passengers. I bought a bright-pink nightgown and robe (for my mother) from a Gypsy woman. A Russian man came through the train with a large plastic bag filled with pocket watches. I bought one that was engraved with a likeness of Saint Basil's Cathedral in Moscow for my friend Erich in Bad Kreuznach.

I had no idea where we were, or what the current time was. Looking at my watch didn't help. I didn't know if it was a.m. or p.m., so I couldn't convert the time. I should have worn my twenty-four-hour watch. The train moves as if it has been polarized. Sometimes it goes on that way for hours, making me sleepy, no matter what time it is.

When the train stopped for ten minutes I stepped off. I didn't find a vendor selling potatoes or dumplings, but one had a tray of candy bars. I bought a Snickers bar and a bottle of the sour milk that is something like Kefir, which made my coffee taste terrible. It was back to black. I'll bet they have cream or milk in soft class, if there *is* a soft-class carriage on this train. I haven't seen one; the attendants won't let me walk through to look, and I don't have time to walk down the platform to the end of the train when we stop. I need the time to find food.

Today is the eighth day; the train will arrive in Vladivostok, the end of the Trans-Siberian line. We have been traveling close to the Chinese border since yesterday, and we'll follow it all the way to Vladivostok. I ate everything I had left, which wasn't much. I ate the rest of the health crackers and a chunk of brown bread smeared with mustard. It was my last packet of mustard, still available only because I couldn't make "soup" with it, as I had with the catsup packets. I didn't make soup with it because I remembered that mustard mixed with water is an emetic. I finished my two-liter bottle of soda too; I could replenish my supply in Vladivostok. The only thing I didn't consume of my stock was a bottle of tonic water that tasted terrible.

All the food and drink drove me to the WC. The door was open, and an attendant was beating and twisting the spigots off with a hammer and some sort of pliers. There was no water anywhere. Shaking her head at me, she closed the WC and locked it from the outside. Arrival in Vladivostok was still an hour and a half away. There was nothing I could do, but wait.

The beautiful snow I had expected to be awaiting me in Vladivostok was nonexistent. It was raining, but I had seen plenty of snow the last few days. The yellow train station is striking. Its arched portals and windows lend it a palatial look, but the lacy ironwork atop the roof looks like art deco. Not sure how far it was to the Hotel Vladivostok, I paid twenty dollars for a taxi. We drove for about six blocks. The driver let me out at the edge of the parking lot (in a mud puddle). As it pulled away, the taxi splashed me with muddy water. Welcome to Vladivostok. No matter, it didn't lessen my enthusiasm. I have wanted to visit Vladivostok for a long time.

My room was on the seventh floor. Someone was using a jackhammer on the wall outside my room. First the toilet, and then a nice hot shower; it had been eight days of sponge baths (mostly ice-cold) on the *Trans-Siberian*. There was no water coming from the sink spigot. The toilet didn't flush. I stepped out into the hall and called out, "Hello! Hello!" No one was about. The noise from the jackhammer was deafening. I went down the hall to talk to the key lady. She speaks English, but I spouted out in a mixture of English and Russian. She understood.

"There is no water in Vladivostok, Madam. This evening."

"Do you mean there is no water in the Hotel Vladivostok, or not in all of Vladivostok?"

"No water in all of Vladivostok. This evening, eight o'clock."

"I have to use the toilet, and I have to take a shower. I have been on a train for eight days. Can I find water in another hotel?"

"No water. I will show you how to flush the toilet. I will come to your room."

She brought me a red bucket half-filled with water, and a granite cooking pot to dip it out with. I laughed politely, barely managing to hold back a guffaw. As I closed my door behind her, I began laughing hysterically. Welcome to Vladivostok. It was "whining time." I let the tears flow for a few seconds, then, ashamed of myself, I laughed again. I hadn't cried when I was lost, beaten or injured. Why did I cry because I couldn't take a shower?

I wondered where she got the water if there was no water in all of Vladivostok. Anyway, it was a relief to use the WC again. I tried to improvise; I showered with a squirt bottle of disinfectant soap that needs no rinsing. It stung. I rinsed with the bottle of tonic water. It was carbonated. Then I was sticky. I dressed and went down to the concession stand in the lobby. They had only carbonated mineral water, but it was better than nothing. I rinsed myself again. Then I was tingly. If the rain hadn't stopped I would have stood nude on my balcony and rinsed. The jackhammer was still blasting away.

I walked through the muddy streets, glad to be in Vladivostok. At one of the outdoor markets two old ladies in black coats and babushkas got into a fistfight. They had to be at least eighty years old. When the short one smacked the tall one square on the nose, I butted in. I said, "Stop it! You are hurting each other!" They both stopped fighting and looked at me. The short one walked away. The other one stood there, with her hand over her nose. I walked away, almost feeling the stares from the patrons.

A flea market was set up on the sidewalk across from the train station. I bought a wreath made from vines, and a pinecone from an old man. He said he goes into the Siberian Forest to collect them.

It was a long time before I noticed the pain in my toes. I was freezing, and I was worried about frostbite. I looked for a restaurant; I needed a cup of tea. All the signs were in the Russian alphabet (a slight variation on the Cyrillic), but I know that restaurant is pronounced almost the same, although it is written in the Russian alphabet as *"Pectohpah,"* which, if converted to the Roman (Latin) alphabet would be *Restoran*. I walked for several blocks but didn't see a *pectopah*.

One building had a large sign showing a beautiful golden samovar. It must be a tearoom, I thought, so I went in. There was a turnstile just inside the door. I tried to go through. Speaking to the cashier, I said in Russian, "I am a vegetarian. Do you have any macaroni?" Such a tirade of chastisement! I was in a museum, and they were exhibiting samovars at the time; hence the sign on the building. The crazy American had struck again.

Boy, did I need a cup of tea. My feet were so cold I could hardly walk, although I was wearing my cotton-lined boots. Finally, I saw a shop with tables. Why didn't it say *Pectopah?* Perhaps it wasn't a restaurant, but a coffee shop, a snack bar or a bakery/deli. I'll have to check my Russian dictionary. I had a piece of cake, and coffee. With cream! Best of all, the room was warm.

The water came on in the early evening. I showered as quickly as I could; I was afraid the water would go off at any time. It sure felt good to sleep in a regular bed again.

I went downstairs to breakfast, and found the restaurant closed. I went back up and asked the key lady where I should go. She said Americans eat in the bar on the eleventh floor. I had read the sign in the lobby inviting foreign tourists to "stay on the eleventh floor where you will be looked after by us in very comfortable rooms." It was written in English. Why was I on the seventh floor then?

I sat down in the bar on the eleventh floor. Only one other person was there for breakfast. The waitress told me to leave; only eleventh floor guests would be served. Back to the key lady. She brought me back up to the bar, and questioned the waitress. After a quick argument between them, the key lady took me to the basement Sushi Bar. It was locked, but she knocked and yelled until a sleepy-eyed woman answered the door. After another quick argument I was seated at a long table covered with a white tablecloth and set with white porcelain dishes. The Sushi Bar is there mainly for the many Japanese tourists and business people that flock to Vladivostok. The decor was pure Japanese, done in surprisingly good taste.

The woman who had answered the door went into a back room. I wondered if she had gone back to bed. In about ten minutes she reappeared, dressed in a white shirt and black skirt. I gave my vegetarian speech in Russian, adding that I would like something hot to eat. She brought me tea, bread and butter and sliced cucumbers. Then she came back with a bowl of rice and a bowl of hot oatmeal, asking me to choose one. It was kind of odd sitting alone in a large Japanese restaurant in Vladivostok eating oatmeal, but it was a breakfast I won't soon forget, if only because of the difficulty in getting breakfast at all.

The Sea of Japan is down the hill and across the street from my hotel. It was frozen solid, and a few Russians were walking on it. I wanted to walk on it too, but after I had told my husband about walking across the Nahe River when it was frozen, he was upset, and I promised him I wouldn't walk on any more frozen rivers. But this isn't a river; it's a sea. I wouldn't be exactly breaking a promise. Gingerly, I picked my way, step by step, as far out as I dared. Japan is across the sea. A little farther north is the Sea of Okhotsk, and a little farther south is the Yellow Sea (the Chinese call it Hwang Hai). All three are arms of the North Pacific. They all flow into each other. And all are connected to the Bering Sea. It was as though I was walking on all of them. Vladivostok is very near the Chinese border, and North Korea is not far away. It was thrilling. A Japanese photographer, who motioned for me to move out of the way, interrupted my thrill. The other ice-walkers were nowhere in sight. Thinking the ice may be breaking or something, I walked back carefully toward the shore, only to find that the Japanese man wanted me out of the way so he could photograph his Russian model out on the ice. The frozen sea stretched for miles, but he wanted to pose her in the spot nearest the bench that held his gear, and I was in the line of fire. The blonde model faced the shore, bent slightly from the waist forward, stuck her rear end out, and made a *moue* that would have made Marilyn Monroe envious. It was too much. I walked back over the ice, stood behind her and mimicked the pose and the *moue*. The photographer fussed a bit, and motioned for me to move again. Enough fun for today anyway; I started walking back to shore. Too bad I couldn't piece together an appropriate phrase from the Japanese words my sister had taught me. But, using a perfect blend of Japanese and English, I said, "Sayonara, jackass!"

I stored my luggage at the station; it would be hours before my train left. There is an old locomotive outside the station. A man from the railways gave me permission to climb up the steps of the locomotive to pose for a picture. He snapped a couple of shots for me.

After a few more hours of walking, my feet were freezing again. I went into the Sea Terminal, a building next to the train station that comprises shops, restaurants and the waiting room for ship passengers. A snack bar overlooks the waiting room below. My coffee was served in a tall glass, piping hot, but as usual, it was made the Russian way, sweetened with plenty of sugar. I drank it anyway.

The decorative fountain in the center of the lower floor is made of brass flowerets, forming a large golden rose. Water pours forth through lights in the flowerets. Viewing it over coffee had a relaxing effect on me; I was no longer so tired. I went out to the harbor on Golden Horn Bay (*Bukhta Zolotoy Rog*). Unlike the sea, the bay was not frozen; it is kept clear by icebreakers. Some ships must be sailing; I had seen passengers waiting in the terminal. A few ships of the old Soviet Navy were moored in the bay. From 1948 until 1992, Westerners were barred from Vladivostok, mainly

171

because of the ship activity. Now, ice permitting, passenger ships carrying people from all over the world arrive and depart from the harbor, the Navy ships in plain view of the passengers. I knew better than to take a photo, though.

Concerned that the luggage office may close before time for the train, I went back to retrieve my things. In the train station I sat in the waiting room on the lower floor near the boarding platforms. The old man who had sold me the wreath and the pinecone came and sat by me. His hair is snow white, and his eyes are actually the color of turquoise stones. We had a limited conversation in Russian. His wife had died, and to supplement his meager pension he gathers the pinecones and the vines to fashion the wreaths. He said, "It is cold in the forest. That is why I carry this blanket with me." It was a wool Army blanket that matched his overcoat. He was wearing the gray felt boots that many Russians wear.

According to my itinerary copy, Intourist had me booked on train # 7 to Irkutsk, but my ticket said train # 1, which is the *Rossia* on its return to Moscow. It would be three nights of repeat travel with 4,113 kilometers unaccredited. I don't know which train I'm on, but it's going to Irkutsk.

Just as I was entering my compartment, three young men came into the corridor. One of them said, in Russian, "Don't be so slow. Move!" He seemed to be joking, so I smiled and said, "OK!" They all smiled, and two of the men slapped the third one on the shoulder. He was the traveler; the others were there to see him off, and they were teasing him about being alone in the compartment with me. It didn't seem to matter that I was older; it was enough that I was foreign. Somehow that made me desirable. They didn't know I understood the conversation. Like most Russians, they assumed I was German (I was surprised they were still smiling). It was only after the two visitors detrained that I spoke in Russian to the train passenger. "*Ya Amerikanski.*" He spoke English, so I didn't have to use more of my Russian, although it has gradually improved. He leaned forward from his bottom bunk (opposite mine). Brushing his dark hair away from his forehead, he pointed to a small black satchel, and said, "May I open this?"

"Well... yes. It's *your* satchel."

"But it is a cat! A meow! Can I let the cat out?"

"Yes. Go ahead."

"I am a soldier, and I take my cat with me everywhere. We have been to visit my parents, and now we go back to my camp."

Slowly, a black and white cat with yellow eyes slithered out of the satchel. "This is Katiya." The soldier took a litter pan from another bag and slid it under his bunk. Katiya behaved pretty well at first. She jumped up on the empty bunk above her master and

172

began washing herself. After I had slept for a couple of hours she leaped from her bunk onto my face. The compartment was dark; I thought I was being attacked. My scream didn't even wake the soldier. I shooed her away and covered my face with the blanket. When she gave a repeat performance, I added a pillow to my protection, and hoped I wouldn't suffocate in my sleep.

From daylight on, the cat ran into the corridor each time the train stopped. She tried to get off the train. I was a nervous wreck, but the soldier didn't seem to worry.

The train had stopped in the same towns on the way east to Vladivostok. This morning, at one of the stops a little old lady came running up to me and said, "Snicker! You Snicker!" She wasn't laughing at me; she was reminding me that I had bought a Snickers bar from her on the way east. She kept pointing at me, and saying, "Snicker!" until I boarded the train. I wasn't sure if she was trying to sell me another Snickers bar or was just happy to see me again.

The Intourist Hotel in Irkutsk is on the Angara River. What a view! Snow covers the ground and trees, but it seems warmer than Vladivostok. My hotel room was warm enough too; I slept well.

I had read about the old wooden chalet-like houses in Irkutsk. Many of them have been torn down, but I managed to find a street that was still home to several of them. The gingerbread trim on the gables, windows and porches looks like something out of *Hansel and Gretel.*

Then I went in search of toilet paper. On the trains it isn't always replaced when it runs out, and I had exhausted my personal supply. I checked in several stores, and found none. There was a grocery store a few blocks from the hotel. I walked in and through the turnstile with only a nod and a smile toward the three clerks (two women and one man). I wasn't ready to be recognized as a foreigner until I checked for toilet paper. One of the women came to help. I tried my Russian, "*Ya roulon toalyetna bumagi.*" They didn't have any toilet paper, but the other woman joined us, and asked me to say it again, but not because my Russian wasn't understood. They were just surprised and pleased (and probably amused) to hear me say it. After a brief conversation about my travels, I said, *Dosvidaniya,* and walked toward the door. The man hurried over to me, and asked me to repeat my request for toilet paper. As near as I could figure, the hug he gave me was because I had asked for the paper in Russian. I still had no toilet paper, but I felt proud of myself, and a little less lonely.

There was a message for me from Intourist. My train for tomorrow had been canceled; I would have to leave around midnight, on an overnight train to Novosibirsk, then take a train to

Alma-Ata, Kazakhstan, my next overnight stop. It was uncertain whether the hotel there would have a room for me when I arrived a day early.

I had the afternoon to explore Irkutsk. I carried a red shopping bag, packed with a warm corduroy vest, a plaid shirt and a pair of gloves. They were things I no longer needed; I planned to give them to a homeless person, should I chance to meet one in town.

One man (obviously a wino) was picking through the commercial trash bin in an alley I happened to pass. I offered the bag to him, with the clothing still in it. He didn't understand, and went on looking through the trash. Unpacking the bag, one item at a time, I put each one on top of the trash, and picked it back out again. Then I offered it to the wino. He understood, and accepted each of them. He put the vest on immediately. I put the shopping bag in the trash bin, and then retrieved it, to show him that I didn't want it. We had an audience. A man came out the back door of a building carrying two Styrofoam cups of coffee and two sandwiches on a paper plate. He had thought I was a wino or a bag lady. It did look as though I was picking through the trash. I gave the wino both sandwiches, but I drank the coffee as I walked back to the street.

At 11:30 p.m. a taxi was waiting to take me to the station. Inside the station several different men offered to help (for five dollars) with my luggage. The woman behind the ticket window called me over. She warned me not to speak to anyone, and suggested I stand near the ticket window until the train arrived (at 1:00 a.m. local time). A young woman was sitting on the windowsill near the door, crying. She kept falling onto the floor; she was very drunk. Two policemen came in and took her away. Every few minutes of the next hour I saw drunken men stagger in and out of the station, sometimes one alone, sometimes two or more together. The woman behind the ticket counter seemed concerned that I was in the middle of all the commotion. She had no way of knowing that I had witnessed much more serious goings-on in train stations in Europe. Still, it was a long hour.

When I started down the steps to the platform, one man grabbed my satchel and another my suitcase. "Two dollar! Two dollar!" I agreed; they wouldn't let go of my luggage. The woman at the ticket office yelled at them, but I didn't understand her, and the men ignored her. The two men carried my luggage down the steep concrete steps to the tunnel, put it down and left me to carry it up the next flight. It really didn't matter; I have managed even more luggage on my own. An older woman was sweeping the tunnel, and saw them run up the steps. She came over to help me. I saw her looking at my fancy mesh shopping bag. I think she was intrigued by the French designer's name imprinted on it. When we reached the top of the stairs I gave it to her. A wide smile brightened her face.

It was the first time I was assigned a top bunk, but it was only for two nights. I kicked my shoes off and began the climb on the narrow metal bars of the ladder. They hurt the bottom of my arches. A blonde Russian woman had taken the bottom bunk on the opposite wall. Her dark-haired husband slept above. An old Kazakh woman had the bottom bunk under me.

The attendant brought me a sheet, pillow, mattress pad and blanket, but I refused them. I recently heard that the bedding wasn't washed after each use. The towel I had thought was to use at the sink in the WC was to place over the pillowcase, which may have been used by a previous passenger without being laundered. Rather than explain that to the attendant, I said the bedding always slips off onto the floor, so I didn't want it. It does, so I told half the truth. The vinyl bunks are thin, and without the pad they seem too hard, but compared to sitting up all night, I rate them four stars.

A woman from Intourist met me at the station in Novosibirsk. We were picked up by a man driving a black Mercedes, and driven to a multi-storied hotel. The woman brought me a cup of black coffee, and told me to rest. I sat in a wide armchair. After a delay of several hours I was given a train ticket for train # 226 to Alma-Ata, Kazakhstan and driven back to the station. The driver carried my luggage to the train, and into my compartment. I was alone in the compartment. In the morning word got around that an American was traveling in hard class. Whenever I stepped into the corridor, children came and stood beside me. People spoke to me in Russian and German. If I stood looking at the schedule posted in the corridor, others came to look, and watch me.

In the afternoon we stopped in a country village, but there were no vendors on the platform. Three little boys were playing kickball with a jacket. They had rolled it into a ball, and tied the sleeves around it. Sheep were lying on the ground near the boys. I didn't see even one blade of grass. The ground was dirt-brown, with tiny patches of dirty snow along the wooden fences. Most of the route was through desert. Late in the evening of the next day, an Uzbek man took the bunk across from me. He spoke to me in English. He was returning to Uzbekistan, where he is a member of the Ministry for Internal Affairs. Tomorrow I will be in Alma-Ata.

Chapter 23
Kazakhstan: Free Man's Land

Fortunately, they had a room for me at the Hotel Otrar in Alma-Ata, but it meant two overnights instead of the one night I had paid for. The Otrar is more expensive than any hotel Intourist had booked for me. I was hoping that since I didn't stay two nights in Irkutsk, they would transfer the payment to the second night in Alma-Ata.

I was the first guest in the restaurant in the morning. The choice of food here is amazing. While waiting for news of my next train, I sat in the lobby reading a brochure about the Tien Shan, which means "Heavenly (or Celestial) Mountains" in Chinese. Peak Pobeda (Pik Pobedy) is 24,406 feet high, the highest in the Tien Shan. It is the northernmost peak to reach more than 20,000 feet. Peak Hantengri (20,991 feet) is close to Alma-Ata, where Kazakhstan borders with China and Kyrgyzstan. The twenty-one-mile Muzart Glacier descends from Hantengri. According to my brochure, snow leopards live in the Tien Shan.

Good news! I could stay another night without extra charge, and catch the train I was originally booked on. When I asked the receptionist to return my passport, she said she would keep it for another day, since I wasn't checking out. I hurried out to see something of Alma-Ata (also called Almaty). Alma-Ata means "Father of Apples," and Almaty means "Apple Place." Kazakhstan (Qazaqstan) means "Free Man's Land." The Kazakhs had been under Russian rule since the sixteenth century, but now they are free again, although they have chosen to be part of the Commonwealth of Independent States. Alma-Ata is no longer the capital of Kazakhstan. In 1997 Astana (also still called Agmola) was designated as the capital.

My brochure listed a museum on the same street as my hotel. I stopped by one of the kiosks in the park across the street and asked if the pink building in the middle of the park was a museum. The woman said it was, and tried to sell me an umbrella. The rain was only a fine mist; I didn't need an umbrella. As I entered the building a woman began yelling at me in Russian. She was complaining about my head being uncovered. It must be a mosque, or a cathedral. I must have misunderstood the woman at the kiosk. I didn't see any pews; worshippers were standing in a group around the priest.

About a dozen people stood in a line near the exit. I noticed that the women in the line were not wearing headscarves or hats.

Assuming that they were separated from those who properly covered their heads, I joined the line. When some of the people started giving money to those standing in my line, I realized I had joined the beggars, waiting for alms. Shamefaced, I darted out the door. The rain was coming down hard then, but people were gathering outside, where a van with loudspeakers was parked. I stood on an embankment above, listening to the beautiful music that came out over the loudspeakers. A woman was singing a hymn in a voice that made me understand the meaning of "hauntingly beautiful." When the singing stopped, the bells began to ring. The pitch was high and tinkly, like the sound of an old-time music box. The bells didn't just ring the hour; they played a lively tune.

The peaks of the Tien Shan glow in the sun. I can see some of them from the park, the street, and the window in my room. They are completely covered (all year) in snow and ice. The highest peak is iced in sparkling white. Next to it, a peak is glazed in shiny apricot, looking much like a giant cone of orange sherbet. Credit for the changing of colors on mountain peaks is attributed to alpenglow, seen on mountain peaks at sunrise and sunset. Alpenglow is a derivative of the German word, *Alpengluhen* (Alps glow). I can think of only one word to describe the Tien Shan. Awesome. Later in the evening, I watched the changing colors of the peaks until darkness eased them away.

Katiya, one of my roommates

Chapter 24
The Last Hurrah

Train # 7, the *Kazakhstan*, will take me to the finish line. Somewhere between Alma-Ata and Moscow I'll break the mileage record. I figure I'll pass the milestone close to the Kazakh/Russian border. Much of the route runs through the Kyzyl-Kum (Qyzylqum). Kum and qum mean desert. The Kyzyl-Kum is mostly covered by sand, and its name means "Red Sands" in the Turkic languages. Surprisingly, gold is found there, and people manage to raise livestock in certain areas of the desert.

It was difficult to understand the Kazakh conductor. I wasn't sure if he was speaking Kazakh or Russian, but he signed my document.

Three Kazakh men entered the compartment. The one who chose the bottom bunk across from mine began to take his clothes off. It is a normal thing to do on Russian trains. Everyone changes to sweat suits or other comfortable attire as soon as they set their luggage down. After hanging his slacks and shirt up, he pulled on a dark blue jumpsuit over his red boxer shorts and undershirt. Two more Kazakh men came in, and set paper plates of chicken, rice and salad on the table. I moved into the corner of my bunk, near the door, to make room for the others. Passengers lucky enough to have a bottom bunk suffer the inconvenience of moving every time someone wants to eat (which is often). They offered me some of the chicken. I surprised them by answering in Russian. They would learn later how limited my Russian is. I excused myself, and let them have full use of the table and my bunk. When I came back in, the grease from the chicken had soaked through and stained the tablecloth. Vodka bottles had been shoved under the table and the lower bunks. One of the men was drunk.

I wondered if all five of them were planning to sleep in the four-bunk compartment, but at the next stop, the conductor took them all to another compartment at the end of the corridor. He showed a pretty young Kazakh woman to the bottom bunk across from mine. Her short, shiny black hair was smoothed back over her ears. She was wearing a long black skirt and a rainbow-striped silk shirt. Just as she pulled off her high black boots, the conductor came in and asked her to follow him. I figured I would have the compartment to myself, but in a couple of hours she came back in, changed to a blue-and-white print nightgown, and began to read a book.

Sometime in the night, one of the crew came in and got into bed with the woman. He didn't take his clothes off; he just slipped under the blanket with her. I was embarrassed, but there was nowhere for me to go. I turned my face to the wall and pretended to sleep. The only noises I heard were whispered words. Then someone coughed, just above my head. Looking up, I saw the drunken Kazakh man. He was leaning over the edge of the upper bunk, gazing down at the crewman and the woman. I could no longer pretend to sleep; I put my shoes on, and stood in the corridor until the crewman came out. I could have sat on one of the tiny foldaway seats in the corridor, but I was afraid I would doze off, and fall onto the floor. The drunken Kazakh slept on the bunk above mine. His four companions filled the compartment at the end of the corridor.

At dawn the young woman detrained. The water in the samovar was already hot. I sat on my bunk and drank a cup of coffee. Suddenly, the drunken Kazakh came down from the upper bunk and went to join his friends. Later I heard music coming from their compartment. One of the men invited me to the compartment to hear the music. We stood in the corridor; there were six men sitting on the lower bunks. Three of the men were playing guitars, and one was playing a potbellied, stringed instrument called a "dombyra" that resembles the lute, and the American "taterbug." They sang a Kazakh folk song for me.

New occupants joined me in my compartment. A sandy-haired Russian man took the top bunk across from me, and his wife took the bottom one. Her brown hair curled softly around her face. Both of them were slightly stout. The woman was decidedly top-heavy. They introduced themselves as Gennady and Tammara. Speaking a mixture of Russian and German, we learned a little about each other. They had been sent to Kazakhstan to work, many years ago. The recent changes in the former Soviet Union have given them hopes of moving back to Russia. They were on their way to Moscow to search for employment. Tammara asked me about the TV soap opera, "Santa Barbara." When I told her I had been to Santa Barbara, California many times, she said her friends would envy her, because she had met me. I promised to send her a souvenir from Santa Barbara. As soon as they changed into sweat suits, out came the greasy chicken, wrapped in newspaper. After I declined to share it, Gennady gave me a chunk of delicious homemade bread with butter.

As I stepped out of the dining car, a young blond-haired man asked (in German) if I was an American. He said his name was Sergei, and he wanted to bring his friend Konstantin to my compartment; they were going to Germany, and wanted some information. I agreed, and in an hour they came in. Konstantin has dark hair and eyes; he reminds me of a young Sean Connery. Using a mix of German and Russian, I gave them the information they needed. Sergei was divorced, but Konstantin's wife and small

179

son had remained in Kazakhstan. If all went well in Germany, he would send for them. Konstantin admitted he had been a KGB officer. He said he never did anything against anyone; he had worked in an office.

When we stopped in the early afternoon, I snapped a picture of the vendors and passengers outside the station. I converted the Russian letters to the Roman, and came up with "Qyzylorda" as the name of the town. Feeling brave, I took another picture at the next stop. This time I even managed to get part of the train in the picture.

At the next stop I ran into the station and asked for toilet paper at the kiosk. I was mistaken for a German again; the vendor said, "*Ja, toiletten papier!* " Then I hurried (we supposedly had twenty minutes) to see what was offered at the huge flea market behind the station. Most of the household items were old, but not antique. I didn't dare look for food in the nearby kiosks; I have had to board the train many times as it was pulling away. Today was no exception; three of us had to run to catch it, jumping on before it picked up speed. I almost dropped my precious toilet paper.

Another flock of Gypsy vendors boarded the train. While my seatmates were in the dining car, one of the Gypsies came into the compartment. She tried to sell me one of everything in stock. Each time she brought out another item I repeated a different Russian phrase. "No, thank you." "I don't want any." "Sorry, I don't have room in my suitcase."

She wouldn't stop. Finally, when she insisted I buy the black leather jacket she held up, I spoke the only other phrase left in my Russian vocabulary: "I am a vegetarian!" That did it, she ran out of the compartment.

In the evening Konstantin gave me a pink scarf, striped with gold threads that he had bought from one of the Gypsies. I gave him a silver key chain for his wife.

I checked the envelope that Intourist had given me in Alma-Ata. My passport and visa were missing! I searched through every inch of my luggage and my papers. At first I suspected theft, but I had carried the envelope in my neck pouch at all times. My passport must be at the hotel in Alma-Ata; I should have checked the contents of the envelope before I left the hotel. I can't help wondering why they kept my passport and visa, but gave me my travel vouchers and train tickets.

At every stop, Gennady and I ran to find a phone. We found phones at two of the stops, but there wasn't enough time to wait for the hotel receptionist in Alma-Ata to look for my passport.

Crossing borders in this part of the world without proper documents is probably impossible. When I am worried, I eat. But there was no time to buy potatoes or ice cream when we stopped;

I had to find a phone. I pigged out on bread and grated beets in the dining car.

The next time Gennady reached the hotel in Alma-Ata by phone, the receptionist assured him that my passport and visa would be on the next flight to Moscow, and delivered to the Hotel Bellegarde. She had no suggestions to help me get across the borders to Moscow without the proper papers. I couldn't help wondering if it was time for my "dream of soldiers" to come true.

Trying not to worry, I stood in the corridor when we passed through Aqtobe, still in Kazakhstan, but getting close to the border. Martuk is listed in my timetable as the border checkpoint. But, my timetable doesn't list all the stops, so I have to wait and see. I was looking out the window, ready to celebrate the last mile of the way with a cheer for myself. I was about to break the record, somewhere around Martuk.

Sergei came down the corridor and said, "The border guards and customs agents are already on the train. They are coming to us!" At his suggestion, I went into the compartment and sat on my bunk, allowing Konstantin to intercept them, and speak on my behalf. Two men came in with Konstantin. They were smiling! They shook hands with me. One of them asked why everyone had bedding except me. Through Sergei, I related my story about the mattress and blanket slipping to the floor in the night. They found it amusing. One of them patted my hand as he bid me good-bye. I couldn't believe how easy it had been. Konstantin had told them that he was KGB, and had checked my papers. He also told them about my rail record. By that time, the train had crossed my milestone; we were in Russia. It was impossible to recapture the excitement, but I was happy. I have broken the record, and crossed two borders without a passport or visa. And, without my nightmare of the stone customs building coming true. I stood looking out the window in the corridor, amazed that I had finally accomplished my goal. I tried to feel like myself, like a housewife from Arkansas, USA, but I couldn't. Instead, for a moment, I was an intriguing stranger, traveling across the world, without a passport. I have a "title" now; I am the "Holder of the World Record of the Most Unduplicated Rail Miles." I can shorten that, and print it on a T-shirt, and on my business cards. I feel famous.

Chapter 25
In Moscow without a Passport

The outskirts of Moscow were in view. It had been a long ride. A bargaining session with taxi drivers outside the Kazanski Station got me nowhere. The asking price from the station to the Hotel Bellegarde was an exorbitant fifty dollars. One driver (out of the goodness of his heart, no doubt) offered a "bargain fare" of forty dollars. Sergei spotted me, and helped me out. He talked a driver into taking me for fifteen dollars. For another five, he would (after dropping me off) take Konstantin and Sergei to the Smolenskaya Station for their train.

Konstantin and Sergei carried my luggage into the lobby. I felt that my thanks were sadly inadequate, considering all they had done for me. An offer of money wasn't necessary; Konstantin and Sergei have plenty. They had been saving for years for such a trip, yet never fully believing it would ever be possible for them to visit the West. I stepped back out onto the sidewalk with them; it was time to say good-bye. I hugged them both. They waved, and Sergei threw me a kiss from the window of the taxi.

I ate heartily from the breakfast buffet before I left for Red Square. I didn't go inside any of the buildings; I just walked around admiring the cathedrals and the Kremlin. At Saint Basil's Cathedral (Cathedral of the Intercession) I compared the etching on the pocket watch I had bought for Erich to the outline of the cathedral; it was a good likeness.

Just before noon I returned to the hotel to check with Intourist. My passport had not arrived. I asked if I could have my train ticket to Chop (Cop) in Ukrainia. There had been a shift change since I last spoke with Intourist. The woman I had spoken with earlier was polite and helpful, but her replacement was too busy to write my ticket. I was to come back in three hours. But, I had to vacate my room; checkout time was noon. Without a passport, visa and train ticket, I couldn't leave. I stored my luggage and headed for the Arbat, a famous pedestrian zone. Despite the cold, vendors were out in full force. I bought a hat with earflaps, and several sets of the Russian nesting dolls, called *Matryoshka* (Little Mother). I couldn't resist buying a set with the newest "star," Mikhail Gorbachev, painted in bright colors. The tiniest doll was a likeness of him as a child. The others showed the main changes in his life. The fifth and final one portrayed him (without the famous birthmark) holding the new Russian flag.

As the air warmed a little, it began to rain. I ducked into a huge tent for a cup of Turkish tea. Then, hoping for good news, I went back to the hotel. My passport was not there. It was time to worry; something wasn't right. In answer to my request for a train ticket, I was told, "I have no time for you now. Sit down and wait." I sat. In fifteen minutes the woman came to me and said she had an errand to run; she'd be back in twenty minutes. She came back in thirty minutes, wrote me a train ticket to Chop, and advised me to go to the American Embassy for a new passport. It was past worry time; it was panic time. I felt my throat constrict.

Luckily, the embassy was only a few blocks away. But, without my passport and visa I couldn't verify my identity. A young man joined me in the waiting area. "What about a drivers' license?"

" I am here to ride trains, so I left it at home."

" I can't issue a passport without a picture ID."

Rummaging frantically through my purse and my backpack, I came upon a Xerox copy of an old visa. My picture was on it. "Will this do? It's all I have. Please!"

At first he started shaking his head, then miraculously (I had prayed for a miracle), he agreed. I could have a passport! I waited for someone to take the required photographs. Credit cards or foreign currency were not accepted. I barely scraped together the eighty American dollars to pay for the pictures and the passport. Now, we had the visa problem to solve. The young man called the Intourist desk at my hotel. Someone there would give me a new visa. I felt the weight lift from my chest. I hurried back to the hotel, only to be refused by the same woman who had finally written out my train ticket. How much was I expected to endure?

" I was told at the American Embassy that someone would give me a visa. An official called you from there. I have a new passport, but I need a visa."

" We are too busy to write you a visa. You may leave without one."

"You know I cannot leave Russia without a visa. I will wait. When will you have time?"

"We will not have time at all. You will not have a visa." It was all the Ugly American could take.

" I am going back to the American Embassy and report that you refuse to issue me a visa."

She didn't look up from her paperwork. There was nothing to do but walk away. For now. Stress makes me hungry. I went back to an Italian restaurant I had seen in the Arbat. It looked Italian. It felt Italian. The young blonde waitress spoke to me in English. I had the best spaghetti in Russia. It tasted Italian. The waitress brought me a frothy green drink in a wineglass, compliments of the house.

Back to the hotel. The Intourist officer wouldn't talk to me. She made one phone call after another. When I tried to get her attention she told me to sit down, and wait.

In a few minutes I stepped up to the desk again, prepared for another dose of rudeness. "May I please have a visa now? My train leaves tonight."

"No, we are too busy to write you a visa."

"If you don't give me a visa, I can't leave Russia. You will have to give me a job at the Hotel Bellegarde!"

"You will not have a visa! Sit down!" I sat, but only to reconnoiter. I changed my tactics; I would be sweet (actually saccharine).

"I want to leave an address where my passport can be mailed when, and if it arrives."

I wrote down my address in Bad Kreuznach and (smiling sweetly) handed her the paper.

"We do not mail things to Germania."

"What will you do with my passport? You cannot keep my passport. I am an American citizen. I want my passport!" I was no longer even pretending to be sweet.

"If you want your passport you may come back to the Hotel Bellegarde for it!"

"If you don't mail my passport to Germany, where I will be staying, then that means you are keeping my passport. I will go to the American Embassy in Moscow, in Frankfurt and in Washington, and I will tell them you are keeping an American passport."

"What do you mean?" She was getting the message.

"I mean I will tell them that you are keeping the passport illegally. I will also go to the Russian Embassy in Frankfurt and in Washington, and tell them." That seemed to intimidate her a tad. She made a quick phone call; it must have been to a higher authority, because her attitude toward me changed. She almost smiled when she said, "We will send your passport to Germania." I thanked her, and asked if I could have my visa. "No. You may not." I sensed it was the end of all conversation between us. I gave up, and went out the door. To my surprise and delight, the rain had turned to snow. Beautiful, soft, soothing flakes of snow were falling, turning Moscow into something out of *Doctor Zhivago*. Too bad I couldn't stay. Or perhaps I could; I might not be leaving without my visa. I was still trying to come to a decision on that. Meanwhile, I needed to mail postcards; the post office was only a few blocks away.

The snow was coming down harder as I walked back to the hotel. What a beautiful sight the Moscow River and its bridges are in the snowy night. The lights on the bridges add a soft glimmer to the whiteness of the snow and the blackness of the river. I had come to a decision; I'll take a chance; I'll leave without the visa.

Chapter 26
Westward Ho!

I retrieved my luggage and went out to find a taxi. Four taxi drivers were standing on the sidewalk in front of the hotel. My train would leave from Kievskaya Station, about four blocks away. That didn't stop the drivers from trying to charge fifty dollars. Hah! I declined when one lowered the price to *twenty* dollars. I said, "I can see the station from here; I will only pay five dollars (that's all I had, and they didn't want Russian money). If I didn't have this luggage, I would walk." No takers. None of them felt sorry for the old American Babushka. They laughed. I was wearing my backpack; I picked up my satchel from the snowy sidewalk, took the pull strap on Tagalong, and started toward the station. When I got almost to the bridge the youngest taxi driver caught up with me. He jumped out and put my luggage in the trunk; he would take me for five dollars.

Train # 9 to Chop (Cop), on the Ukrainian/Hungarian border was waiting. It pulled away just after 9:00 p.m. I had two overnights to worry about getting out of Russian territory without a visa. At least I have a passport. I welcomed the luxury of a hard-class compartment to myself.

As we drew near the Russian/Ukrainian border I pretended to sleep, hoping to be passed over by the customs officials and border guards. It didn't work; the Ukrainian officials requested my papers. I handed one of them my passport, and showed the other one my Xerox copy of an old visa with a different picture and passport number on it. I watched as my passport was stamped with the Ukrainian entry seal. Both of the men smiled as they handed back my "papers." What a surprise! Now I had only the worry of getting out of Ukrainia, at Chop. Hungary doesn't require visas for American citizens.

We arrived in Chop at six o'clock on the second morning; it was the last checkpoint on my route to the West that requires a visa to enter or exit. I followed the crowd off the train, and into the station to Passport Control. The official gave my passport (I had the Xerox copy of the old visa inside it) a cursory check; one obstacle passed. The customs-check line was next. A big burly man wearing a Russian hat with earflaps motioned for me to come to the head of the line. At his request I lifted my luggage onto a long wooden table. He spoke English; I could explain the visa problem if necessary.

"Any souvenirs? What did you buy?"

"Nothing in Ukrainia. In Moscow I bought a hat like yours, some

185

nesting dolls, and T-shirts."

"Show me the T-shirts."

That worried me; they were printed with funny pictures and sayings about communism. I showed the least offensive one. On the front of it Lenin presides over a pair of golden arches. Pointing his finger, he was saying, in Russian, "You go to McDonald's!" The customs man laughed. I hesitated before showing the next shirt. The Russian initials for the KGB were emblazoned in the center in front. He turned the shirt to read the back. It depicted a woman in a red headscarf with one finger across her lips. She was saying, "You say nothing! To nobody!" I was sure he would confiscate the shirt and send me back to Moscow. But, after all, he was a Ukrainian; I shouldn't have worried. He loved it. Still laughing, he waved me through without looking at my passport.

There was one more problem to face. My EurailPass is valid in Hungary, but I didn't have a train ticket for the short distance to the Hungarian border. I was denied access to the train I had taken from Moscow, because I didn't have a berth reserved. I didn't need a berth once we crossed into Hungary; carriages with seating would be hooked onto the train, but the conductor said I would have to take the local train across the border. I didn't have time to purchase any Ukrainian currency. The conductor on the local said five American dollars would cover the ticket. I thought I had used all of my dollars in Moscow, but I found four singles in my pocket. The conductor accepted them. I was on my way to the West.

In Zahony, Hungary I transferred to an overnighter to Budapest. I think it was the same train I had taken from Moscow, but with seating carriages added. As soon as I settled in, I folded the arms down on the seats on the left side of the compartment; I was planning to stretch out for the night. I sat by the window on the left side of the compartment, waiting for the conductor to sign my document. A young man came in and sat down, leaving one seat free between us. There are four seats on each side in second class; I wondered why he didn't sit in the fourth one, next to the door, leaving two seats between us. Most passengers try to leave as much space as possible between themselves and others, especially on overnight trains. Another young man entered, and sat across from me. The two men seemed to know each other. After the conductor had made his rounds, a tall dark-haired man from the next compartment opened the door and smiled at me. He spoke to the man who was sitting one seat over from me. I was not familiar with the language. He squeezed his bulky body between the man and me. The newcomer spoke English to me. I couldn't place the accent, but he definitely wasn't Russian.

"Do you have American money? I have never seen dollars. Show them to me."

"No, I haven't." It was hard to believe he had never seen dollars before. I was in for some sort of trickery, and I suspected that my two seatmates were in on it.

"Do you have German Marks?" I said I didn't, but he didn't stop there.

"You are going to Budapest. You must have Hungarian Forints. Show them to me."

I knew he didn't believe me when I said I didn't have Forints either, but he left the compartment. Several times within the next few minutes he came to the door of my compartment and looked at me.

The conductor had gone to the sleeping carriages and locked the door between them and the seating carriages; I was on my own. I no longer felt safe in the presence of my seatmates, and I was unsure of the further intentions of the dark-haired man from the next compartment. There have been many reports of con artists and thieves traveling on trains between countries. Some of them rob tourists for a living. I took my luggage with me, and went as far down toward the locked sleeping carriages as I could. The seating compartments were full; I stood in the corridor most of the night. Toward morning I spotted the conductor. He led me to an empty compartment on the other side of the sleepers. By then, I needed coffee more than sleep.

I arrived an hour too late for the train that would take me to Vienna in time to catch one to Mainz, Germany, with connections to Bad Kreuznach. There was no way I could make it to base tonight. I caught the next train to Vienna, and connected to a train to Cologne, where I had a couple of hours to wait for the *Airport City,* an express train that would stop in Bingerbruck on its way to the airport in Frankfurt. Other than a few railway workers, I saw only winos and beggars in the station. In times past, it would have been safe enough to lean against a wall or sit in the waiting room in the middle of the night in the Cologne Station; now I felt I should stay alert. Arrival in Bingerbruck was at 3:30 a.m. After a two-hour wait, I caught a train to base. I was home free.

Chapter 27
At Journey's End

My rail pass is valid for another two weeks; I set out to make extra miles. Just two trains took me to Paris from BK. Soldiers were patrolling the train station, probably because of another bomb threat. I took an overnighter to Perpignan, France, with credit for the miles as far as Toulouse.

I had planned to take the famous "Little Yellow Train" from Perpignan to La Tour de Carol, France, near the border of Andorra, but my timing was off. Instead, I got back on the same train and went on to Barcelona. There were a couple of routes into France from Spain that would give me partial credit. I stood looking at the schedule in Barcelona Sants Station; it was difficult to decide between the two routes. The train over Pamplona would give me a few hundred kilometers. The one over Hendaye was one I had taken before, but from Hendaye to Paris the conductor had refused to sign; perhaps I would be lucky enough to ride with a different, more accommodating conductor. If so, I could claim over 800 kilometers. But, what if the same conductor was aboard? Then I would have zero kilometers to claim. I solved the dilemma by taking the train to La Tour de Carol from Barcelona; I would have beautiful daytime scenery, and if I couldn't connect to Paris I would spend the night in a hotel. La Tour de Carol is a delightful little mountain village.

After an early dinner, I took a night train back to Paris, earning credit only up to Toulouse.

For once, I had time to enjoy Paris. My first stop was Montmartre, to see the *Sacre-Coeur*, Church of the Sacred Heart. Its stark-white exterior fairly sparkles in the noonday sun. A funicular railway goes up, but I needed the walk up the steep steps. From the wall in front of the church one can see for miles. The city of Paris stretches below, looking like a bas-relief map.

In Montmartre I spied a small Italian restaurant. Knowing that I could almost always trust the Italians to have meatless pasta, I walked in and waited to be seated. A man and a woman (the owners) were eating spaghetti at a round table. It was the time between lunch and dinner. I had overlooked the *Ferme* (Closed) sign on the door. Perhaps because I was a tourist, they seated me anyway. They had left the door unlocked because they were expecting a delivery. My table was in front of the picture window; I could people-watch through the sheer lace curtains. Although I ordered "a la Americaine," just a plate of spaghetti and a basket of bread, I was forgiven. The man brought me a carafe of wine, compliments of the house. He lit the candle on my table and turned the radio on. I enjoyed classical music with my meal. After the delivery, the door was locked. Several would-be patrons saw me sitting by the window and tried the door, but I was the only privileged guest today.

It wouldn't seem like Paris without seeing the Seine River and its beautiful bridges. I walked along the left bank of the river for a long time, stopping to rest outside Notre-Dame Cathedral. The grotesque gargoyles seem out of place on a holy edifice. My brochure dates the building of the cathedral back to 1163. It was built on the site that had previously borne a Gallo-Roman Temple, a Christian Basilica, and a church. In the seventeenth century the bell in the south tower was recast. Some foolish women of Paris threw their jewelry of gold and silver into the molten bronze, after being told by the workmen that the precious metals would give the bell a purer tone.

While window-shopping on the famous boulevard, Champs de l' Elysees, several different men stopped me, and offered me money. I didn't need to understand French to know what they wanted for their money.

It wasn't amusing anymore; I kicked the third creep in the behind as he walked away. He turned, and said, in English, "That is the way they do! They walk slowly and stop to look in windows." I was shocked. He meant that I was behaving like a prostitute! Why do the brochures and travel guides tell tourists where to window-shop if only prostitutes do it? Hey, I wasn't wearing a leather micro-miniskirt with thigh-high boots or a thong bathing suit with spike heels. I was wearing jeans, a plaid shirt and running shoes. Determined not to let the jerks ruin my special day, I walked on. Later, near the Gare du Nord (North Station), another man offered me money. "No" wasn't enough; he followed me along like a puppy dog. I called him a bad boy, "*Mauvais Garcon!*" Then I used my best French. "*Je suis une Americaine!*" I am an American! That didn't deter him. I tried "*Je suis une touriste!*" He was still close behind me. In desperation, I said, "*Je suis une clouchard!*" Boy, that shocked him; he turned and ran. "*Clouchard*" is the French name for the bums and winos that sleep in cardboard boxes in alleys or under bridges, and I had convinced him I was one. From Paris I caught the last train to Frankfurt; tomorrow I will be back at base. I had inadvertently made a wise decision when I decided against traveling from Barcelona over Pamplona or Hendaye; both of the trains had crashed that same night. I would have been a loser either way. But for now, I am a winner. I have 79,841 miles documented.

Epilogue

I wouldn't be finishing out my current EurailPass or adding any more miles. On arrival in Bad Kreuznach from Paris, I was greeted with bad news. My mother was in a hospital in Corbin, Kentucky, near death from congenital heart failure. Icelandair could get me out of Luxembourg to Baltimore the next day.

From Baltimore/Washington International Airport, I took the Metro to the Greyhound bus depot for an overnight trip to Corbin; the train doesn't go there and the closest airport is eighty miles away. The next day in Corbin, I took a taxi to the hospital. While I was en route, my mother had a stroke. Family members were already at her side. She was able to speak briefly to each of us. When I told her I had broken the world record, she said, "I prayed for you." Those were the last words my mother spoke.

Mother died the next morning. I had come to the end of my rail journey, and my mother had come to the end of life's journey.

Afterword

My daughter flew in from California to join us in a celebration train ride on the Arkansas and Missouri Railroad from Van Buren to Winslow, Arkansas. The conductor signed documents for all the family members, attesting to the rail miles they rode with the new record holder, me.

It was July 1997 before I knew for certain my documents had been approved by Guinness Publishing. I was listed in the 1998 *Guinness Book of World Records*. My title is official. Now I am a champion.

Guinness Publishing didn't print my record in the 1999 edition. I was assured that I am still the record holder, and I may be listed again in a future edition. When the listing of all records is completed on the Internet, I will be on it.

Since I completed my journeys, Amtrak's *Pioneer* and *Desert Wind* have been canceled. The Sears Tower in Chicago is no longer the tallest office building in the world. The Petronas Towers building in Malaysia now holds the record.

My previous passport was sent from Moscow to the New York Intourist Office. It arrived home before I did.

I used the following rail passes on my journey to the world record: two 15-day Eurail FlexiPasses, one 2-month EurailPass, one thirty-day EurailPass, one 3 month EurailPass, three PolishRail Passes, one European East Pass, two Romanian Rail Passes, one Bulgarian rail pass, one BritishRail Pass, one Irish Rover Ticket, one Swiss Pass, three thirty-day All Aboard America tickets, and one 12-day Canadian Flexi Pass. Many regular rail tickets were also purchased.

Dzhusaly, Kazakhstan